Prisoners' Work and Vocational Training

Most prisoners serving in British prisons are required to work. Does this work help them to serve their sentences, and does it help them to get employment when they are released?

Prisoners' Work and Vocational Training portrays the various kinds of work and vocational training courses provided for prison inmates, and compares them with work and training outside prison. It describes what satisfactions and responsibilities the prisoners get – or do not get – in their work and how the process is viewed by the staff who supervise them. A significant part relates prisoners' experiences of work to their efforts to find jobs after being released, and shows that the link between unemployment and crime, while real, is not simple.

Based upon original research and shedding light on a crucial area of activity in the rehabilitative work of prisons, this book reveals that although the Prison Service has tried hard to make prisoners' work relevant to the outside world, it has potential to do more. In order to improve prisoners' employability, and therefore their prospects of eschewing crime, prisons must address not only their work needs but also other personal needs in an integrated way.

Prisoners' Work and Vocational Training is essential reading for those studying criminology, prison and probation studies as well as for prison staff, probation officers, social workers and careers advisers.

Frances Simon has worked as a researcher in the New Zealand Justice Department, the Home Office, NACRO and the Department of Law at Brunel University. She is the author of *Prediction Methods in Criminology*, which won a prize from the International Society of Criminology, and is co-author of *Unemployment, Crime and Offenders* and *Training Young Offenders*.

Prisoners' Work and Vocational Training

Frances H. Simon

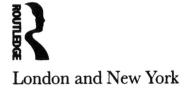

London and New York

First published 1999
by Routledge
11 New Fetter Lane, London EC4P 4EE

Simultaneously published in the USA and Canada
by Routledge
29 West 35th Street, New York, NY 10001

Typeset in Baskerville by Routledge
Printed and bound in Great Britain by
Creative Print and Design (Wales), Ebbw Vale

British Library Cataloguing in Publication Data
A catalogue record for this book is available from the British Library

Library of Congress Cataloging in Publication Data
Simon, Frances H.
Prison work and training/Frances H. Simon.
Includes bibliographical references and index.
1. Prison industries Great Britain. 2. Convict labor Great Britain. 3. Prisoners Employment Great Britain. 4. Ex-convicts Employment Great Britain. I. Title.
HV8931.G7S56 1999   98-35094
365'.65'0941 dc21   CIP

ISBN 0-415-14676-3 (hbk)
ISBN 0-415-14677-1 (pbk)

For Nicholas
and in memory of John

Contents

List of tables

Foreword

Prison work, which is what this book is about, runs parallel to prison education and vocational training. 'The primary purpose of prison work', writes Frances Simon at page 184, 'should be to fit prisoners for work outside.' I would go further. Prison work, prison education, vocational training, are to aim at reducing crime by turning as many prisoners as possible into useful citizens.

The majority of prisoners are young men with inadequate education and family life. They are likely to spend the next half-century in our community, and we do not want them to prey upon us for any longer than is inevitable. We do not want them in despair to be stealing to buy drugs and drink, and wrecking our motor cars and frightening the old. If they are to be fitted for work outside, in a society where unskilled work is going to be hard to find, then they will need efficient education and training. Without this background their work will be dim and of the kinds described by Frances Simon as most common in the past: sewing clothes and maintenance tasks.

Frances Simon deals with prisoners' work in English prisons. I suspect it would be valuable if someone of her skills would now look at the more advanced industrial prisons abroad. The German prisons, where a factory is introduced by an outside company and prisoners are taught to perform skilled jobs for which they are properly paid, are prime examples of combining training for the future with useful work. Coldingley failed as an industrial prison, due, says Frances Simon, to lack of long-term planning. I suspect that a major cause of failure was to treat prisoners as ordinary factory workers, but pay them only as prisoners. Despite some improvements, the principle of realistic pay does not seem to have been wholly accepted by the Prison Service.

A main difficulty in prison work and education is lack of money. Where a Government cuts the money for prisons, but leaves it largely to prison governors to decide where the axe will fall, it cannot fall on security or health. It inevitably falls on education and, through reducing education, to lowering the levels of work.

I very well remember the Prison Service giving evidence to Lord Woolf and myself that work in prison should be run as a profit-making business, and that the only way to achieve this result was to restrict wages. We disagreed. Our aim was to help prisoners learn how to get and hold jobs after release. Frances Simon brings back the brave days of the Woolf Report and indeed summarises the history of work in prison over centuries and in specific and varied prisons. It will be a necessary study for those who in the future try to put Woolf into real effect and help the young and older prisoners to achieve a measure of self-respect and to hold decent jobs.

Sir Stephen Tumim
Her Majesty's Chief Inspector of Prisons 1987-95

Preface

This book is intended as a contribution to public understanding of some of the things that go on in prisons, especially the work that prisoners do and the vocational training that some of them undertake. It is based largely on research which was commissioned by the Home Office and carried out by Brunel University during 1992–4, with the addition of later material. Any views expressed are the responsibility of the author and are not necessarily shared by the Home Office or any other agency.

The research was originally conceived in the context of Prison Service policy development following the Woolf Report, and the emphasis in the 1991 White Paper *Custody, Care and Justice* that 'work should have a central place in the life of the prison'. The book examines prisoners' work and training with regard to their value for achieving part of the Prison Service's statement of purpose: 'to help [prisoners] lead law-abiding and useful lives in custody and after release'; and it takes into account major changes which have occurred since the early hopes generated by the Woolf Report and which now jeopardise the prospect of accomplishing that purpose. In carrying out the study with my colleagues, and in drafting the book, I have tried to work in the spirit of Woolf, and in the interests – according them equal weight – of the Prison Service, prisoners, and the public.

Frances H. Simon
Centre for Criminal Justice Research
Department of Law
Brunel University

Acknowledgements

An appreciation: Dr Claire Corbett

In drafting this book I have been indebted to my colleague Claire Corbett, Director of the Centre for Criminal Justice Research at Brunel University. Claire helped to plan the original Home Office funded study on which much of the book is based, and from 1992 she shared in the fieldwork, data coding and shaping of our research report, of which the Home Office published a summary (*An Evaluation of Prison Work and Training*) in 1996. Although she did not take part in gathering the later material she has always been at hand as adviser, critic and friend, and with her agreement I have written 'we' throughout. Her suggestions did much to improve the text, and she has my warm appreciation.

Many people helped with the research or in other ways, and gave generously of their time, information and advice. It would not be practicable to mention more than a very few individually, but they include:

- the governors of Channings Wood, Highpoint, Holloway, Kirkham, Liverpool and Maidstone Prisons, and nearly 300 other people who, when we first met them, were in those prisons as staff or inmates;
- representatives of the outside employers referred to in Chapter 3, the training schemes referred to in Chapter 5, and seven Training and Enterprise Councils;
- representatives of several colleges, voluntary bodies and other organisations;
- a great many people in Prison Service HQ, and especially Mr Roger Fisher, Head of Prison Enterprise Services in 1996, and Mr John Ditchfield and Ms Diane Caddle, both of the Research and Statistics Directorate;
- Dr Silvia Casale;
- several members and former members of Brunel University, including Professor Keith Smith, Head of the Department of Law in 1992–4, and especially Dr Bonny Mhlanga, Research Fellow, who worked with me in 1992–3 and during that time made a substantial contribution to the fieldwork.

The author and publishers thank the following for permission to reproduce copyright material: the Controller of Her Majesty's Stationery Office for extracts from Crown copyright material; Oxford University Press for extracts from M. Grunhut, *Penal Reform* (1948) and from R.D. King and K. McDermott, *The State of Our Prisons* (1995); Professor R.D. King for an extract from R.D. King and R. Morgan, *The Future of the Prison System* (Gower, 1980); the Prison Reform Trust for an extract from P. Robson, 'Learning from scratch' (*Prison Report*, 1996, no. 36); the Penal Affairs Consortium for extracts from *Prisons – Some Current Developments* (1996); Mrs M.J. Wurr for an extract from HMP Holloway Board of Visitors, *Annual Report 1995*; the Reader's Digest Association for an extract from D. Ramsbotham, 'Why we need to reform our prisons' (*Reader's Digest*, January 1997); *The Independent* newspaper for extracts, 1996–7; Dr Ros Burnett for an extract from R. Burnett, *The Dynamics of Recidivism* (1992); Professor John Braithwaite for extracts from J. Braithwaite, *Prisons Education and Work* (Australian Institute of Criminology, 1980); Routledge for an extract from I. Crow, P. Richardson, C. Riddington and F. Simon, *Unemployment, Crime and Offenders* (1989); the Department of Corrective Services, New South Wales Government, for an extract from J. McHutchison, *NSW Corrective Services Industries and Offender Post-Release Employment* (1991); the Department of Corrections, New Zealand, for an extract from K. McLaren, *Reducing Reoffending: What Works Now* (1992); the Howard League for an extract from R. Tilt, 'Rights, risks and rehabilitation 1996' (*Criminal Justice*, 1996, vol. 14, no. 4).

1 Introduction

PURPOSE AND SCOPE OF THIS BOOK

Most prisoners serving sentences in British prisons are required to work. What kinds of work do they do, and why? How does prison work compare with ordinary work outside prison? What training do the prisoners get? What do they think of their work? Does it help them to serve their sentences, and does it help them to get employment when they are released, especially now when the world of work is changing?

This book is addressed to people interested in the criminal justice system, including practitioners and others, who have a general awareness of prisons but would like to know more about what goes on inside them. Although most prisoners have to work, prison work is a relatively neglected subject in the literature of imprisonment. Few studies have been made of the nature of prison work, the ways in which prisoners as individual people experience it, and the extent to which it meets their needs. This book, much of which is based on a study carried out for the Home Office by Brunel University, is intended as a contribution to public understanding.

We focus on matters affecting prisoners and ex-prisoners at a personal individual level, not on wider structural factors though some are mentioned in discussion. At appropriate points reference is made to findings from other studies. The Brunel research has much in common with one or another of them on various topics, but it also has some extras (as well as being more up to date). We give more attention than most other writers to describing and analysing prisoners' own views of their work. We make direct comparisons between kinds of prison work and examples of their counterparts outside. Perhaps most significantly, our study includes a follow-up in which people who were first interviewed while working in prison were interviewed again after their release, to enable us to examine how far prison work and training affected their subsequent job chances. And we discuss our findings in the light of national economic and employment trends, to evaluate the usefulness to prisoners of prison work and training in the 1990s.

Our concern is with prisons in England and Wales, which contain approximately 85 per cent of all prisoners held at any one time in the UK and which are administered by the Prison Service (answering to the Home Secretary). Except for the historical section of this chapter and for parts of the book concerning the general prison population, we refer to adult prisoners, which in the prison system means those aged 21 and over and who comprise about 85 per cent of the total. And we focus on people confined under sentence. Prisoners on remand (or awaiting trial) are not required to work, and many have no work offered them in prison. Sentenced prisoners are approximately 75 per cent of the total.

This first chapter begins with a short historical survey of prison work from the eighteenth century onwards. It shows that over the years the purposes of prison work, as officially perceived, have been many and various, and the emphasis given to one or another has shifted back and forth with the changing currents of penal philosophy. The history helps to form a background for the research, because part of our project is to explore what the purposes of prison work should be. Following the history and coming to the present decade, we consider what the Woolf Report[1] said about work and how Prison Service policy has developed since then. We look at recent major changes affecting the Service, including the rising numbers of prisoners, tighter security, budget cuts and other matters which could influence inmates' opportunities for work and training. Then we summarise the methods of the Brunel study, and the chapter closes by indicating the structure of the rest of the book.

A SHORT HISTORY OF PRISON WORK[2]

Prison work in the eighteenth and nineteenth centuries

Prisons, as establishments for the confinement and punishment of convicted offenders, developed during the eighteenth and nineteenth centuries from the older institutions of the workhouse, the house of correction and the local jail. From the time of John Howard in the 1770s there was extensive and recurrent debate as to how the twin objectives of reformation and deterrence could be achieved. Howard and his fellow reformers, shocked by the squalor and idleness of the local jails, advocated a regime in which the chief elements would be solitary confinement (in clean conditions), religion and hard work. These three themes predominated in the prison system well into the nineteenth century, though the relative importance of work, its rationale and the forms it took, varied with time and place.

Howard believed that the prison cell should induce reflection and repentance, and that that process would be aided by the discipline of hard labour. The 1779 Penitentiary Act, which he helped to draft, envisaged work 'of the hardest and most servile kind, in which Drudgery is chiefly required', such as sawing stone, rasping wood or chopping rags. At Gloucester Penitentiary, built by G.O. Paul in 1784 as one of the first in a wave of new local prisons, the emphasis was more on solitary confinement with work given as a relief from it. Sounding a different note, Jeremy Bentham argued from 1791 that his 'panopticon' design for the ideal prison would not only provide surveillance but also enable the place to run as a profitable factory, turning its inmates into self-disciplined workers who would welcome work as 'a cordial'. Though Bentham's architectural ideas bore fruit in many of the new prisons which were built in the following decades, the government in 1810 finally rejected his panopticon on account of its exploitation of captive labour for private gain. In this they were much influenced by Paul's view that a penitentiary was not a factory, and that a prisoner's work should be a penance for sin.

During much of the nineteenth century the system continued to be a diverse mixture of establishments, but the central government was gradually gaining influence over local prisons and building big national ones (like Millbank Penitentiary which opened in 1816 with space for 1,000 inmates). The Gaols Act 1823 stated the principles which were intended to apply to all: the purposes of a prison were to keep prisoners in custody, preserve their health, improve their morals, and deliver the right amount of punishment to the convicted; this was to be done by 'due Classification, Inspection, regular Labour and Employment, and Religious and Moral Instruction', though the Act did not specify how. The great debate between the proponents of the 'silent system', in which prisoners worked together but were not allowed to communicate with one another, and the 'separate system' which kept them strictly apart working silently in their cells, was eventually resolved in favour of the latter, and culminated in the opening of Pentonville in 1842.

By this time, as a response to rising crime and increasing numbers of prisoners since the 1820s, prison regimes had become harsher. The treadwheel was common, as were the bread and water diet and the rule of silence. Ignatieff[3] has graphically described a typical day in the life of a Pentonville inmate: twenty-three hours spent alone in his cell, eight and a half of them working at his cobbler's bench or loom to make prisoners' boots or cloth for their garments; one hour for chapel and exercise, all the time masked and separated from his fellows; a monotonous diet of bread, cocoa, gruel and stew; and for leisure, pacing his cell and reading the Bible. Indiscipline was punished by the lash or by confinement in a dark basement, and at night inmates could hear the screams of others unable to bear the solitude. Crawford, one of the first prisons inspectors, wrote in 1834 that work was a comfort to prevent insanity.

From 1848 public works prisons gradually replaced transportation, and offenders sentenced to penal servitude went to them after an initial period in solitary confinement. At these prisons most convicts worked mainly in association, and the work, while still hard labour under strict discipline, could be more varied and healthy. At Portland the prisoners quarried stone, built a breakwater and later mended roads and railways for the Admiralty. At Dartmoor they constructed buildings, they farmed and reclaimed land, and they worked in several manufacturing industries including clothing and footwear, hammocks and mailbags, as well as in domestic and maintenance tasks. Prison labour built Wormwood Scrubs. Du Cane, first chairman of the Prison Commissioners after 1877, wrote that the purposes of convict labour were deterrence, reform (by instilling good work habits and a knowledge of honest trades), and – fortunately accompanying the first two, he said – helping to make the prisons self-supporting.

However most prisoners, whose sentences were of weeks or months rather than years, served all their time in local prisons. In the 1860s the locals had between them a diversity of work: Ruggles-Brise[4] describes how while some relied on the treadwheel and oakum picking, others were vigorously engaged in manufacturing, including the use of commercial travellers to sell the goods and the payment of incentives to both staff and prisoners depending on trade. But the Prison Act of 1865, following a crime wave and official views that prisons were too soft, led to increasing severity and emphasis on punishment, with religious reformation becoming less important. The 1877 Prison Act brought all prisons under central government control, and by the 1880s (when the prison population totalled about 18,000) the work being done by most prisoners was intended as mainly punitive and deterrent. First-class hard labour, to which nearly all male prisoners were put for at least the first month of their sentence, typically comprised the treadwheel or the crank. As the majority of sentences did not exceed one month, such labour would have been many prisoners' only experience of prison work. Those serving longer in local prisons would eventually be given other work such as picking oakum, making mats or mailbags, sewing prison clothes, or domestic and maintenance tasks. Female prisoners were typically employed in picking oakum, knitting and needlework, or washing and mending clothes. Except for the treadwheel and the laundry, most work was done by the prisoner alone in his or her cell, for between nine and ten hours daily. Pay, in the form of a gratuity on discharge, was a maximum of ten shillings, which might be earned by a prisoner who had served at least six months.[5]

The Gladstone reforms and the new century

The oppressive prison conditions of late Victorian times were considerably ameliorated by the Gladstone Report of 1895,[6] which led to change in many features including work. During the next two decades treadwheels were taken out and the spaces filled by workshops where prisoners worked together; staff were paid extra for instructing them, and some power machines were installed. Cranks were disposed of, and oakum picking gradually reduced (though it occupied a few prisoners till the 1930s). There was a drive to obtain industrial work, largely from other government departments, and in 1898 the Comptroller of Industries listed over thirty kinds of articles being made. From 1902 trade training was given to some young inmates of convict prisons and to lads at the new borstals, while at the local prisons inmates increasingly spent more of their working hours in association and fewer alone in their cells. However, the Gladstone Committee's recommendation that a prisoner should be able to earn something continuously during sentence was not adopted, and by 1913 the gratuities had stopped, being replaced by a scheme of direct grants to discharged prisoners' aid societies.

The Prison Commissioners' views on the purposes of prison work at this time may be gauged from the following passage from their 1906–7 annual report:[7]

> Every effort is made…to obtain means of employment, which shall not only be remunerative, but shall furnish in its execution the occasion of teaching some sort of industry to the prisoner which, if it may not directly conduce to his employment in that particular trade on discharge, will, at least, give him the habit of applied labour, the absence of which quality is the principal predisposing cause to a life of crime.

Sufficient work, however, was not always readily procured, and the majority of prisoners were thought capable of only simple tasks. Mailbag sewing was heavily relied on, especially for work in cells; in 1908 the Comptroller of Accounts and Stores, referring to the Post Office, said, 'That great Department is, without doubt, our sheet anchor in the matter of prison employment.'[8] World War I brought prisons plenty of work making war supplies, but from 1920 it was a different matter, and by 1931 there were not enough orders, even for mailbags, to keep all inmates occupied.

The 1932 inquiry

In 1932 a Departmental Committee was set up 'to review the methods of employing prisoners and of assisting them to find employment on discharge, and to report what improvements are desirable and practicable'. Their report[9] indicated a thoroughgoing inquiry. Though sympathising with the prison authorities' difficulties in employing unskilled short-term inmates ('this incompetent and changing crowd of workers') they were firmly of the view that the primary aim of prison work should be the reformation of the prisoner: 'In making our proposals we have borne in mind that the main object of prison employment should be, not the exploitation of prison labour so as to secure a return to the State, but the rehabilitation of the prisoner.'

The Committee pondered whether a prison sentence could be utilised to teach prisoners a trade they could use on discharge ('a question which has been constantly put before us') and concluded that this was practicable only for a small minority; for the rest, 'the most that can be done is to provide work which will accustom a prisoner to habits of industry and to the speed which is required in outside employment'. They also considered whether, as many witnesses suggested, prisoners should be paid outside wages with deductions for board and the maintenance of dependants. They concluded that this was not practicable either, but they recommended a general scheme of wages for prisoners based on systematic work measurement as developed in outside industry. The thrust of the Committee's recommendations was twofold: a drive to obtain more work, and the vigorous pursuit of industrial efficiency. Workshops should be overhauled and rationalised; work should be speeded up; instructors should be more numerous and better qualified; the larger prisons should have industrial managers, and so on. Over the next five years much of this was carried out. New workshops were put in, with modern power machines and safety equipment; all prison farms were given tractors; and by 1938 fewer than one-third of the prisoners employed in manufacturing were on mailbags (though this proportion rose again in subsequent years). Earnings schemes spread to many prisons, with average pay for piece-workers at about seven pence a week.[10]

World War II

The Second World War forced prison industries to make big changes, some of which held pointers to the future. The need for skilled workers stimulated training: Maidstone Prison, for example, pioneered a six months' training course in engineering fitting for selected inmates, who on release were quickly placed in skilled jobs by the Ministry of Labour. Private employers become involved with prisons through the war effort: at rural prisons some inmates went out daily on bicycles to work for local farmers, who paid the prison authorities Agricultural Wages Board rates while the inmates received their usual prison pay. Other prisons, under similar financial arrangements, sub-contracted labour to employers making war supplies on government contracts, and the firms' representatives supervised the work in prison workshops.

Prison reforms in the 1950s: treatment and training

Substantial changes in prisons followed the 1948 Criminal Justice Act. Sentencing was restructured and prisons were classified as local, central or training ones. Inmates' living conditions improved in many ways; staffs expanded to include psychologists and other specialists; local education authorities supplied teachers to run evening classes in every prison. In all this the watchword was 'treatment and training', in the spirit expressed by Rule 6 of the Prison Rules:[11] 'The purposes of treatment and training of convicted prisoners shall be to establish in them the will to lead a good and useful life on discharge and to fit them to do so.'

According to the Commissioners the basis of inmates' training was personal influence on their characters by prison staff, and the material basis of training was work.[12] Fox, the chairman, quoted with approval Grunhut's statement: 'The object of prison labour in a rehabilitative programme is twofold: training for work and training by work.'[13] So in the central and training prisons work opportunities expanded. New workshops included, for example, light engineering, furniture-making, plumbing and electrical wiring, and staff shifts enabled the shops to operate a full working week. Prisoners did much of the building work which renovated disused jails and military camps to increase the number of Prison Service establishments from forty in 1946 to seventy in 1956. Animals from prison farms won prizes at agricultural shows. Vocational training courses, aiming increasingly at City and Guilds qualifications, spread from borstals to adult prisons, and at the end of 1959 769 prisoners were studying for them. Several prisons had pre-release courses to advise inmates on coping with life after discharge, including employment matters, and in 1953 the first pre-release hostel opened at Bristol, where a very few selected men in the last stage of a long sentence went out daily to ordinary jobs. (At this time the average prison pay was about three shillings a week.)

But as well as these substantial improvements there were problems. The prison population doubled its pre-war level, approaching 30,000 by the end of the decade, and the refurbished jails and camps could not immediately meet the need for accommodation. The result was great pressure on the local prisons, exacerbated in regard to work by a shortage of staff, insufficient workshop space, a severe decline in government orders, and trade union opposition to prisoners working outside the walls as they had done during the war. In 1952 the working week in local prisons rarely exceeded twenty-two hours, and – as in succeeding years too – mailbags were being made by hand while sewing machines stood idle in order to spin out the work. Efforts to get orders from private firms met with some success, but much of the work was low grade, such as dismantling meters or sorting bristles for brushes. The problem was seen as the perennial one of getting enough work to occupy the majority of prisoners, who because of short sentences, lack of aptitude or other reasons, would not receive industrial training.

The 1960s: another inquiry

At the end of 1959 the government appointed an Advisory Council, chaired by an industrialist (Sir W. Anson), 'to advise on the organisation and management of industries in prisons and borstals, including the supply of sufficient and suitable work; the development of other forms of employment for inmates; the industrial training of inmates; and related questions'. The Council's guiding principle was their belief that 'suitable work, if properly organised, is a most valuable part of a prisoner's training', and over the next five years they produced three reports.[14] Like their predecessor of thirty years earlier they emphasised industrial efficiency, which they felt was essential to good training, and they criticised the prison authorities' approach as uncertain and half-hearted. While acknowledging the difficulties of local prisons, they nevertheless thought much could be done to give the great majority of prisoners training for industrial work. 'Most jobs in modern industry which may be open to prisoners on discharge are jobs requiring not so much specific skill in a trade as general experience in modern industrial techniques and conditions.'

The Council thought that prison workshops should be run like modern factories, and they made extensive and detailed recommendations to that end. And prison industries, they said, should be mainly ones requiring only short training and not too much space, like tailoring, woodwork and (especially in local prisons) metal recovery; the more skilled trades like printing and engineering fitting should be kept for training prisons. Orders should be sought from private firms as well as government departments, and prisoners' pay (while still at pocket-money levels) should have differentials reflecting skill and effort. Finally the Council proposed a pilot of practically all their recommended measures in the shape of an industrial prison, and this eventually led to the opening in 1969 of Coldingley (about which more is said later).

Much was done during the 1960s to implement the Council's recommendations. But despite new management structures and many other changes in the system, local prisons were still in difficulties, aggravated by the rising prison population, which in 1969 passed 34,000. That year in local prisons mailbag sewers were still the largest employed group, at 18 per cent of all male workers and 28 per cent of those engaged in prison industries. The Radzinowicz sub-committee of the Advisory Council on the Penal System formed the view that British practice in regard to prison work was generally far below the best overseas, and said that while recent efforts and current planning were impressive actual progress was slow. 'We are convinced that the prison service as a whole is still not paying enough attention to prison industries.'[15]

Nevertheless the 1960s were, on the whole, a period of official optimism in the higher reaches of the Prison Service. Rule 6 had been raised in 1964, with a slight change in wording, to pre-eminence as Rule 1,[16] the authorities looked forward to guidance from a new research programme, and in this context it was stated that the most important aim of the current developments in prison work was 'that offenders in custody shall be given training and experience that will fit them to get and keep jobs on discharge'.[17]

Disillusion

But in the 1970s optimism shrank. Research on penal treatments, especially the reviews by Lipton, Martinson and Wilks[18] and Brody,[19] gave rise to the belief that 'nothing works'. The prison population was still rising, passing 40,000 in 1975. That year the Prison Department's annual report spoke of 'a more flexible view of penal treatment' and the following year it said frankly that the primary function of prisons was 'humane containment'. Despite continuing improvements in some prisons, the decade saw repeated demonstrations and violent disturbances by inmates and unprecedented industrial action by prison officers. These convulsions led to the setting up of the May Committee, whose report in 1979[20] expressed the views that 'confusion about objectives has been a significant cause of the present malaise' and that 'the rhetoric of "treatment and training" has had its day and should be replaced'. Instead, the Committee proposed the concept of 'positive custody', and saw the primary purpose of prison work as keeping inmates occupied.

In these circumstances the managers of prison work struggled. Efforts were made to raise the quality of workshop products and to sell more on the open market. In 1971 the industrial workshops showed a profit for the first time (farms and gardens had always been profitable) and they managed it again in 1972 and 1974, but otherwise they ran at an increasing loss. The 1977 annual report contrasted Category C training prisons, which offered inmates a diversity of semi-skilled employment and a full working week, with local prisons where orders were hard to get, officers were often called away to other duties, inmate turnover was rapid, and mailbags were still relied on as 'pick up and put down' work. King and Morgan, who had given evidence to the May Committee, wrote in 1980:[21]

> In spite of valiant efforts to introduce work-study and incentive earnings schemes in recent years, the fact remains that most prisoners are under-employed, on tasks of little real value, in conditions that are a parody of the outside world. Productivity remains low, and earnings are pitiable. Education classes, like vocational training schemes, reach only a minority of the prison population.

During the 1980s the Prison Service tried to redefine its objectives, at a time in penal philosophy when the 'treatment model' had given way to 'just deserts'.[22] In 1983 the Prisons Board made a statement of the task of the Service[23] which, while not formally replacing Rule 1, was more narrow and managerial in tone, focusing on the efficient use of resources to keep prisoners in custody, to provide for them as full a life as possible (including among other things work, education and training) and to enable them to retain links with the world outside. Ian Dunbar's influential 1985 report *A Sense of Direction*[24] held that a good prison system should be based on treating staff and inmates as individuals, maintaining good interpersonal relationships and keeping inmates active; but it did not say what should be the aim of the inmates' activity apart from implying that it would aid security and control. And the problems persisted. The population continued to rise, reaching 48,000 in 1985, and prisons were overcrowded despite another large new building programme. In their report for that year the Prisons Inspectorate said, 'We were drawn to the inescapable conclusion that substantial parts of the system were wholly pre-occupied with survival.'[25] Industrial action by staff and disturbances by inmates recurred, and in 1989 King and McDermott, after comparing facilities for prisoners, including work, in 1985–7 with what they had been fifteen years previously, were writing of 'the ever-deepening crisis'.[26]

The Prindus affair

Meanwhile, prison industries had been racked by scandal. In 1984 the Comptroller and Auditor General reported 'evidence of serious irregularities in dealings with contractors by the Directorate of Prison Industries and Farms' (DIF, trading as Prindus).[27] Police and others investigated. Six DIF staff, including the commercial manager, were suspended; three of these were charged with corruption and acquitted; all six resigned or were retired early. The House of Commons Public Accounts Committee, inquiring into the affair in 1986,[28] reported a 'catalogue of inefficiency and bad management' which had led in 1984–5 to losses and bad debts of around £20 million, including £15 million through dealings with one particular firm. What had happened was that in the 1970s pressure to get work for prisoners had induced the workshops side of DIF to expand considerably their trade with private companies, taking on contracts which they had not the ability to manage. The Committee's report spoke of 'a crucial lack of sound financial and management control and information' and 'serious and fundamental misjudgments', while the chairman, commenting on evidence from the Home Office, said, 'This is a most unedifying picture of lack of control which could lead to fraud and corruption.'

Vigorous remedial action was taken. The Prison Department introduced tight financial controls for prison industries, shook up the management of DIF, which was now renamed Prison Service Industries and Farms (PSIF), considerably reduced their involvement with private companies, and set about closing the most uneconomic prison workshops. During 1986–7 forty-two workshops were closed, reducing the number of industrial employment places for inmates from 14,204 to 12,863. Even so, only 66 per cent of these places were taken up, a proportion which remained much the same in the next two years. The National Audit Office reported in 1987[29] that good progress was being made towards controlling losses, but that big differences existed in management and workshop efficiency even between prisons of the same type, and that the Home Office lacked a long-term plan for prison industries.

Coldingley industrial prison

Lack of long-term planning is well illustrated by the history of Coldingley Prison.[30] Coldingley was opened in 1969, in response to the recommendations of the Anson inquiry, as the first industrial prison in Britain: a purpose-built, Category B 'training' establishment whose regime centred on a full industrial working week for inmates. It had two light engineering workshops making steel shelving and road signs, and a commercial laundry, all well equipped and staffed, the products being sold to outside customers. Prisoners worked eight hours a day, five days a week, and interruptions were not allowed: other activities, like education and visits, had to take place outside working hours. Pay was based on the usual prison rates, though somewhat higher to reflect the longer working week. Prisoners sent to Coldingley were selected as being thought likely to fit in with the regime. Trade training was not given; an official press release[31] explained: 'The purpose is to accustom men to working eight hours a day in modern factory conditions and so enable them more readily to lead a good and useful life on discharge.'[32]

By 1986, when the Prisons Inspectorate first visited Coldingley, things were changing. One of the four wings was now being used for prisoners on remand, few of whom worked, while only half the convicted inmates worked in the laundry or the workshops. The forty-hour week still operated, but there was pressure to alter it by non-industrial staff who had little opportunity during their own working day for personal contact with inmates; probation officers in particular felt that Coldingley's population now included more men who had problems needing specialist attention. And the prisoners lacked motivation to work, saying that the pay differential had been reduced and they received very little more for forty hours than inmates in other prisons who worked half as long.

In 1993 the Inspectors went again, and reported that the concept of an industrial prison had not been followed through. Coldingley was now neither an industrial prison nor a proper training one. The workshops' week had dropped to twenty-eight hours, the machinery was out of date, and financial planning was inadequate. About a third of the prisoners who were supposed to be at work were lounging about the wings or reporting sick. Education was now available in the daytime, but it was not linked with the industrial work. Morale among staff and prisoners was low. The Prison Department should decide, said the Chief Inspector, whether Coldingley was to be 'a normal training prison with a full range of work training, education and other activities' or a profitable industrial prison which motivated carefully selected inmates to work by paying them near-industrial pay. 'At present the prison is in a muddle and there is no consistent thought as to where or how it is going.'[33]

At a further visit in 1995 the Inspectors found great improvement on the industrial side. 'The resurrection of production industries from its moribund condition to its present buoyant state was a success story.'[34] The two workshops and the laundry now usually worked at a good pace with a seven-hour day, they had incentive schemes allowing prisoners to earn up to £30 a week through team productivity bonuses, and they were about to show a profit. The governor was aiming 'to establish Coldingley as a pilot industrial prison'. But at present it seemed that management effort had been focused on this at the expense of the rest of the regime, and the Inspectors were very critical of many aspects of the prison. Moreover, the industries still occupied only half the inmates, the others could not earn nearly so much, and it was said that many prisoners sent to Coldingley were unsuitable for the industrial work.

In its Corporate Plan for 1996–9[35] the Prison Service stated its intention to develop Coldingley as an industrial prison, thus returning to the project of nearly thirty years earlier. The vicissitudes of the intervening years show clearly the lack of planning to which the National Audit Office referred in 1987, and the ambivalence towards prison work which the Inspectors reported in 1988 (quoted below).

A mixed picture

By the end of the 1980s the annual reports of the Prison Service and the Inspectorate, read together, were giving a mixed picture of what was happening in prisons. A major development was the implementation from 1987 of 'Fresh Start', the new staffing scheme which the Home Office hoped would lead to industrial peace. Another event was the adoption from 1988 of the now well-known statement of purpose: 'Her Majesty's Prison Service serves the public by keeping in custody those committed by the courts. Our duty is to look after them with humanity and help them lead law-abiding and useful lives in custody and after release.'

And some good things were happening. Daytime education had expanded, more vocational courses were running, and National Vocational Qualifications

(NVQs) were slowly being introduced into prisoners' training in several kinds of work (beginning with catering, farming and clothing manufacture). Physical education was enabling more inmates to gain certificates which might help some find jobs on release. More establishments (eighty in 1988–9) were running officer-led pre-release courses, and prisoners were increasingly involved in voluntary work and other activities which kept them in touch with community groups outside.

But a principal finding by the Inspectors in 1988 was the great variation between individual prisons, even between some of the same type, in their provision for inmates. In physical conditions, staffing ratios, medical facilities and various aspects of regime the Inspectors found a great lack of consistency. On employment, they noted the under-use of workshops, great differences in the quality of work provided, the short working hours, interruptions for other purposes, and variable procedures for placing inmates in work. In summing up they said:[36]

> All of these problems – the lack of enough work in the prison system, staffing problems, unrealistic workshop criteria, the failure to make the best use of inmates' skills, the daily interruptions – reflect the ambivalence with which the role of work in prisons is seen.

Looking at prison history from the late eighteenth century up to the beginning of the 1990s, we see that prison work has been regarded in different ways at different times. Its purposes have been variously seen as: redemption from sin; an aid to discipline; teaching the virtues of labour; maintaining prisons; running them as profitable factories, or at least reducing their costs; alleviating the rigours of incarceration; building public works; punishment; deterrence; imparting good work habits; imparting trade skills; 'treatment and training'; and just keeping prisoners occupied. And every now and then one has a sense of *déjà vu*. Treadwheel, crank and oakum picking have long vanished, but down the years the same basic questions recur. Should prisoners work? If so, at what kinds of work, and for what reasons? How far should prison work resemble outside work? How far *can* it do so? Every two or three decades there has been an official inquiry into prison work, or into the wider prison system in which it takes place. The Gladstone Committee of 1895, the Departmental Committee of 1932, the Advisory Council of the early 1960s, the May Committee in 1979 – not to mention other critics like the National Audit Office or the Prisons Inspectorate – have all deliberated on the problems of prison work, within the other complexities of imprisonment and the shifting currents of penal philosophy.

So we come to the current decade and its landmark for British prisons: the Woolf Report. We consider what Woolf said about work, how the government responded, and what has happened since.

THE WOOLF REPORT AND AFTER

The disturbances of April 1990 which led to the Woolf Report were described by its authors as 'the worst series of prison riots in the history of the British penal system'. A basic cause, they said, was uncertainty springing from 'insufficient clarity about what the Prison Service should be doing and how it should do it. This affected the way prisons were run.' Discussing what the role of the Service should be, the authors saw it as one part of the criminal justice system, sharing with other parts 'a special responsibility for maintaining law, order and justice in society'. In prisons, they said, security, control and justice were fundamental, interdependent and must be kept in balance. Justice required humane conditions and fair dealing with the prisoner. And since one implicit purpose of the criminal justice system was to reduce crime, 'The Prison Service should therefore, as part of its role, be seeking to minimise the prospect of the prisoner re-offending after serving his sentence.'[37]

The authors endorsed, for sentenced prisoners, the Service's statement of purpose. They made it plain that they were not advocating a return to the 'treatment model' of imprisonment, but that

> the prison system...should give each prisoner every opportunity to serve his or her sentence in a constructive way....We must ensure that the Service makes proper use of the time which a prisoner spends in prison, and the best use of the money available for keeping him or her there. The aim must be to reduce the likelihood of prisoners re-offending after their release.

A prison regime should, among other things, encourage the offender to take some responsibility for himself in prison, give him an opportunity to obtain skills towards future employment, enable him to keep links with his family and community, and prepare him properly for his return to society. The Report's recommendations for dealing with prisoners amounted, said the authors, to 'a substantial agenda for reform'.[38]

Woolf on work

The Report dissented from PSIF's view (stated in evidence to the Woolf Inquiry) that it should run like a business aiming at a profit.

> We propose that workshops should instead be seen primarily as part of a planned programme of activities and opportunities for prisoners...the choice of industry and the capital invested should be strongly influenced by the need to provide constructive and purposeful employment in farm and workshop for as many prisoners as can usefully be deployed. It should be influenced also by the need to find work which is likely to assist the prisoner to find employment after release.[39]

Work opportunities should cater for a range of abilities among inmates, and domestic work should not be used as a long-term assignment. There should be a greater variety of arrangements for providing work: outside employers and Training and Enterprise Councils should be involved as advisers (as was already happening in some prisons); local firms might be invited to set up in prison work-shops; there should be schemes (as some prisons already had) for inmates to produce goods for charity. Moreover, the Report proposed that 'education should be given an equal standing to work within the activities of the prison'; prisons should have a planned programme which 'should bring together work, training and education in a way that provides the most constructive mix for the prisoners who are to be involved in it'.[40]

Governors should have the freedom and responsibility to provide and manage work at their own prisons, with PSIF withdrawing to a role of central adviser, consultant and supervisor. Prisoners' working hours should be more like those outside. On pay, the Report recommended that inmates should be able to earn more in order to meet some of their obligations and needs. Initially the Service should aim to raise pay to an average of £8 a week, and in the longer term rates should be much higher, so that prisoners could help maintain their families, contribute to the support of victims, perhaps pay towards their upkeep, and obtain extra facilities for themselves. 'A realistic wage would be a way of ensuring that the prisoner takes greater responsibility for himself in prison and outside.'[41]

The Home Office response to Woolf

This was set out in the White Paper *Custody, Care and Justice*,[42] published seven months after the Woolf Report. Woolf was broadly accepted:

> The Government...has examined closely each of the 12 central recommen-
> dations in the Report and all of its 204 supporting proposals. The Woolf
> Report describes the recommendations as signposts setting the direction for
> the Prison Service in the years ahead. The Government has accepted the
> direction set by those recommendations. It has accepted the principal
> proposals which identify the route to follow.[43]

The White Paper aimed to provide 'a coherent and consistent strategy for the Prison Service', and reading it shows that the Home Office planned to adopt a great deal of what Woolf had advocated, though they warned that it would take years to achieve and would depend on the resources available. They accepted Woolf's view of the Prison Service as a part of the criminal justice system, and in relation to the statement of purpose they saw the Service as having three central obligations, stated 'in order of priority, and indeed of ascending diffi-culty': to implement the court's decision (to imprison the offender); to provide a positive regime in prison; and to prepare the prisoner for release. Chapter 7 of the White Paper was devoted to 'Programmes for Prisoners', setting out inten-tions for giving all prisoners 'an active day'.[44]

On work, the White Paper's emphasis was somewhat different from Woolf's. While stating that programmes should aim 'to produce as full a range of activities and opportunities as the available resources will allow', it did not agree that education and work should have 'an equal standing'. Para. 7.25 said in part:

> The activities must be relevant to the prisoner on release and create as normal a working life as possible. It follows that work should have a central place in the life of the prison and that convicted prisoners should normally be expected to work....Daytime education should focus on providing basic education and skills and on encouraging and providing vocational training. Prisoners in full-time education should be enabled wherever possible to complete their courses. Other education activities must not be seen as alternatives to these provisions or to participating in available work.[45]

Thus the Home Office opinion was that for most prisoners work was a fundamental requirement. Para. 7.22 set out the official view on the purposes of prison work:

> Work has a central role in the prison regime. It ensures that convicted prisoners contribute to the cost of their upkeep by helping with the running and maintenance of the prison and by providing goods and services in prison industries and on prison farms. The prison day needs to be arranged to make best and fullest use of the work available. Workshops allow industrial skills to be practised; farm work offers externally recognised qualifications. The pace and type of work should be closer to work in the community. Experience of regular work in prison can be a useful preparation for seeking a job on release.[46]

It was intended, said the White Paper, to improve quality in prison workshops by introducing British Standard 5750; to consider pilot schemes increasing the involvement of private employers; to enable governors to improve the management of their workshops and to identify potential local sources of work; and to extend considerably prisoners' access to NVQs through workplace training, education and other activities. On pay, the Service would initially aim, when resources allowed, at Woolf's suggested average of £8 a week, and would explore ways of funding higher pay levels from workers' increased productivity.[47]

The House of Commons Employment Committee

In mid-1991 the House of Commons Employment Committee, inspired by the Woolf Report (which had been published in February) considered prison work and employment for ex-prisoners, taking evidence from a range of concerned organisations including the Prison Service.[48] By the time the Committee reported in November *Custody, Care and Justice* had been published, and the Committee took this into account in their own report. Their recommendations emphasised several themes, among which were: the importance of sentence planning and focusing on prisoners' needs; increasing working hours and pay to more realistic levels; the importance of giving prisoners training, whether by education or work ('ideally, there should be no place in the prison system for work which exists merely to pass the time'); more help to prisoners to move into jobs or training on release; and that the Prison Service should set target dates for their intended improvements.[49]

Replying to the Committee's report, the Home Office and the Employment Department largely reiterated the relevant proposals of the White Paper and indicated current progress.[50]

Developing policy and practice on prison work

From 1992 Prison Service HQ was active in developing policy and practice. In the middle of that year a policy statement issued to governors[51] on 'the nature and balance of regime activities' included among other key points the following:

> All prisoners should take part in constructive activity. For convicted adult prisoners this should be work for most of their sentence. Therefore a substantial majority of daytime activity places – for adult sentenced prisoners – should be work based.

The statement set the following criteria for judging prison work:

- Is the work experience realistic compared with that likely to be found outside, in terms of: acceptance of responsibility; hours of attendance; production processes/technology; interaction with others (supervisors, workmates); incentives for good work/penalties for poor performance; chances of the inmate getting that kind of job outside; the pace of work?
- Does the work fit the aptitude of the prisoners concerned (demanding enough, but not too demanding)?
- Does the work teach specific trades or skills which are sought after by outside employers? Is there opportunity for those who gain such skills to acquire qualifications and can skills already possessed be maintained and accredited?
- How much does the work contribute to the upkeep of the establishment or of the prison system (net cost or contribution per place of the work activity concerned)? (The assessment needs to take into account the extent to which the activity concerned makes cost-effective use of existing assets.)
- Does the work generate earnings which the offender can use: for the upkeep of his or her family; to pay compensation to the victim of his or her offence?
- Can the products of the prisoners' work be used to support charitable causes?
- What other positive regime activities are available to make full use of the prisoners' day, and how does their cost compare?

Later a PSIF document,[52] repeating this list, said it was in descending order of priority, thus implying that the degree to which prison work is like outside work, and the extent to which it prepares prisoners for outside jobs, were seen as more important than its contribution to maintaining the prison system. This relative emphasis is an interesting contrast to that implied in para. 7.22 of the White Paper (quoted on p. 15), which gave first mention to contributing to the cost of the system and last mention to preparing the prisoner for employment on release.

The Prison Service annual report for the year ending March 1993 described existing practices and several new developments which were in line with the recommendations of Woolf or the House of Commons Committee, including:[53]

- a new pay scheme from December 1992, raising the average prison pay from about £3.30 a week to £6;
- pilot schemes at selected prisons, paying selected inmates more realistic wages with deductions for board, savings and tax;
- pilot schemes for involving private firms directly in employing inmates;
- co-operation, at several prisons, with Training and Enterprise Councils for the benefit of inmates;
- the increasing availability in prisons of NVQs for various kinds of training;
- schemes to allow prisoners near release to work outside in ordinary jobs;
- several schemes, including prison jobclubs funded by the Employment Service, to give prisoners more help in moving into work or training upon release.

In addition to all this, responsibility for providing and managing work was gradually devolved to individual prisons, with PSIF, later renamed Prison Enterprise Services, offering central advice and support as Woolf had recommended.

Such, in brief outline, were the Prison Service's hopes and intentions for prison work in the year or so immediately following the Woolf Report. As the White Paper had warned, much of what Woolf had recommended would take years to achieve, and from 1993 onwards official indications of progress were given in the Service's annual reports and in other documents such as the annual business plans.

RECENT MAJOR CHANGES

The developments in prison work described above took place in a context of rapid and major changes in the Service. From January 1993 it had a new Director General, Derek Lewis, a former businessman. Addressing his senior managers he said: 'I have a broad and simple brief to continue – and I hope accelerate – the reforms recommended by Woolf and outlined in the *Custody, Care and Justice* White Paper. And to improve value for money.'[54] A new 'mission statement' for the Service was issued, which reiterated the existing statement of purpose and then set out 'vision, goals and values'.[55] From April 1993 the Service became an executive agency instead of a department of the Home Office. A three-year corporate plan and a one-year business plan (both to be updated annually) were promulgated, along with performance indicators to measure how far goals were being achieved. (For example, the goal 'provision of positive regimes' was to be measured partly by the average number of hours per week prisoners spent in purposeful activities, one of which was work.) Plans were made to devolve more power to establishments, and a code of standards was prepared. By November 1993 Ian Dunbar, addressing the annual Prison Service conference, said that the Service had found a sense of direction and that Woolf had been a turning point. 'Following Woolf and the White Paper, we have never had such a pragmatic programme and such a profound sense of direction....We do have a very much better Prison Service now.'[56]

But since then there have been other changes, some of which have continued the direction welcomed by Dunbar while others have worked against it. Several have had significant potential for affecting prisoners' work and training, and we now look at these matters one by one. (Whether, and how, they actually affected work and training are addressed in later chapters.)

Tighter security

From the beginning of 1995, following the escape from Whitemoor in September 1994, the heavily critical Woodcock Report[57] on that matter in December, and the escape from Parkhurst in January, the Prison Service turned attention and resources towards preventing further escapes. Prisons had more fences built, both round the perimeter and internally between sections of them, as well as investing in more hardware and dogs; staff spent more time counting and searching prisoners; staff training emphasised greater security awareness; other procedures were stepped up. In December 1994 the Director General had set 'security first and foremost'[58] among the Service's priorities for the coming year, and the 1994–5 annual report said: 'We have refocused our attention and energies so that security is *the* key area for both immediate and future concern.'[59]

The pressure to concentrate on security became even greater after the publication in October 1995 of the Learmont Report[60] on prison security, which like Woodcock was in many parts severely critical. Amid public uproar the Home Secretary (Michael Howard) sacked Derek Lewis as Director General, and eventually Richard Tilt, a former prison governor who had been the Service's director of security, was appointed in his stead.

Clearly, if prisoners' movements are restricted and staff are preoccupied with surveillance, opportunities for work and training in prison may be diminished. In addition, from April 1995 the arrangements for allowing certain prisoners temporary release on licence were replaced by more restrictive ones which reduced the number of licences granted by 40 per cent.[61] This would be expected to decrease inmates' opportunities, for example, to have work experience or training courses outside the prison.

Increasing prison population

In 1991, the year of the Woolf Report, the prison population averaged 44,800 (in round figures, and excluding prisoners held in police cells). For 1992, 1993, 1994 and 1995 the figures were 44,700, 44,600, 48,600 and 51,000. Details showed that, after a welcome drop to around 42,000 at the end of 1992, the population rose steeply (apart from the usual seasonal dip each December), mainly due to the increasing use, from 1993, of custodial sentences by magistrates' and Crown Courts and of longer sentences by Crown Courts.[62] By July 1996 it exceeded 56,000. The Home Office had estimated in March 1995 that the level of 56,000 would not be reached until the year 2002;[63] a year later they thought this would happen in the year 2001;[64] but still the number of prisoners rose faster than the projection. By spring 1997 the population was 60,000 and still climbing.

Women prisoners, while only about 4 per cent of the total, increased in numbers much more quickly than the men. Between 1992 and 1996 the male prison population increased by 20 per cent but the female one rose by 43 per cent, while the annual number of receptions rose by 24 per cent for males but 44 per cent for females.[65] This had particular implications for Holloway Prison, as will appear in Chapter 2.

It is obvious that such rapidly increasing numbers must put a great strain on prison staff. In almost every month in 1994, 1995 and 1996 the total number of prisoners exceeded the total number of prison places available ('in-use certified normal accommodation')[66] and as always it was the local adult prisons that bore the brunt of overcrowding. The chairman of the Prison Governors' Association said in September 1995, 'Prison overcrowding destroys positive regimes. In an overcrowded prison, staff and management time is devoted to basic survival.'[67] One would expect the adverse effect on work and training to be worst at local prisons, but there could be consequences at other prisons too, if staff had to cope with a greater turnover of prisoners because of the pressure to find spaces somewhere in the system for the swelling numbers.

Privatisation

Privatisation of parts of the Prison Service, a process which gathered pace from mid-1992, could take any of three basic forms. The first was the contracting out of particular functions, such as escorting prisoners to court. Referring to the latter, Prison Service HQ said, 'It will relieve prison and police officers of a non-core task and enable them to concentrate on core duties,'[68] although it also led to a reduction in staff posts. To the extent that core duties involve assisting inmates to take part in work and training, prisoners would be expected to benefit. Another function which has been contracted out is prison education services, which include a good deal of the vocational training prisoners receive. Until 1993 all these were provided by local colleges of further education through contracts with local education authorities. But after that year, for each prison any interested body could tender direct for the supply of prisoners' education, and while some contracts were let to the same providers as before, others went to different ones. The transition involved demoralising uncertainty for prison teachers, but it was conceivable that the new system, once it had settled down, might have some advantages for prisoners. A national curriculum was devised, including a core curriculum of basic skills, information technology and 'life and social skills'. In 1996 the Chief Education Officer said that the contractual relationship between the Service and providers had 'encouraged goodwill, clarity of purpose and the development of effective practice'.[69]

The second form of privatisation was the 'market testing' of a whole existing prison, inviting bids for its management from private bodies and from the existing staff. The first such case was Manchester, narrowly won by its own staff in 1993. The Prisons Board intended to select other existing prisons for market testing, and the Director General explained that these would be 'those where the most scope for performance improvement exists and where there is the least evidence of progress'.[70] Thus the prospect of market testing could, in theory, spur existing prisons to improve their regimes, including training and work, for inmates.

The third method of privatisation was for the private sector to manage (and in some cases, design, build and finance) a new prison from its outset. The first such was Wolds, which opened in 1992, and there have since been several more, the Home Secretary having announced in September 1993 the intention to have twelve privately run prisons, or about 10 per cent of the total. This book does not cover work and training in privately managed prisons. But we may note the statement of the Prisons Board (accompanying the Home Secretary's announcement) which explained its approach to the role of the private sector in providing prison services. Competition was seen as a stimulus:

> The Board is committed to securing continuing and lasting improvements in standards, quality and value-for-money across the whole of the prison system in England and Wales....Carefully managed, operating to a common code of standards and measured by the same performance indicators, private sector involvement can provide creative and constructive competition which will be to the ultimate benefit of the prison system as a whole.[71]

One would therefore hope that private involvement in prisons would, directly or indirectly, lead among other things to better work and training opportunities for inmates generally.

Sentence planning

Assessment by prison staff of a new prisoner's needs, followed by efforts to help him or her address them during sentence through whatever facilities the prison could offer, had been going on for many years in some prisons, for some prisoners. But from 1992 the Prison Service tried to put it on a regular basis by a national scheme of sentence planning, in response to proposals of the Woolf Report[72] and to the new sentencing structure brought in by the Criminal Justice Act 1991. Sentence planning was introduced in October 1992 for all sentenced Category A prisoners and for all others who were sentenced to four years or more from the first of that month, and in autumn 1993 it was extended to all prisoners sentenced to a year or more.

The aims of sentence planning, in the words of the Prison Service, were:

> to make the best use of the time people have to spend in custody, to reduce the risk of their re-offending and to help them lead law-abiding and useful lives in custody and after release. It links work on helping prisoners to tackle their offending behaviour with planned experience of work, training and education. It provides opportunities to review the prisoner's progress throughout the sentence. It is also the mechanism for co-ordinating work done in prison with work done with prisoners who will have a period of compulsory supervision after release.[73]

In 1995 a joint working party of the Prison Service and Probation Service carried out a review of sentence planning and found that the working of the national system was very patchy.[74] During the next year it was revised, and 1997 saw the introduction of the redeveloped scheme which is described on p. 209.

One would expect that sentence planning, once properly in operation, would not only affect decisions in regard to individual prisoners about what work and training they would undertake during sentence, but would also influence the programmes of work and training that prisons provide. These matters are discussed in Chapter 7 in the light of our research findings.

Inmate development programmes

Under this heading we include mainly those prison activities designed directly to help prisoners address their offending behaviour, in line with the intention expressed in *Custody, Care and Justice* to 'give sentenced prisoners every opportunity to acquire the skills and resolve necessary not to commit further crimes'.[75] Of course in earlier decades probation officers, psychologists and psychiatrists in some prisons worked with small numbers of inmates towards that objective, as did counsellors from outside agencies especially in relation to alcohol and drugs abuse. Increasing numbers of prison officers were trained to participate. But in 1991 the Prison Service began a substantial effort to expand and co-ordinate such work and to encourage a multi-disciplinary approach to it by prison staff.

That year saw the introduction of a nationally devised treatment programme for sex offenders, which by 1995 was running in twenty-two selected prison establishments to which prisoners could be sent in order to take it. The sex offender programme comprised a period of intensive assessment, a core treatment programme, then lasting about 140 hours (seventy sessions), a booster (relapse prevention) programme, and a variety of other modules depending on the individual offender's needs.[76] By 1992 other courses for prisoners had been developed in anger management and in cognitive skills, the latter based on the 'Reasoning and Rehabilitation' training for offenders developed by Ross *et al.* in Canada.[77, 78]

This growth continued in subsequent years. The 1995 review of sentence planning found that prisons between them were running courses on a great variety of subjects, including among others alcohol and substance abuse, anger management, relationships, sex offending, motor vehicle offending and domestic violence. In 1996 Prison Service HQ was planning for the accreditation of offending behaviour programmes, and that the number of inmates completing an accredited programme a prison provided would be one of a prison's 'key perfomance indicators'. This development and its implications are discussed on p. 210.

Besides such programmes, many prisons had for some years been running pre-release courses, often known as pre-release and inmate development courses. These offered prisoners near release information about employment, housing, benefits and so on, but also some training in social skills, self-presentation and avoidance of offending. Prison education classes could also include social skills. All these things, together with work, vocational training and education, were regarded by the Prison Service as helping to provide positive regimes for prisoners, and they contributed to the Service's key performance indicator of the number of hours spent in purposeful activity.[79] The reason for mentioning them in the present context is that we shall argue later that work and vocational training on the one hand, and programmes addressing offending behaviour on the other could, *if* adequately provided, be mutually reinforcing in helping ex-prisoners to avoid further crime.

Incentive schemes

In 1995 the Prison Service announced a 'national framework for incentives and earned privileges'.[80] This developed from pilot schemes that had been running in several prisons, and the intention was to have the national framework in place throughout the system by the end of the year. It set three levels of facilities which prisoners could earn 'through responsible behaviour and participation in hard work and other constructive activity'. These were: basic level, the minimum to which all inmates were entitled (unless removed as a punishment for indiscipline); standard level; and enhanced level, which carried extra rewards for superior conduct. An alternative name for the scheme was 'differential regimes'.

The three levels were linked to four kinds of facilities or 'key earnable privileges': access to private cash (limited, for convicted prisoners, to a weekly maximum of £2.50 at basic level, £10 at standard, and £15 at enhanced); extra or better visits; eligibility to take part in enhanced earnings schemes; and opportunities, for certain groups only, of community visits (i.e. going with their visitors outside the prison). In addition, two other facilities might be available in a part of a prison where all inmates had reached the same level: inmates could wear their own clothes, and have more time out of cell for association. The aims of the national framework were stated as follows:

> To ensure that privileges generally are earned by prisoners through good behaviour and performance and are removable if prisoners fail to maintain acceptable standards; to encourage responsible behaviour by prisoners; to encourage hard work and other constructive activity by prisoners; to encourage prisoners to progress through the prison system; and to create a more disciplined, better controlled and safer environment for prisoners and staff.

Individual prisons were required to devise their own incentive schemes within the national framework, so there was room for local variation. It can be seen that a scheme might relate to prisoners' work and training in two ways. Inmates' motivation to work, at whatever task they were set, might be encouraged by hope of promotion to a higher level; but also, access to particular kinds of work, or training courses, could be one of the incentives in a local scheme.

Budget cuts

In its Corporate Plan for 1995–8, published in May 1995,[81] the Prison Service had planned to reduce unit costs by 8.6 per cent between 1994–5 and 1997–8, apart from spending on security measures to implement the Woodcock Report. However, following the Chancellor's Budget statement in November 1995, prison governors were told at the end of that month that, after allowing for spending on Woodcock and on the new drugs strategy,[82] they had to reduce costs by an average of 4–5 per cent a year, or about 13.5 per cent altogether, in the three years from April 1996. The Prison Governors' Association immediately issued a statement saying, 'The budgetary settlements announced by the Prison Service today clearly indicate that there will be insufficient money in 1996 for Governors to deliver effective regimes.'[83]

The Director General, at a conference in December of governors and senior managers, stressed 'the importance which I attach to maintaining the balance between security and control on the one hand and rehabilitation and justice on the other, and the importance of supporting continuity and stability in the system', and said that cutting regimes should be the last resort in the effort to reduce costs.[84] The 1996–9 Corporate Plan outlined a varied programme for achieving economies, and its section on regimes set a target for 1996–7 of ensuring that prisoners would spend on average at least twenty-six and a half hours a week in 'purposeful activity', as against the average of just over twenty-five hours achieved in the previous year.[85]

Despite such indications of official determination and optimism, it is hard to believe that inmates' work and training might not suffer from the financial constraints, especially when these pressures came on top of those caused by the rising population and the increased concentration on security. One of the cost-cutting measures in 1996 included a plan to lose about 1,500 prison staff posts by voluntary redundancy and early retirement, in which the officers most likely to be paid off were among the longest-serving and most experienced.[86] Moreover, the budget cuts were imposed at a time when, following Woolf,[87] individual prisons were gradually being given more financial autonomy[88] (a process loosely spoken of as 'governors' budgets'). As a result each governor had the freedom to decide, within limits, how to achieve the required saving at his or her own prison, and one of the consequences could be that some prisons cut provision for inmates' education or training while others did not. In 1996 the Chief Inspector was severely critical of this unplanned, piecemeal approach to economy.[89]

THE BRUNEL STUDY

This was conceived in 1992 as an evaluation of the work and vocational training done by sentenced prisoners at adult prisons, with specific objectives as follows:

1 To describe the nature of prison work and work-related training at a sample of prisons, and to compare it with work and training in the same industries outside prison.

2 To describe the employment experiences of a sample of prisoners leaving prison establishments, and to examine how their experiences on release correlated with the work and training opportunities offered to them during sentence.

3 To describe how prisoners experienced and perceived the work and training they did in prison, in relation to (a) the totality of their sentence and their confinement while serving it, and (b) their work and training careers before sentence and after release.

Information for the research was gathered in several ways which are summarised below. A more detailed account of most of the research methods has been published elsewhere.[90]

Visits to prisons

Six large prisons participated in the study: Channings Wood (Category C), Highpoint (Category C), Holloway (local, female), Kirkham (Category D), Liverpool (local) and Maidstone (Category B). (No dispersal prison was included.) These six, having populations of between 400 and 1,100 inmates, were chosen by agreement with the Home Office so as to include between them prisons in all security categories except Category A, with examples of male and female, open and closed, local and training establishments, and having a broad geographical spread; and to offer a wide range of work and training courses for inmates. Training prisons (which hold roughly half of all adult males in the prison population) were over-represented in the sample, but this was not inappropriate for a study focusing on work and training.[91]

All the main kinds of work employing inmates across the six prisons were studied, including seven types of industrial workshop supported by Prison Service Industries and Farms (as it was then), farm and gardens work, and non-PSIF work including kitchens and other domestic tasks, building maintenance ('the Works') and some other jobs employing fewer prisoners, like orderlies and clerks. Altogether the kinds of work studied included all those which employed at least 1 per cent of working prisoners in the population (except for light engineering which was not carried on in any of the sample prisons: see p. 62 and Table 1), plus some smaller ones. Training courses studied included four types of construction industry training course which at the time were run by Works departments, and eight other types of vocational course run by education departments.

Academic (non-vocational) education, at basic or higher level, was not part of the study's focus. But at each prison we noted the arrangements for providing it, and the education officer was among prison staff interviewed. Our sample of 178 inmate interviewees, described below, included fifteen who at the time were occupied in daytime education and whose opinions could be compared with those of others occupied in prison work. All inmates interviewed were asked briefly about any experience of prison education, and this was taken into account in some of the analyses of post-release employment.

At the six prisons the researchers observed sessions of work, training and some other activities (e.g. labour allocation boards), studied documents, and interviewed staff and prisoners. The staff interviewees were a purposive sample selected as key informants, and at each prison they included the governing governor (or deputy),[92] some senior managers, prison officers of several grades, education and probation officers, instructors of inmates at work (whom we refer to as work instructors), and tutors in charge of training courses (whom we refer to as trainers, without at all implying that the work instructors did not train). Altogether 108 staff were interviewed.

A total of 178 inmates in the six prisons were interviewed, being those who consented (and were available) out of 251 who were asked (so the response rate was 71 per cent). The prisoners asked were chosen to include all those serving sentences of between one and ten years and who were within one to three months of release, and a random selection of others who were near the middle of a sentence of between four and ten years. Priority was given to those near release so as to yield a pool large enough to achieve a good sample of follow-up interviews later (see p. 27), and long-termers were included to give some representation of people whose release dates were some years off. People serving sentences of less than a year were excluded because of their probably limited experience of prison work or training during the current sentence, and those serving over ten years were also excluded. The obtained sample of 178 comprised 134 prisoners near release and forty-four long-term ones.

These 178 people included fourteen women and twenty-seven people of ethnic minorities. Fifty-five per cent were under 30 years old and 83 per cent were under 40. Forty-one per cent had been imprisoned for acquisitive crime (burglary, theft, fraud, etc.) and 35 per cent for violence or robbery. Eleven per cent had been sentenced for drugs crime, but interviews with some of the burglars revealed that their activities had been drugs-related too. Thirty-seven per cent were serving sentences of no more than eighteen months, 34 per cent between eighteen months and four years, and 29 per cent over four years. Two-thirds had had at least one previous custodial sentence and 37 per cent had had at least three. As regards occupational background, 37 per cent were classed (by the researchers) as skilled workers, 43 per cent as semi-skilled and 20 per cent as unskilled. Each of these groups contained some people who had been unemployed before coming into prison; altogether 41 per cent of the sample had been wholly or largely unemployed during the previous twelve months.

Various tests were carried out to see how far the sample represented the adult prison population generally.[93] In regard to age and the proportion of ethnic minority inmates there was a fairly close match. The sample had a higher proportion of women prisoners than the population due to the inclusion of Holloway, but at 8 per cent they were still a very small group.[94] In regard to sentence length the sample, through being weighted in favour of people near release, had rather more with sentences of eighteen months or less than the population, and there was a corresponding difference in the types of offence for which they were imprisoned: the sample contained relatively fewer people imprisoned for violence and sex offences and more imprisoned for burglary, theft or fraud. Nevertheless all the main types of offence were represented in the sample. And as in the National Prison Survey,[95] a majority of the research sample had some degree of occupational skill.

At the time of interview 150 of the inmates in the sample were assigned to various kinds of prison work, thirteen were in vocational training courses, and fifteen were in other daytime education classes. The immediate focus of the interview was on this occupation and the respondent's perceptions of it, and experiences of other prison work and training during this or any previous sentence were also explored. Other topics included biographical data (especially employment history outside prison), other aspects of prison life and (for those near release) hopes and plans for release.

As well as the interviews with 178 inmates, brief chats about prison work and training were held with 139 others during some of the activity sessions, and this material contributed to the findings.

Follow-up of ex-prisoners

The 134 people interviewed in prison near their release date were asked if they would give the researchers a second interview three months after coming out. All but five were willing in principle, but various practical difficulties later reduced the number who were reached. Eventually eighty-eight follow-up interviews were held, most of them between three and five months from release, when many of the respondents were scattered far and wide in England and Wales.[96]

The follow-up sample was thus 66 per cent of those originally targeted. A comparison between them and the other forty-six people suggested that the eighty-eight were perhaps slightly 'easier' cases, but not much. Both groups had a substantial proportion of people with considerable criminal records. Compared with released adult prisoners in general, the eighty-eight were fairly representative in respect of age and gender; their distribution of broad types of offence was fairly similar except that they included more people who had been imprisoned for burglary and robbery, and fewer imprisoned for offences like motoring crime and criminal damage, owing to the exclusion from the inmate sample of people sentenced to less than one year.

The main focus of the follow-up interviews was the person's history of job-search and employment since release. Other topics included any plans for training, financial circumstances, further offending and the respondent's perceptions, in retrospect, of his or her time in prison.

Visits to outside employers

Twelve outside firms were visited, corresponding to ten of the main kinds of work studied in the prisons (see Chapter 3). At each visit the researcher observed production processes and interviewed at least one manager. (Shopfloor employees, who may be considered as outside counterparts to prison inmates, were not interviewed.) The interviews covered many of the same topics as had been explored with prison staff (especially work instructors): the organisation of the work, and conditions including hours and pay; recruitment methods and expectations of new recruits; training given and levels of skill acquired; motivation and discipline; and the labour market in that industry. Managers were also asked whether they would employ ex-prisoners.

The twelve firms were a haphazard sample, having only one or two of each kind (and within the research timetable no more would have been practicable). It is not possible to say how representative their views were (for example, on the employment of ex-prisoners). Nevertheless the visits yielded valuable data to compare with prison work. It happened that at least six of the firms were noticeably high-class examples of their kind, which was no bad thing for the research in view of the emphasis in prison industries on high quality, as will be seen later.

Other information

Visits were made to four large providers of training under the government's 'Training For Work' scheme (formerly called 'Employment Training'). The researcher interviewed staff at each one and a few trainees at two of them. The schemes were selected as ones which were willing to take ex-prisoners along with other clients, and the information gathered in the visits was used in two ways: to compare with training in prisons, and as background to the questions in the follow-up study about the use made of such training schemes by ex-prisoners.

Discussions were held with senior staff of the local Training and Enterprise Council nearest to each of the six prisons, and with one other London TEC. Topics included the kinds of work and training done at the prison, provision of training outside and the local labour market. Additional background information on work in farms and gardens, and in the leather and clothing industries, was obtained from two training colleges and a trade association. These bodies also facilitated some of the visits to outside firms.

Updating and additional material

The fieldwork so far described was carried out in 1992 and 1993, when the Prison Service's new policies for prison work, described on pp. 16–17, were just beginning to be put into effect (though some features, such as prison jobclubs, already existed). So what we saw then was largely a pre-Woolf picture of prison work, which might be regarded as a baseline against which the new measures, once bedded in, could be assessed. During the spring of 1996 we revisited the five male prisons in order to update our material. These were shorter visits: we did not talk with inmates or observe work sessions. But we held long interviews with senior managers responsible for inmates' work and training, and talked with other staff including education and probation officers. We were given much documentary material, and held some supplementary discussions by telephone. We told interviewees of our 1992–3 findings for their prison, and sought to learn what had changed since then, especially in regard to the arrangements for work and training but also on related topics such as sentence planning and inmate development programmes. Among other things, we looked for any impact of other factors mentioned in the last section – tighter security, rising numbers, privatisation, incentive schemes and budget cuts. Holloway Prison was not included in these updating visits, but some information was gathered from published sources.[97] All this updating information, together with reports of the Inspectorate, has been drawn on to supplement and modify, where relevant, our earlier data.

Additional material for the research was supplied in 1996 and 1997 by various sections of Prison Service HQ, especially in relation to regime monitoring, the development of NVQs, the work of Prison Enterprise Services, pre-release provision, sentence planning and offending behaviour programmes. This enabled us to put data from the six prisons into a national context, so that although much of the book is based on what was learned from them we also indicate, at appropriate points, the general provision for prison work and training throughout the system.

A note on the use of interview data

The research findings in total came from a variety of data. Some depended to a large extent on what prisoners and ex-prisoners told us in confidential interviews, and we deliberately took no steps to check the personal information they gave us against other sources, feeling that to do so would have been a breach of trust.[98] This meant that some of the interview data was of variable quality.

In the interviews with prisoners the primary topic – prison work and training – was relatively non-threatening. Many inmates seemed glad of the opportunity to talk to the researchers: they answered with apparent frankness and some were reflective and thoughtful, offering insights and suggestions which we took into account. Other people were more reticent. In the course of conversation inmates told us about other aspects of prison life, and no doubt some were trying to impress us while other matters were concealed. Some biographical data was probably subject to selection, exaggeration, distortion or failures of recall, but prisoners are not alone in this respect. Probably some prison staff also were careful in what they said to us. Most interviews with inmates lasted about an hour but some, especially at Liverpool, had to be shorter because of the prison routine, and not all the desired topics could be covered with every informant.

The follow-up interviews were usually more relaxed than the prison ones, with many of the respondents talking very freely (even when, as occasionally happened, other family members were present). Some people may not have remembered all that was said to them by, for example, staff at jobcentres or probation offices, so that our findings may understate the service actually offered by various agencies. On the topic of further offending, some interviewees were naturally reticent, and we have had to omit from some analyses in Chapter 6 twenty-four cases in which we think the interviewer did not gather sufficient information (though it is not suggested that all those people would have been recorded as offenders if we had learned more). On the other hand, some people volunteered information even before the interviewer had raised the matter, while others seemed relieved to talk about it once the topic had been broached.

If our figures on prisoners' and ex-prisoners' situations are taken as objective measures of fact there will be some gaps. But a major concern of the study was with people's experiences as they themselves perceived them, which is what is likely to influence their attitudes and behaviour. Self-report data has a respectable place in criminology: see, for example, Hirschi *et al.* (1980)[99] and the useful discussion by Graham and Bowling (1995).[100] By integrating what inmates and ex-inmates told us with what was learned from prison staff and other people, and with what we observed ourselves, we hope we have produced a balanced picture of prison work and training, using both qualitative and quantitative data.[101]

PLAN OF THE BOOK

This first chapter has set the scene for the rest. We began by surveying the history of prison work from the eighteenth century to the present decade, noting the shifting variety of its stated purposes within the prison system and the changes which have taken place in the latter. We looked at what Woolf said about prison work, at the development of official policy and practice since then, and at how the principle that 'work should have a central place in the life of the prison' may have been affected in the last few years by other major concerns like security. Then we outlined the methods used in the Brunel research which is the main basis of the book.

Chapters 2, 3, 4 and 5 are mainly descriptive, gradually building up the evidence on which our analyses and arguments in Chapters 6 and 7 are based. Chapter 2 comprises pen pictures of each of the six prisons which participated in the research, to give the reader an idea of what they were like to live and work in. Topics include the types of prisoners held, the atmosphere of the prison, the occupations available to inmates and the means by which they were assigned to them, and some other features of the prisons' regimes which were important in relation to inmates' work and training.

Chapter 3 is introduced by an examination of what prisoners wanted by way of occupation during their sentence. Then after summarising the national provision of prison work the main part of the chapter describes particular kinds, largely as we saw them at the six establishments visited. We describe what the workers did, how their tasks were organised, and how they felt about their work. Ten of these pictures are followed by the examples we saw of similar work in outside industry, with comments on the comparisons. Several other types of prison work are also described.

Chapter 4 examines general features of work in prison, including the working atmosphere and relationships, the amount of responsibility given to prisoners, and their degrees of job satisfaction. We look at what the work instructors aimed to achieve with inmates, and what contact they had with their industries outside prison. The benefits of prison work to prisoners, and its resemblance to outside work, are examined from the viewpoints of staff and inmates. And we present the findings of an exercise measuring the perceptions by staff and prisoners of the purposes of prison work, which in the light of the history sketched in Chapter 1 is a fundamental question.

Chapter 5 addresses vocational training in prisons. It describes the development of NVQs, the training courses available at the six prisons, problems of co-ordination and continuity, and the levels of skill inmates achieved. We compare prison courses with four outside training schemes, and describe a special scheme which ran for a few years at Channings Wood. We list a number of practical suggestions for improving training which were offered by staff and inmates.

Chapter 6 begins by considering what things could help ex-prisoners avoid crime in future. Then it follows the fortunes of the eighty-eight ex-prisoners in the research sample during their first few months in the outside world. After looking at ways in which the six prisons prepared inmates for release, we examine the success or otherwise of the eighty-eight in finding work, relating this both to their pre-sentence work records and to the work and training they did in prison. The first part of this analysis is statistical, showing what effect the prison experience had on subsequent employment once the pre-prison experience was allowed for. The second part is qualitative, looking at ex-prisoners' attempts to use their prison experience and at various factors which influenced their efforts. Further sections of the chapter are concerned with people's financial circumstances during the follow-up period, whether they committed further crimes, and links between these matters and unemployment. Finally we report how the ex-prisoners looked back on their time in prison: whether they felt they had learned anything useful from it, and what they wished it had done for them.

Chapter 7 pulls together all our material and discusses the implications. We argue that the centuries-old confusion about the purposes of prison work continues today, and that neither the public nor prisoners are well served by this state of affairs. We maintain, from evidence, that the primary purpose of prison work and training should be to help prisoners (those who want it, and most do) to get work on release; and that if this aim is given priority it will also make prisons easier to manage, as inmates are occupied in ways which they feel give them worthwhile opportunities.

The chapter draws on published surveys and economic forecasts to consider the changing world of work: the kinds of jobs available and the skills and qualities successful job applicants require. We examine prison work and training in this light, looking at the relevance of prison work to outside job prospects, the vocational training prisoners receive, and how far prisons equip them with the personal competence needed for success in the world of work. We argue that prisons have good potential, at present largely unused, for training inmates. Ideas are put forward for improved linking of vocational courses with prison jobs, and for making better use of the potential of the instructors who play a central role in working prisoners' daily lives. We discuss how outside employers and TECs can contribute, and we advocate a scheme, here termed employment throughcare, which would enable prisoners to make the best use of opportunities and which would fit well inside the Prison Service's framework for sentence planning. Then we broaden the discussion by invoking 'what works' principles, and argue that if they were applied to prison work and training these could really become a significant factor in helping prisoners to become law-abiding citizens. In concluding, we discuss the crisis facing the Prison Service as the 1990s draw to a close, and appeal for the change of public attitudes necessary to allow the Service to do constructive work.

2 Six prisons

INTRODUCTION

Prisons are all subject to the Prison Rules and to central control by Prison Service HQ. They vary according to their function, size and security classification. But each prison also has an individual character stemming from its locality, history and tradition. Since 1993 the scope for individuality has increased, following the recommendation of the Woolf Report that governors should be given more responsibility for managing their own prisons. By 1995 governors had a good deal of autonomy in regard to business planning and budget control,[1] and at the time of our updating visits in 1996 this devolution was continuing. Thus, within limits, governors could respond in different ways to the recent pressures and changes described in Chapter 1.

The six prisons which participated in the research were chosen for their representation of a range of features, as stated on p. 25, but they also illustrate the individuality just mentioned. This will become apparent in this chapter, which offers the reader a brief description of each prison. Our purpose is to convey some idea of what they were like to live and work in, and especially to show the different arrangements each had for providing prisoners with the work and training which we examine more generally in Chapters 3–5. Here we indicate what occupations were available at each prison, how inmates were steered into them, and what choices people had. We also look briefly at two other features of the prisons' regimes: incentive schemes, which are relevant to the consideration in Chapter 4 of prisoners' motives for working; and inmate development programmes which, it will be argued in Chapter 7, should be integrated with work and training to give inmates the best prospects of becoming responsible citizens.

The descriptions start with what we saw in 1992–3 and note any relevant later changes up to the time of our visit in 1996. They will illustrate how governors were beginning to implement the Prison Service's policy on work and training following the Woolf Report and *Custody, Care and Justice*, and how their efforts were affected by increasing security, budget cuts and other constraints.

As well as the types of work and training listed below for each prison, all the prisons employed some inmates in kitchens, gardens, Works departments (building maintenance), cleaning and other domestic duties, and as stores assistants, orderlies and clerks. All the prisons offered general education to some inmates.

CHANNINGS WOOD

Population and buildings

Channings Wood Prison in Devon was a Category C establishment holding about 580 male prisoners. In 1992 nearly all of them were serving sentences of more than eighteen months; about half were serving more than four years, and between forty and sixty were lifers. By 1996 the population had changed slightly: the great majority still had sentences of at least one year but there were more short-sentence people than previously, and the proportion serving four years or more had dropped to about two-fifths. Many Channings Wood prisoners had come there after serving the first part of their term in more secure prisons.

The prison was modern and largely purpose-built, with five two-storey cell blocks, workshops and other buildings set in spacious ornamental gardens. One cell block with 112 places was a Vulnerable Prisoner Unit (VPU) for men segregated for their own protection under Rule 43, many of whom had come to Channings Wood from other prisons in order to undertake the national Prison Service programme of treatment for sex offenders.

At the time of our first visit in 1992 the prison was surrounded by a high perimeter fence of steel mesh. The VPU and its garden, and the workshops area, were fenced off from the rest, but otherwise inmates could move freely about the grounds and the atmosphere was fairly relaxed. By 1996 the perimeter fence had been solidified into a wall for part of its height and topped with a 'beak', and all the cell blocks and the administration building were separated from one another by steel mesh fences. One of our inmate interviewees in 1992, R609 who had Category D status and was due for release soon, told us that on summer evenings he liked to go for a solitary run right round the edge of the grounds (inside the perimeter fence); he enjoyed the exercise, the views of the Devon countryside, and the feeling of getting away from other prisoners for a little while. If he had been at Channings Wood four years later he would not have been able to do that. After the internal fences went up inmates still generally moved about without escort and were expected to get themselves to wherever they needed to be, but they had to wait at each fence for an officer to unlock the gates. All inmates had 24-hour access to sanitation, and most were unlocked from their cells for about ten hours daily.

Work, training, education

There were three production workshops in 1992: a machine sewing shop known (as in other prisons) as 'the tailors', making garments; two woodwork shops (the woodmill, for machining, and the assembly shop) making furniture; and a laundry. By 1996 there was a fourth shop doing light unskilled assembly work. The laundry and the woodmill were reserved for inmates of the VPU. Daytime training courses in 1992 included arts and crafts technology, business start-up, building operatives, catering, computers, horticultural mechanics, industrial cleaning, and painting and decorating. By 1996 the building operatives course had ceased, and the horticultural mechanics course had been replaced by one in metal fabrication and welding (some of it on horticultural machinery). VPU inmates did not have access to these courses, but a separate computer course was included in the VPU's daytime education programme. Inmates' daily hours in most kinds of work were between five and a half and six hours, and about five hours in education and training courses. Altogether prison managers felt that a good range of activities was provided, and in 1995 their opinion was endorsed by the Inspectors, who spoke of 'an impressive variety of training and work opportunities'.[2] By 1994 NVQs were available in most kinds of work and training courses, including physical education, and we were told in 1996 that despite financial pressures a good NVQ budget had been preserved. In the week of our updating visit 64 per cent of all the prisoners were occupied in work, 8 per cent in training courses and 21 per cent in other education, with the remainder accounted for in other ways, including induction as described in the next section.

Between mid-1992 and spring 1995 Channings Wood ran an unusual training scheme, 'Options For Learning', funded by the local Training and Enterprise Council. Chapter 5 describes it in detail. Its special features were that for each participating prisoner it combined prison work and training with personal support and vocational guidance in an individual plan, and enabled the trainee to earn extra money which was put aside for his release. Unfortunately it lapsed after three years when the TEC withdrew the funding.

Assignment and choice

For a new arrival at Channings Wood the first week was an induction period in which the rules were explained, immediate problems addressed, and information given about the various activities. In 1992 the system was that during induction the new inmate was expected to go around the prison and 'find himself a job', i.e. find out whether any occupation he was interested in had a vacancy. The following week he appeared before the labour board, comprising senior representatives of departments of the prison providing occupations for inmates, which then decided where to place him. However closely (or not) the board asked him about his past experiences, preferences and future plans, he was likely at first to be placed in work to meet the prison's needs rather than his own, and in many cases this meant the tailors' or the wood assembly shops, where there was pressure for production and there were usually vacancies. (The tailors at that time, though not necessarily later, was the most unpopular job in the prison.) Other people might be taken on in workplaces of their choice if they had skills that happened to be needed there (e.g. the kitchen or Works). Most Rule 43 inmates could choose only between the woodmill and the laundry, though a few could work as cleaners or gardeners within the VPU.

A man lacking basic educational skills would be allowed to go to education if he wanted to, but most others wanting education or a training course would have to wait. All the courses had waiting lists, and an inmate had the best chance of getting a place eventually if he put his name on the list and then kept on asking, while doing other work in the meantime. Acceptance for a course vacancy would also depend on whether, at that stage, the applicant still had time enough to do all or most of it before his expected date of release, and not all had.

This system of expecting the new inmate to find out what was available and to ask for it was seen by staff as encouraging personal initiative and responsibility, but it also meant that the ignorant or less persistent were likely to miss out. A contrast is provided by the following cases:

> R613: ('What information did you get when you first arrived here?') 'Ha! you've just got to find a job, or you end up in the tailors.' R was a skilled painter; he asked the Works for a job, passed their painting test and was taken on.

> R509: 'After a week we went to the labour board and they asked, "Have you found yourself any employment?" and as far as I was concerned, I didn't know what jobs there were, where they were....They don't say, well, you can go down to where the work units are....I wasn't sure how this prison worked or anything....I suppose I might have liked to do some of the courses, but there's a waiting list, so I'd be waiting a month or more, then whatever time was left, I wouldn't have had enough time to get to the level' [for qualification]. R was sent to the tailors.

Nevertheless, the labour board would often look sympathetically on an inmate who applied for a 'change of labour' after doing a three months' stint in a workshop without complaining, and efforts were made in many cases to arrange for someone wanting a course to get it sooner or later. Among the thirty-one Channings Wood inmates in our main interview sample were ten for whom at least one occupation there had been arranged to fit in with their past work skills or experience, other work or training during this sentence, or plans for the future; and twenty-three were at the time of interview in an occupation which, at least to some extent, they had chosen.

By 1996 there was a different system of placing new arrivals. During the induction week the inmate received plenty of information, including among other things a description of the incentive scheme (see next section) and a sheet listing the various occupations on which he could indicate any preferences. Then he was simply assigned to an occupation by the Labour Control Unit (LCU) (which had replaced the board) and was expected to stay there for three months before asking for a change. Usually he was assigned to 'primary labour' which meant the tailors or the wood assembly, though if he was needed elsewhere (e.g. Works or gardens) he went there. At our updating visit LCU staff said firmly, 'The needs of the establishment are paramount,' and the information sheet made that plain. All the courses still had waiting lists, and despite the policy that a man wanting basic education could go straight into it without having to be in a workshop first, at the time of our visit the basic education classes were all full and could not accommodate any of the new inmates who were going through induction that week.

After his first three months the inmate had a choice, if there was a vacancy in what he wanted. Our impression early in 1996 was that, as before, the majority would sooner or later have at least one of their preferences met from within the range of occupations available at the prison. But although most Channings Wood prisoners had a sentence plan drawn up for them, usually after they arrived there, this seemed to have little systematic influence on their assignment to work, though for people serving at least four years a man's plan might help him get into a vocational training course later on.

Incentive scheme

Channings Wood's scheme of incentives and earned privileges began at the end of 1995. To the three levels in the national framework (see p. 22) the prison added a fourth, 'Cat. D enhanced', by which the forty or so inmates with Category D status had their own accommodation in a small building apart from the main cell blocks and were given extra freedom. It was intended that eventually levels 1, 2 and 3 would also each be accommodated in their own areas. The facilities or 'privileges', of which differing degrees distinguished the levels, were various: besides those set out in the national framework they included, for example, access to education, training courses and the gym.

Work was related to the scheme in two ways. First, in all cases except level 1 (basic regime), the supervisor of an inmate's work or other daytime occupation normally wrote a report every month on his performance and behaviour, and these reports contributed to the three-monthly reviews at which senior staff would consider him for promotion to the next level. (Demotion involved more and quicker procedures, and inmates on the basic regime were reviewed more often.) Second, work opportunities differed between the levels. Level 1 prisoners, of whom there were only two at the time of our updating visit, were given light assembly work in their cells, like fixing chains on to sink plugs. At level 2, the standard regime where most new arrivals at Channings Wood started (unless they had already been on level 3 in their previous prison), an inmate could apply for any occupation within the prison except kitchen and orderly jobs. At level 3 (enhanced) he was eligible for any inside occupation and could be considered for work on supervised community projects. At level 4 he was eligible for prison work outside the gate (which included some Works maintenance, some gardening and work in the officers' mess) and for community work.

Most of the prison's population were on levels 2 or 3. However, one of the national framework's 'key earnable privileges', that of participating in an enhanced earnings scheme, was not available at Channings Wood as no scheme of enhanced or 'real' wages had yet been introduced. Prison pay for all jobs was based on an average of £7 a week; the minimum for inmates at work was £4 and some people, such as kitchen workers, might earn over £12. Inmates achieving a full NVQ received a bonus.

At the time of our updating visit the scheme of differential regimes had been in place less than four months and was still settling down. Potentially the combination of carrot (levels 3 and 4) and stick (level 1) could have a marked effect on inmates' behaviour at work. We were told that the atmosphere in the tailors' workshop, which formerly had functioned as something of a 'sin bin', had improved considerably, due partly to the existence of the basic regime and partly to the efforts of one of the instructors there. (This is further mentioned in Chapter 3.)

Inmate development programmes

The VPU at Channings Wood was a regional centre for the national sex offender treatment programme which by 1994 was well established. A pre-release course in its own building (later taken over to house Category D inmates) had been described by the Inspectors in 1990 as 'a centre of excellence'.[3] But by the beginning of 1996, apart from the sex offenders' programme which usually kept going, offence-focused work with prisoners had been erratic for several years, and the pre-release course had stopped altogether. This was mainly due to a chronic shortage of prison officers through much absence on sick leave, a problem to which the Inspectors repeatedly drew attention.[4, 5] In mid-1996 things were beginning to improve after new staff had been appointed and trained. A resettlement course and a course in anger management, each lasting four to five days, had been started, though staff said that neither yet ran often enough to meet the demand. Counsellors from outside agencies, as before, ran sessions on alcohol and drugs awareness. Prison managers hoped to expand the provision of these courses and to start others on relationships and assertiveness. Inmates attending education classes were offered training in social skills, and in 1996 the education department began a course called 'New Horizons' which was said to be very popular. It included vocational guidance, and to that extent was an attempt to fill the gap left by the demise of the Options For Learning training scheme (p. 34).

HIGHPOINT

Population and buildings

During the period covered by this research Highpoint Prison in Suffolk was, like Channings Wood, a large Category C prison for men. At the time of our first fieldwork visit in May 1992 it held about 700; when we went again in January 1993 to interview most of our inmate sample there were 200 fewer (as the national prison population had temporarily dropped), and by the time of our updating visit in March 1996 the number had risen again to 650. Highpoint accommodated prisoners with all lengths of sentence above a very few weeks, including lifers, and about a quarter were serving not more than eighteen months, which resulted in a noticeable turnover. In early 1996, on average twenty-three prisoners a week were coming into Highpoint and the same number were leaving. Most men received at Highpoint stayed till their discharge, and many came from the London area.

Physically the prison was in two parts separated by a main trunk road (the A143). The smaller part (North) had modern two-storey living blocks in which inmates shared two to a room and were free to move about, the blocks being locked at night. North had its own kitchen and other facilities, and also the prison administration buildings. Across the A143 (and ten minutes' walk away) was the larger main prison (South), with four modern two-storey cell blocks, kitchen, workshops and education buildings. North and South each had sports-fields and gardens, South's including polytunnels for growing vegetables. Both North and South were surrounded by high steel mesh fences. South had a double perimeter fence as well as internal fences separating its various sections. Most of the prisoners in South, which held 70 per cent of the population, were unlocked for up to twelve hours a day. All inmates had 24-hour access to sanitation.

Work, training, education

In 1992–3 South prison had two large production workshops for tailoring and light assembly, and a small jam factory run by the gardens department. The large education department, as well as offering general education, ran training courses in computers, engineering skills, motor mechanics and printing. North prison had no production workshops but there were some education classes, and the Works department in North ran five construction industry training courses: bricklaying, carpentry, electrical installation, painting and decorating, and plumbing. In most daytime occupations Highpoint inmates at that time normally worked about five and a half hours a day.

By early 1996 there had been some changes. The light assembly workshop had been moved to North, and South had a new welding shop where inmates made prison gates. South had taken over the bricklaying course, and in North the electrical course had ceased (though the other three Works courses ran as before). A new course in physical education skills was running in both North and South. But the biggest change was that, in response to budget cuts, South was to lose sixty of its general education places from 1 April in order to save money, leaving just twelve places for inmates who needed help with basic literacy and numeracy. In South also, inmates' hours in most daytime occupations had been reduced to about four a day or sixteen a week.

At the time of our updating visit about 64 per cent of the prison's total population were occupied in work. Most of the courses and some of the workplaces offered NVQs.

Atmosphere

Senior Highpoint staff talking with us in 1992 described management's philosophy for the prison as open and liberal, with strong efforts to promote good staff–inmate relationships. At the same time there was a tradition of inmate under-employment which had not been fully overcome. Until the previous year, though the education department had always been strong there had not been nearly enough other occupation, and inmates had had a choice of education, some work, or remaining unemployed. In 1991 new workshops and training facilities were put in and unemployment was officially no longer an option. But the physical layout of the prison, as well as its past history, hindered co-ordination between the various departments and the enforcement of some of the rules. Inmates (as at Channings Wood) could move about without escort and were supposed to get themselves to work (though officers had to unlock gates for them). But the few who were determined to avoid work could often manage to, by taking advantage of wing officers' changing shifts and the reluctance of some staff to spend time chasing attendance among the unwilling. Problems were compounded by the high turnover of short-stay inmates. At our first visit one staff member said the prison was just beginning to emerge from a state of 'wandering disorganisation'. By 1993 things were beginning to be tightened up, though still our sample of forty-seven inmate interviewees contained two who had been unemployed (by their own choice) for all their stay.

Four years later it was different. Security was the watchword, and in South prison there was much more control. Officers lined the routes along which inmates walked to work, and had strict routines for manning sentry points, locking and unlocking gates, counting and checking, while from the workshops staff reported by telephone the numbers received and made sure they tallied. So officers were busier and had more knowledge of where prisoners were and why. We were told that some inmates welcomed the closer supervision of movements because it had reduced bullying: for example, a secluded path previously unwatched and known as 'muggers' alley' was now safer.

Under these routines there was less opportunity to evade work and in that sense unemployment was reduced, though the detailed timetable for officers' duties meant that inmates' working hours were actually shorter. But the prospect was looming of large-scale unemployment from April 1996 due to the closure of

South's main general education section, and at the time of our updating visit managers were considerably exercised as to how to deal with it. What with this, as well as other problems (including the loss of all evening classes in South), morale in the prison was said to be low.

Assignment and choice

Induction for a new inmate comprised a stay of up to two weeks in one of the South blocks, where staff explained (among other things) what occupations might be available and asked for his preferences. From our interviews with inmates it seemed that in 1993 the amount of information they received could be very much 'pot luck', but by 1996 a clearly written information pack was available. The induction officer took the newcomer's details to the labour board (the inmate himself was not invited), the board decided where he should go, and soon afterwards he went there. In 1992–3 requests for education were usually granted, but by 1996 this was seldom possible. Acceptance for a course depended on vacancies and most had waiting lists. Admission to North prison, with its more relaxed conditions, depended on passing security tests and was linked with the incentive scheme (described in the next section); we were told in 1996 that a man applying to do one of the courses in North had a 70 per cent chance of getting there eventually. Because of the waiting time, short-sentence people in particular were likely to miss out on course places. And as at Channings Wood there was pressure to keep the production workshops manned, so new arrivals could end up in the tailors or (in 1993) the light assembly.

Nevertheless prisoners' choices were considered, requests for a change of work seemed to be granted fairly freely, and thirty-five out of our forty-seven interviewees were, at the time of interview, in an occupation for which they had asked. But it appeared that, as at Channings Wood, sentence planning (in 1996) had little to do with the matter.

Incentive scheme

Highpoint's incentive scheme, established in mid-1995, had four levels linked to the location of prisoners' living quarters. The basic regime (level 1) was in one of South prison's four cell blocks, which also accommodated the induction unit, the few inmates on Rule 43 and the segregation cells. All new prisoners arriving at Highpoint were put on the basic regime while they remained in induction, but then they would normally move to either of two other blocks in South which had the standard regime (level 2). Later they could aspire to promotion, either to North prison whose regime was known as 'standard-plus' (level 3) or to the enhanced regime (level 4) in the remaining South block.

In addition to the national framework the four regimes were distinguished mainly by degrees of facilities and comforts like association, choice of menu for meals and cell furnishings. All prisoners above basic level were allowed to wear their own clothes if they wished, though we were told that many preferred to wear prison garments while working. Links between regime level and work were not as strong as at Channings Wood but there were some. People on the basic regime while going through induction did not work and received unemployment pay of £2.50 a week. Others on the basic regime were there through demotion, and they had to work where they were told with no choice. Inmates on standard regime, and standard-plus in North, could apply for any type of work available except where there was only minimum supervision. Those on enhanced regime were eligible for any work, including Category D work (e.g. in the officers' mess outside the gate) if the inmate himself had Category D status.

In practice, we were told, the labour board and the various work instructors tried to arrange matters so that most workplaces had a mixture of inmates on different levels. But there was also competition to get the 'best' workers, and it usually turned out that about 90 per cent of the labour force in the kitchen – a workplace essential to the prison's morale – were on the enhanced regime.

Promotions and demotions took into account reports of the inmate's diligence at work as well as other behaviour, and men on the basic regime were reviewed every three months. Like Channings Wood, Highpoint had as yet no facilities for enhanced or 'real' wages. Pay varied between £4 and £13 a week, depending both on the type of work and on the worker's skill and achievement; in the tailors, the light assembly and the welding shop pay was decided (within the £4–£13 range) by piece rates.

Staff said that the existence of the basic regime had removed the tendency for one workshop to be regarded as a repository for awkward prisoners. Previously the assembly shop had been seen in something of that light, but now that it was in North prison it had better workers, many of whom were in it only while waiting for a course vacancy. In 1993 a manager had told us that new arrivals had to be 'cajoled and massaged' into staying in the workshops, but now the incentive scheme had taken over. At the same time, said staff on our updating visit, the fact that men on any one level in the scheme were housed all together in one block reduced the desire of some to try for promotion: they got used to their surroundings and being with their friends, and the basic regime wing was said to be very untidy.

Inmate development programmes

Probation officers and psychologists in 1993 were doing offence-focused work with some inmates though with little input from prison officers, while an officer-led pre-release course ran erratically. An 'employment focus' course (see Chapter 6) sprang up later in 1993 with a year's funding from the Employment Department, but later declined when the prison did not continue the funding, and by 1995 the pre-release course had also stopped.

However, by spring 1996 matters were looking up. The pre-release course was about to start again, and the probation department was running a co-ordinated programme of offending behaviour courses each lasting three to four days and focusing on anger management, alcohol awareness and drug abuse. During induction a probation officer interviewed every new arrival and looked for those thought to need such a course. In accordance with the sentence planning rules first priority was given to men with a sentence of at least four years, and then to those with at least one year. There was a waiting list for every type of course.

A later note

In autumn 1996, after the period to which our study of Highpoint refers, the prison changed. In order to relieve pressure at Holloway (see next section) Highpoint North was made into a women's prison, while Highpoint South continued for men as before. Facilities in South for work and training remained much as described on pp. 38–9, and the sixty places for general education were restored. North kept the light assembly workshop and also the three construction industry courses (carpentry, painting and decorating, and plumbing), which were made over to the female prisoners. Staff said that after an initial period of settling down the women took up these courses with enthusiasm, working hard towards NVQs, and that they had redecorated much of North to a high standard.

HOLLOWAY

Population and buildings

Holloway Prison in London was by far the largest women's prison in Britain, serving a wide catchment area. As a local prison it held women on remand awaiting trial or sentence, as well as prisoners of all categories and with all lengths of sentence. About one in eight inmates were under 21, and just over half the population were serving sentences. Many of the latter were allocated from Holloway to other prisons, but others stayed for their full term.

Built to house 517 inmates, Holloway provided over a quarter of the total accommodation for females in the prison system, but over half that of local prisons. In 1992–3 its average population was 456. Over the next few years, as the number of women sent to prison rapidly increased (p. 19), Holloway filled up and then became overcrowded, with 595 inmates in June 1996. This had serious repercussions on the regime, as will be described later.

The prison was a large modern five-storey building designed very like a hospital, enclosed by a high perimeter wall and with lawns and ornamental garden beds. Accommodation for inmates was divided into sections, all with integral sanitation, and most inmates had single rooms. One section functioned as a hospital and another was reserved for mothers with babies. In 1993 most inmates were unlocked for about ten hours a day.

Activities for prisoners in 1993

Our research at Holloway took place in February 1993. At that time work available to inmates included a production sewing workshop comparable to the tailors in men's prisons, and a special workshop equipped with sewing and knitting machines making items for sale for charity. Two other inmates ran a craft shop through which any prisoner could offer for sale an article she made while in the prison. As for training courses, the Works department (which employed inmates as helpers in the same way as men's prisons) ran a painting and decorating course, and the education department ran courses in catering, textiles, hairdressing and office skills, as well as classes in other vocational subjects such as computing, though early in 1993 the courses in painting, catering and hairdressing had been suspended because the trainers were ill or in other difficulties. Working hours for most prisoners were four a day (two morning and afternoon).

April 1993 saw a new venture: the setting up of a training room by a private firm, Reed Employment.[6] Here four prisoners at a time, all with at least twelve months still to serve, were trained by Reed staff in office skills, doing work for local companies and earning £3 an hour (from which they contributed to their prison board and to savings against release). The training room was furnished as a replica of a Reed office and the inmate trainees wore Reed uniforms. Prison managers hoped the scheme would expand and be copied by other firms.

Another special feature was the jobclub outside the prison, which an inmate in the second half of her sentence could apply to attend and through which she might find an outside job before her date of release. If she did find work she would normally be allowed out daily to do it, as were a few other inmates who attended college. The jobclub and working-out scheme are described more fully in Chapter 6.

Besides work and training courses there were many other activities for Holloway inmates, centred on education and personal growth. Some sessions were run by outsiders, co-ordinated by the Activity Centre which was run by prison officers and was a salient feature of the Holloway regime. Probation officers and psychologists helped inmates to address their offending behaviour and other personal problems. Women on remand were encouraged to join in work, education and other activities alongside those serving sentences (though training courses were not open to unsentenced women or those awaiting deportation). No inmates were required to work or train but all were strongly encouraged to participate in some daily occupation. The management's emphasis was on treating the women as individuals, caring for their needs, providing constructive occupation and steering them towards activities which could help them in personal development.

Induction (1993)

Induction of new prisoners took place once a week in the Activity Centre, but they could go there earlier for information on what was available, as well as asking wing staff. Some inmates we interviewed said they had been adequately informed but others felt differently, and their responses suggested that, rather as at Channings Wood, a good deal depended on the newcomer's own initiative. R586, who arrived in Holloway in September 1992, said:

> You don't find out anything really, unless you ask....The only things they tell you is bang-up times, when's dinner, where you can get your bits and pieces from, and what's available. But they don't tell you how to go around [about] it....They just said, there's education available if you ask...they don't tell you how to go about it, how to get it – there is the odd one [staff] that does, and the odd ones are never hardly on [duty] anyway...I've noticed it's the ones that have been here quite a while, it's them ones that don't tell you nothing, because they've got so used to the system, they expect you to know.

By 1993 a comprehensive booklet was available to new inmates describing the prison and its facilities.

During her first week the new prisoner completed a form showing her preference for occupation, and the labour board then placed her in it if possible. Not all got their first choice and a few remained unemployed, at least for a short time. But of the fourteen inmates in our interview sample only two were then in work they had not asked to do (both were wing cleaners).

Later

In 1994 and 1995 Holloway Prison went downhill. Its regime for prisoners drastically worsened, and staff were under great strain.[7] Among the reasons were pressure from the rising population, a more complex mix of inmates, and increased security. Security changes began after three women escaped over the wall in May 1994: the governor tightened the rules, and further tightening came in 1995 and 1996 from national policies, especially after the Learmont Report.[8] Far fewer women were eligible to go out of the prison (e.g. to the jobclub), and women going out for purposes like hospital visits were handcuffed to officers, who had to spend more of their time on such escorts.

The increasing numbers of prisoners being received included more Category A women, more young ones, more foreign nationals, more women with health problems and more who were difficult to manage. Stable prisoners needing less attention were moved out to other prisons to make room for the newcomers. Staff became stressed and ill; there were high levels of sick leave while other officers worked long hours on essential duties to keep the establishment running. Sixty more officers were said to be needed. Managers were swamped by paperwork resulting from the devolution of the budget and other matters from HQ. Officers perceived managers as bureaucratic and insufficiently in touch with day-to-day necessities.

The Activity Centre was often closed, as was the Reed training room. Induction and labour allocation procedures were erratic. The education budget was cut, and classes often shut because no officers were available to take inmates to them. Inmates were frequently locked up for the night from 3.30 p.m. Reporting on all these and other matters, the Board of Visitors said, 'The Board believes that lack of a purposeful regime was profoundly damaging to the ethos of the prison and to the lives of inmates.'[9]

Rats and other vermin infested the prison. In December 1995 the new Chief Inspector, Sir David Ramsbotham, pulled his inspection team out of Holloway prematurely to draw attention to the conditions there, which he later described as 'appallingly indecent' and 'totally unacceptable by any standards'.[10] Security, he said, 'had been taken to absurd extremes'.[11] In January 1996 there was a public outcry following media reports that maternity patients from Holloway were chained to prison officers while attending outside hospital for ante-natal care and during labour.[12]

Later in January the Home Secretary announced a slight easing of the requirement to chain pregnant women, and the giving of some discretion to governors about chaining other patients on hospital visits.[13] In April the Director General said that extra staff had been appointed to Holloway and that pest control and cleaning were in progress.[14] In June the Chief Inspector was reported as saying that the prison was now 'decent and working again, but that there was still a long way to go'.[15] Six months later, while congratulating staff who had worked hard to improve matters, he said, 'The process of returning this very complex establishment to its former position as a seat of excellence has only just begun.' Among his recommendations were that 'the population and multiplicity of functions at Holloway should be reduced'.[16]

Our research results for Holloway in the following chapters refer to the prison's happier times in 1993. It is to be hoped that at least the regime we studied then can be achieved again.

KIRKHAM

Population and buildings

Kirkham Prison in Lancashire, the largest of the 'open' prisons in the system, had over 600 places for Category D men. At the time of our first visit in 1992 the population was about 460, of whom about 60 per cent were serving sentences of up to eighteen months and the rest were in the last stage of a longer term which they had begun elsewhere. In April 1996 the prison was full, with about 45 per cent of inmates serving less than a year and a high turnover of between 400 and 500 a month.

The main part of the prison was on the site of a former RAF camp and used some of the original buildings. Most inmates were housed in long huts known as billets, which typically contained fourteen small double cubicles plus a section for ablutions, thus accommodating twenty-eight men. (In 1996 they were beginning to be replaced by dormitory blocks with single rooms.) The billets were locked at night but the occupants were free inside, and during most of the day they moved freely about the camp to their workplaces or elsewhere, though the billets were locked during working hours to discourage pilfering. Other prison facilities were in low buildings, some of the old hangars housed workshops, and there were extensive gardens and a large number of polythene tunnels growing salads. In 1992 all this was bounded by a low wire fence. By 1996 the fence had been replaced by a stronger one fourteen feet high, which staff said was as much to keep intruders out as prisoners in. Beyond the fence, and still part of the prison, were fields of potatoes and other vegetables, and twenty miles away was the prison farm to which inmate workers were transported daily.

Work, training, education

Work for prisoners included production shops in weaving and woodwork, a laundry, and work in the gardens and on the farm. In 1992 there was a light assembly workshop which later closed. The Works department in 1992 ran a construction industry training course in building operations, but by 1996 this had stopped although Works inmates received some on-the-job training, as did others in a workshop repairing horticultural machinery. The education department ran training courses of two weeks in computers and business start-up, as well as longer courses for people needing general education; in 1992 there had also been a short course in transport (road haulage) but this was later closed. No NVQs were available in 1996 because of budget cuts. Altogether, the industries department (the production workshops and the laundry) provided about one-third of the places for occupying inmates, the farms and gardens department provided another third, and the remainder included all other kinds of work as well as places in training courses and education. A few inmates went out of the prison to help with community projects: in 1996 up to ten a day were doing so, though in earlier years there had been more. The working day for most inmates was seven hours in 1992, and nearer seven and a half hours by 1996.

Assignment and choice

Some Kirkham staff referred to the prison with satisfaction as 'a *working* prison' and certainly the emphasis was on work. At the time of our first visit in 1992 most prisoners had to work, though a few, especially men with a reading age of less than 12, were allowed to spend all their time in education if they wished. When education was contracted out the system changed so that no inmate could do that, but instead 'sessional release' allowed part-time absence from work to attend day classes under arrangements negotiated between the education department and work supervisors. This change resulted in many more prisoners receiving some daytime education than had earlier been the case (and also in the education department being better integrated with the rest of the prison). The training courses ran full-time for their duration. In 1996, on any one day, about one in eight inmates were attending education or a course.

There was a structured induction period during which incoming prisoners received information about the prison and supplied it about themselves. By 1996 the programme had been compressed from several days into one because there were so many new arrivals, and it included a video and a comprehensive information pack (which mentioned, among other things, 'the emphasis on the work ethic'). All newcomers were assessed educationally (by a group questionnaire) but the dexterity test which had formerly helped to select men for weaving or woodwork was no longer used.

Following induction the new inmate appeared before the labour board, comprising the industrial manager and staff from whichever workplaces currently had vacancies. The board tried to take account of the inmate's preference or previous experience (especially for jobs in Works or the kitchen), but the emphasis was very much on filling vacancies in the prison's workforce, and many inmates were given no choice. The experience of R518, who had been a bricklayer and road mender but at Kirkham was placed in the warp preparation workshop (for weaving), was typical of many:

> When I first came in they said…what was I doing outside like, and when I told them they said, like, we'll try and give you something on the same lines. Then they end up giving me cotton.

Sixteen of the twenty-six Kirkham inmates interviewed for the research said they had had no choice about the work they were then doing.

People could later ask for a 'change of labour'. The farm workers were all volunteers from the gardens party, and from 1995 prisoners wanting work outside the fence (which included the farm, garden work in the fields and community projects) had to pass a risk assessment. A man wanting education or a training course could apply at induction or, in 1996, at any later time by visiting the education department in the evening or on a Saturday afternoon. (This was an improvement on the situation that had obtained in 1992, when people who had not applied at the outset were likely to be refused.) In 1996 all inmates serving a year or more (just over half the population) had a sentence plan, usually started (or re-started) at Kirkham, but plans seemed to be more concerned with participation in offending behaviour programmes than with assignment to work, though they could include a training course and the 'employment focus' course before release (see p. 48).

Incentive scheme and pay rates

Kirkham's incentive scheme, which began in 1995, was very close to the national framework, including opportunities to earn enhanced pay (though not 'real' wages). The three levels (basic, standard and enhanced) were differentiated in regard to private cash and visits (as in the national scheme), phonecards, personal possessions (men on level 3 could have their own typewriter and sports gear), and access to certain kinds of work. Only men on level 3 could go out to community work (or to college on day-release). Men above level 1 could be considered for orderlies' jobs and for those with enhanced earnings schemes, though level 3 men had priority for them.

Three workplaces carried enhanced earnings. In the woodwork shop inmates were paid piece rates and could earn between £25 and £60 a week, from which they could keep £15 and had to save the rest. Farm workers were paid £2 or £3 a day depending on task and skill, so that if a man worked seven days a week (as many did) he could earn a maximum of £21 from which he had to save £6. The same two grades of pay obtained in the vegetable preparation room, which was part of the farms and gardens department. No deductions, other than the compulsory savings, were made from inmates' enhanced pay. In April 1996 about a hundred men were on these pay rates.

All other kinds of work carried ordinary pay, varying between about £4 and £10 a week, with an average of £7. In 1992 the weaving shop had had the highest pay rates, including an allowance for dust, but after the equipment was updated (see p. 84) weavers were put on the same pay as others. Staff said that in the jobs with enhanced pay productivity had increased markedly. In 1992 the vegetable packing shed had been something of a 'sin bin' for the farms and gardens department, but since being upgraded and put on enhanced earnings it was said to be full of willing workers.

Each prisoner received at Kirkham was placed on standard level for three months, after which he could apply for enhanced level. Promotions and demotions were considered by a panel of the sentence planning board, the criteria being general behaviour, evidence of constructive activity, constructive participation in a sentence plan (for those men who had one) and (for promotion) three months' freedom from offences against prison discipline.

Inmate development programmes

Probation officers at Kirkham in 1992 were running some groups, especially on alcohol awareness, but the Inspectors commented that much more such provision was needed and that it conflicted with demands from the workshops and the farm for industrial production.[17] An officer-led pre-release course included a session on offending behaviour. By 1996 the prison was providing short courses (between one and three days) in anger management, drug and alcohol awareness, substance abuse (glue-sniffing) and motor vehicle offences, and also a one-day general 'offending behaviour core programme'. These were mainly staffed by prison and probation officers. A manager explained that every year a psychologist spent a day at the prison surveying (by questionnaire) the whole of its population to assess the need for such courses, which were then set up accordingly, the aim being to ensure that Kirkham met the relevant key performance indicator set by HQ.[18] On any one day about thirty inmates were attending one or another of these courses. The pre-release course had been replaced by a two-week 'employment focus' course provided by an outside agency, which any inmate with a sentence plan, and any other who wanted to, could attend.

LIVERPOOL

Population and buildings

Liverpool Prison, known locally as Walton Jail, was one of the largest local male prisons in the country, serving Cheshire and North Wales in addition to Merseyside. As a local prison it received men on remand (who formed about one-third of the population) and men with all lengths of sentence and in any security category. Many were quickly allocated elsewhere even though they might have only a few weeks to serve, while others remained for years. In 1992–3 the prison had officially 931 places and the average population was 1,210; by mid-1996 there were 1,073 places and 1,250 inmates, so overcrowding had slightly eased.[19] Between the remanded and the sentenced men there was altogether a very high turnover: in April 1996 about a hundred prisoners a day were coming in and a hundred were going out (including transfers to other prisons). So staff at Liverpool were extremely busy.

The buildings were five-storey traditional Victorian cell blocks having wings with landings, plus later additions. There were exercise yards, small gardens and internal fences, the whole being enclosed by a high thick wall. In 1992 a big programme of refurbishment was going on and some wings were still slopping out, but by 1996 most of it was complete and all inmates had access to sanitation. Security was strict and most inmates were escorted everywhere they went.

Groups of cells were associated with particular workplaces nearby: thus one section housed the kitchen workers, another housed those in the leather workshop, and so on. One wing was reserved as a VPU with about 170 inmates. In 1992 staff hoped that another wing, then closed for refurbishment, would re-open as Category C accommodation, having a less strict regime than the rest and allowing Liverpool to function partly as a training prison, but this did not happen. For sentenced prisoners the usual daily hours unlocked increased from about six in 1992 to between eight and nine in 1996. Men on remand had less time out of their cells than those serving sentences.

Work, training, education

Work available to sentenced inmates in 1992 (there was then very little occupation for men on remand) included: a light assembly workshop and a laundry, both of which were reserved for the VPU; a leather goods workshop for inmates requiring the highest security; another light assembly shop; a tailors' shop; and two woodwork shops doing machining and carpentry. Training courses included two construction industry ones, in bricklaying and in painting and decorating; and courses in engineering theory, computers, business start-up, and desk-top publishing, while a few inmates attended general education classes. Hours of work in most occupations were about five a day or just over twenty a week. The Inspectors in May 1993 found a total of 704 daytime occupational places available.[20]

By the time of our updating visit in 1996 there were 850 occupational places, and even the remands fared better than previously, about half of them having the opportunity of some work or education. A third workshop doing sewing and light assembly had been added and there were plans for a fourth. Men in the VPU no longer went to an assembly shop but could work in the laundry or go to classes in their wing, while some were cleaners there and a few did assembly work in their cells. The engineering course had stopped but the construction industry ones were offering NVQs, while the education department offered training as part of GNVQ in computers, business studies and leisure and tourism, as well as other subjects. The number of education places had increased to ninety, while a few other inmates received tuition in their cells (and a tiny number could receive vocational guidance from education staff). Hours of work for most inmates had increased to five and a half daily, five days a week.

Assignment, choice and pay

New arrivals were taken to a reception wing where they were given a little information and seen briefly by a reception board. By 1996 each wing was holding one half-day induction session for its new inmates, having no time for more than that with so many people coming and going. Allocation to work was done by the Industries Principal Officer, who checked every day with the workplaces to see where there were vacancies, consulted the new inmate's file and then decided where he should go, largely on the basis of his security classification and length of sentence. Inmates with suitable skills were likely to be spoken for by the Works, and experienced prisoners who 'knew the ropes' and wanted a particular kind of work could let it be known to wing staff. After three months, if he was still in the prison, a man could apply for a change of labour, and in 1992 twelve of the thirty-five in our interview sample were then in occupations which to some extent were of their choice.

Sentence planning, for a man sentenced to a year or more, was rudimentary and usually started afresh by whichever prison received him from Liverpool; Liverpool had no personal officer scheme. A manager said the turnover was such that staff could not plan for a man's future: their aim was to get him settled quickly into any prison job rather than be idle. In 1996 among the sentenced men there might be at any one time perhaps eighty unemployed, some of whom would have just been received. Some inmates waited up to two weeks for an occupational place, and most of the training courses had waiting lists. A few sentenced men, by choice or otherwise, remained unemployed and locked up for most of their stay; there were three such among our interviewees.

No incentive scheme operated at Liverpool, nor were there any opportunities for enhanced earnings. In 1996 inmates' pay was based on a per capita allowance which varied between the workplaces: for example, kitchen workers averaged £8 a week and might earn up to £10, men in the production workshops were paid piece rates averaging £6.80, and those in training or education received £5.60.

Inmate development programmes

Prison officers ran a two-week pre-release course, which included sessions on offending behaviour, though it was not frequent enough to meet the demand and in fact was suspended for most of 1995 because of other pressures. ('If we're short of staff it's one of the first things to go.') A somewhat similar one-week 'awareness' course was held once a month for prisoners halfway through their sentences. There was no treatment programme for sex offenders. The probation department had for some years run groups, mainly on drugs and alcohol addiction, and by 1996 had expanded these into a programme of courses on five topics: drugs, alcohol, anger management, domestic violence and general offending behaviour. Each ran for just three days. Most of them had a waiting list, especially the drugs group for which in April over a hundred men were waiting.

Atmosphere

Liverpool Prison suffered by being a big local one in cramped buildings, where inmates spent much time locked in their cells. Nevertheless the general atmosphere was positive. Several staff referred to a sense of local community and Liverpudlian humour which lightened dealings between staff and prisoners, and this opinion of good relationships was generally borne out by inmates interviewed for our research. A probation officer described Liverpool as 'for a Victorian prison, the best I've come across'.

The range of activities for prisoners, and their working hours, were better even in 1992 than they had been a few years previously, and at our updating visit it was clear that progress had continued despite the failure of the plan to redevelop one section as a training wing. As at Kirkham, it seemed that education services to inmates had improved after being contracted out: whereas in 1993 the Inspectors had commented critically that education resources were seriously under-used,[21] by 1996 the department was much more proactive. Budget cuts had reduced the number of probation officers by two (out of fourteen) but even so a varied programme of inmate development courses was running, though not nearly enough to meet the need. There were no plans to cut workshop activities, and association hours for some inmates had increased. A manager at our updating visit insisted that the only impediment to giving Liverpool prisoners more training was the transitory nature of the population.

MAIDSTONE

Population and buildings

Maidstone Prison in Kent was a Category B prison for about 520 men. Nearly all were long-term prisoners, serving sentences of four years and upwards; about a quarter of them were lifers. Most would have begun their sentence elsewhere and then come to Maidstone for the next stage of it, and would move on to a Category C or D prison before release. Very few prisoners were discharged direct from Maidstone. Compared with that of many other prisons the population was stable and predictable, and the prison was rarely overcrowded.

The buildings were a mixture of ages and styles, with one of the four large cell blocks remaining from the original early nineteenth-century prison and others having been put in at various times since. There were small garden areas and the prison was surrounded by a thick stone wall. Most inmates had single cells, and at our first visit in 1992 a programme of installing integral sanitation was under way and completed soon afterwards. One of the cell blocks accommodating 170 men was reserved as a VPU, fenced off from the rest and with its own garden and allotment area.

Atmosphere

A notable feature of Maidstone Prison was its good relationships between staff and prisoners. In 1992 we observed a good deal of mutual respect: staff addressed inmates politely, there was some use of first names both ways, and inmates were allowed to wear their own clothes. We were told then that the policy was to achieve control by good personal relationships rather than physical means like fences, for which scope was limited in the crowded prison grounds. By 1996, following the national policy of increased security, more fences had been put in and there were cameras on the walls, but still the atmosphere was relaxed and liberal for a Category B prison. When outside the buildings most prisoners moved about under escort, but inside each cell block (wing) the inhabitants were free to go where they wanted during unlocked hours, which in 1992 were about nine a day but by 1996 had increased to nearly eleven. Each wing had a cooking area where inmates could supplement the meals sent in by the main kitchen and a laundrette where they could wash their own clothes, and by 1996 all cells had been wired with 12-volt power so that men could use their radios or tape players.

Maidstone's population included some difficult and demanding prisoners, some of whom had been disruptive in other establishments but found they could settle down at Maidstone. The stable population allowed staff to get to know inmates well as individuals, and in 1996 the Inspectors referred to 'the high quality of relationship between staff and prisoners' as being 'the hallmark of Maidstone's success in maintaining good order.'[22] In mid-1996 the governor's preface to an information pack for new inmates included the words, 'I am fully committed to the ethos of the Prison which is to treat prisoners with respect and give them the opportunity to make decisions about their lives and exercise some personal responsibility.'[23]

Work, training, education

Work at the time of our first visit in 1992 included a laundry and a light assembly workshop, both reserved for the VPU which also had a small unit doing

Braille transcription; and workshops for tailoring and printing. Training courses in the main prison included bricklaying, painting and decorating, welding and sheetmetal fabrication, business studies and office practice, while VPU inmates could learn some of these subjects in evening classes. In both the VPU and the main prison some inmates could have general education full-time. Later there were some changes: the tailors' shop was made over to the VPU and a new workshop known as 'the body shop' making firefighters' dummies was put in, while the bricks course closed down for lack of an instructor.

In November 1995 the Inspectors found that there were not enough occupational places to keep all inmates busy even for the five-hour working day. Some instructors were on long-term sick leave and posts for others remained vacant; inmates were often sent back to the wings for lack of work; there were far too many cleaners who were barely occupied. The VPU shops had enough work, but there were production problems when men went off to attend the sex offender programme. The education department, said the Inspectors, should be better organised and managed: the curriculum was poor, attendances were often low, and classes frequently closed. This inspection took place at a time when budget cuts had just been announced and the governor, with considerable sympathy from his staff, was deliberating on how to implement them. Instructors, teachers and other specialist staff as well as prison officers feared for their jobs. In addition, teachers felt they were held in low regard both by Prison Service HQ and by the contracting college which employed them.[24]

By the time of our updating visit at the end of April 1996 some matters had greatly improved. No prisoners were unemployed, and we were told that although there had been staff cuts inmates' activities had been protected. More contract work had been brought in and the number of places in the print shop (for example) had increased from forty to sixty-six. Another small workshop had opened, at present doing light assembly but intended soon to make articles for charity, while a recycling scheme occupied some of the inmates who tidied the grounds. Indoor cleaners had been reduced in number and prompted to work harder by competitions between the wings. The bricks course was about to start again with the appointment of a new instructor. The full-time courses in office skills, painting and decorating, and welding were still running, while the education department's offerings now included training in business studies, computing, electrical installation and road transport as well as other subjects (though some classes were still not well attended and some were cancelled when teachers were absent). Altogether, in the main prison two-thirds of the occupational places were in work, with the others divided fairly evenly between training courses and education, while for the VPU 89 per cent were in work and 11 per cent in education, and NVQs were available in five subject areas. But the biggest change in 1996 was that from mid-April many more inmates had the opportunity to combine work with education through a revised incentive scheme which is described separately below. Working hours, however, were still barely more than five a day or twenty-three a week.

Assignment and choice

Maidstone's induction programme was described by the Inspectors who looked at it in 1995 as one of the best they had seen.[25] It comprised a week of structured sessions in which staff representing the various activities explained what they were, took the new inmates on a tour of the prison to see them, and answered individual queries as fully as possible to allay anxieties. In 1996 a comprehensive illustrated information pack was available.

Before the revised incentive scheme came in, prisoners often had a free choice between workshops and full-time education, though if they wanted a course they might have to go into a workshop until there was a vacancy. The welders' course was especially popular, and in April 1996 had a waiting list of six months. The labour board made decisions without the inmate being present, but many men got what they had asked for, though for people in the VPU choice was more restricted. A man wanting a labour change did not have to wait three months, as at some other prisons, before applying. In our sample of twenty-five inmates interviewed in 1992 there were several for whom an occupation at Maidstone had clearly been planned to link with some previous experience (during sentence or earlier), though planning for the future was less likely because for many prisoners release was so far ahead. Twenty-one of the interviewees were at that time in an occupation they had asked for.

From April 1996 the 'Options' incentive scheme described in the next section allowed prisoners to a large extent to devise their own individual programmes of daytime occupation. As regards formal sentence planning, every Maidstone prisoner had a plan, though the Inspectors in November 1995 found the system patchy and said that 'sufficient thought, emphasis or training had not been given to the process of converting sentence planning from a paper exercise into a relevant dynamic process'.[26] For men taking the sex offender programme that, of course, was a large part of their plan. For inmates generally it seemed in 1996 that sentence planning focused on slotting them into a course on offending behaviour before the date on which they became eligible to be considered for parole. As at other prisons, it appeared that sentence planning had little influence on most people's assignment to work.

Incentive scheme

Maidstone's incentive scheme from January 1996 largely fitted the national framework, the three levels (basic, standard and enhanced) being distinguished mainly in relation to private cash and visits. In addition, inmates at the basic level had to wear prison clothing and were locked up for the night at 6 p.m. instead of 8 p.m., while only those on enhanced level could apply for certain jobs carrying a little more freedom or responsibility than most others (e.g. 'green band' groundsman, visits orderly and work in the officers' mess). New arrivals at Maidstone began at standard level and could apply for promotion after three months, the criteria covering most aspects of behaviour including diligence at work, attitudes to other prisoners and progress towards sentence plan targets. Demotions were preceded by several warnings, and inmates on basic level were reviewed weekly and offered advice on how to climb out of it. In March 1996 35 per cent of the population were on enhanced level and all the rest were on standard.

Overlaid on this framework from mid-April was the Options scheme. The working week was divided into nine sessions (mornings and afternoons Monday to Friday except Thursday mornings, when the prison was closed down for staff training, searching and other administrative matters). Prisoners on the basic level had to work for all nine sessions. All others had to work for at least six, but could choose to have up to three of their sessions as 'options' in which they attended education classes of their choice or physical education courses (e.g. for life-saving, Community Sports Leader Award or remedial gym), and for these they would receive the same pay as at work (except for any special bonuses). Alternatively, they could take any of their three options as recreational sessions on the sportsfield or in the gym. For men on standard level, one recreation session would be paid and the other two would not, while men on enhanced level would be paid for all three. When a particular activity session became full, others who wanted it would be put on a waiting list and given one of their reserve choices meantime, and people could apply once a month to change their options.

Thus each inmate had his own personal timetable with a mix of his chosen occupations. The purposes of the Options scheme were to give prisoners greater choice in the constructive use of their time, to enable fuller use of the education and PE facilities during the working day and, fundamentally, to facilitate better control in the prison. The scheme had needed a great deal of careful planning and explanation to inmates, but at the time of our updating visit it had been in place for two weeks and managers were delighted by the smoothness of the changeover. Over a hundred inmates had chosen no options (i.e. they wanted to work for all nine sessions), over a hundred wanted to take up the full three, and the rest opted for one or two.

Pay

Budgets for inmates' pay at Maidstone in 1996 were devolved to workshop level: each instructor in charge of a workplace (or full-time course) received a weekly per capita allowance (based on an average for that kind of work) to distribute as he or she saw fit. The highest average was for the kitchen at £12, and the lowest was for training courses and education at £6.75. (As at other prisons, an inmate for whom no work was available would receive £2.50, while men refusing work got nothing.)

Added to these budgets in modest amounts was money which the prison earned from inmates' work on contracts for outside firms. The body shop and the light assembly shop (like those at other prisons) had such contracts, as did the printers and the tailors from time to time. The profits were used to top up wages not only for inmates in those shops but for others who contributed to the running of the prison, so that an assembly worker on piece rates or a kitchen worker on overtime might earn altogether around £15 a week. In addition, some of the contract profits were spent on extra facilities like sports equipment or computers, so that the money was spread around for the benefit of the prisoners. The other prisons in the study earned some money from contract work (especially in their light assembly workshops, for which another name was 'contract services', as described in Chapter 3), but none in 1996 seemed to have as much flexibility as Maidstone in deciding how to use it.

Inmate development programmes

The largest of these was the sex offender treatment programme, managed by the psychology department and with input from prison and probation officers. Besides the core programme (then about seventy two-hour sessions and later expanded) VPU inmates could take other much shorter modules which were available to men in the main prison as well. These courses, typically comprising seven sessions over three and a half days, were on alcohol and drugs awareness, anger management, assertiveness, thinking skills, relationships, social skills, stress management and offending behaviour generally. Representatives of Alcoholics Anonymous and Gamblers Anonymous also came into the prison to help inmates. Most of the short courses were managed by the probation department, which by the beginning of 1996 was running a co-ordinated programme of two or three courses each month. In mid-1996 there was still a backlog of inmates waiting to join one or more, but staff aimed to ensure that each man diagnosed (during induction, and as part of sentence planning) as needing any particular course would receive it before the Parole Board considered his case. Prisoners completing a course received a certificate.

GENERAL

New prisoners sent to production workshops, laundries and gardens often had little choice about the matter, though some had asked for such work. They needed little or no ability, their prior work experience was not usually taken into account, and work instructors knew practically nothing about these recruits before they arrived, though they could reject any who were clearly unsuitable. Kitchen workers were usually 'volunteers' except at Kirkham and Liverpool. Works departments hand-picked their inmate helpers from those who applied, and they looked for people with trade skills or at least aptitude. Inmates who became orderlies were carefully selected after prison staff had got to know them. The same was true of some wing cleaners and other domestics, but as well as that there was sometimes a temptation to 'pad' the cleaning parties with inmates who would otherwise be unemployed.

In most cases inmates could apply for a 'change of labour' after three months or so, if not earlier. There was much more assessment and selection of people for vocational training courses, as will be seen in Chapter 5. Educational opportunities varied between the prisons. At some it seemed that the contracting-out of education had led to rearrangements and inmates having better access to classes, though at Maidstone much of this had been due to the new Options incentive scheme; while at Highpoint in spring 1996 education suffered severely through budget cuts.

The range of occupation for Rule 43 inmates in the three prisons with a VPU was more restricted: in many cases to the laundry, one or two other workshops or education. Full-time vocational training was generally not available, though there were some efforts to alleviate this by evening classes in vocational subjects. Though most Rule 43 prisoners were steady workers, some of them resented the limited opportunities. R626, for example, said, 'You get nothing if you're on the numbers...it's the same at other prisons....Everything must revolve around the main wing, we don't count.'

Taking everything together, it seemed to us in spring 1996 that governors and staff at the five male prisons were, by and large, coping valiantly with the pressures resulting from rising numbers, tighter security and reduced budgets. Incentive schemes were growing, though not all included opportunity for 'enhanced earnings' which was one of the key features of the national framework. The sex offender programme was well developed at Channings Wood and Maidstone, whose VPUs were part of a national resource for it. Other programmes of short courses to help prisoners address their offending behaviour were well under way (though some work of that kind had been going on for many years), but there were not yet enough to meet the need. Sentence planning was patchy, and seemed to be concerned more with fitting prisoners into offending behaviour courses than with guiding them into the most suitable kinds of prison work, despite the fact that most inmates would spend far more of their time at work than on courses.

The six prisons had a good many kinds of work and training in common (to some or all). Others, like the Kirkham farm or the Maidstone printing shop, were done at just one of the six, but some prisons not participating in the research had these kinds of occupation too, as will be seen in Chapter 3. Among them the six research prisons had a large range of work and training for inmates, and Chapters 3 and 5 contain descriptions of them in some detail, to give the reader who may be unfamiliar with prison work and training a picture of what was actually going on.

3 Pictures of prison work, and comparisons with outside

INTRODUCTION

The 1990s were a far cry from the days when the typical prisoner sat in his cell sewing mailbags. In several years the annual report of the Prison Service included glossy photographs showing inmates occupied in a great variety of ways,[1] and in spring 1996 only one workshop in one prison (Leeds) was making mailbags. In this chapter we have two main purposes: to describe various kinds of prison work in some detail, and to compare most of them with examples of similar work in outside industry.

Our pictures of prison work are based mainly on what we learned at the research prisons. We wanted to see what was being done and how: the organisation of the work, the processes and equipment used, the quality of the products, and what training the prisoners received. We were interested in finding out how they felt about their tasks: the kinds of satisfaction they got, and whether they thought the experience would benefit them. Here we describe the different kinds of work separately, while Chapter 4 will bring them together in a closer examination of aspects of prison work in general.

The examples of work in outside industry are taken from our visits to employers. There we watched work in progress and asked managers about organisation and working hours, skills expected of recruits, pay and incentives, training given and the state of the labour market. On these visits we kept in mind the first three of the Prison Service's criteria for judging prison work (pp. 16–17): how realistic it was compared with outside (on a number of measures), whether it suited the prisoners' aptitudes, and whether it imparted skills that outside employers would want. In this chapter each description of an outside example is followed by a short comment comparing it on some points with what was seen in prison, and at the end we briefly draw out several themes which will later be integrated with other material.

To provide a context for the descriptions of work at the six prisons, they are preceded by a section on the provision of work for prisoners in the system as a whole, together with a note on Prison Enterprise Services. But first, since our fundamental interest is in prison workers as people, let us look at some evidence from the research on what they actually wanted.

What prisoners wanted

We asked 150 of our inmate interviewees what occupation they had wanted on arriving at the prison where we met them (out of the occupations carried on there). Nearly half of them had wanted a particular prison job. Their preferences covered a wide range, but the most frequent were for Works, gardens, kitchen or cleaning. Just over a quarter had wanted a vocational training course, and just under a quarter wanted full-time education. Three of the 150 responded by saying that they did not want to work.

By far the commonest reason for people's preferences (given by 60 per cent of 128 who were asked for reasons) was that they wanted to learn some skill, or keep up an existing skill, or use their previous experience (sometimes acquired in an earlier sentence) in that kind of occupation. Other reasons, like passing the time, being with friends, access to prison perks or simply enjoying the preferred activity, were mentioned far less often.

Only seven people mentioned money. Here it may be noted that these interviews took place in 1992–3 before the national incentives scheme was set up, and perhaps if they had been asked three or four years later more prisoners might have spoken about wanting to earn higher pay. On the other hand, as was seen in Chapter 2, out of the six prisons only two had by spring 1996 any provision for enhanced earnings, and only a minority of their inmates were receiving them. The figures in the next section show that nationally such schemes involved relatively few prisoners, while 'real wages' were rarer still. In spring 1996 the national average pay for a prison worker was £7 a week. This was more than most of our interviewees were receiving in 1992–3[2] but still below the £8 a week which Woolf had recommended as an interim level in 1991.[3]

So the majority of prisoners interviewed said they would have liked an occupation in which they could learn a skill or use some existing skill or work experience. From evidence to be presented later, on the popularity of various prison jobs and on inmates' reasons for working in prison, it appears that what has just been said may under-represent the importance of the prison setting, and of prisoners' efforts to cope with it, as a factor in their occupational preferences. Nevertheless, the fact that the majority indicated a wish to learn or practise something useful to them is significant, especially in relation to our consideration in Chapter 5 (pp. 135–41) on the continuity of training and the amount that inmates received.

By the time we met them, seventy-five of our 150 interviewees had been placed in the occupation they wanted. The reasons why the others had not, or not yet, were various: for example, the prison gave them no choice, there was no vacancy in the course they wanted, or their expected length of stay was too short. Figures in Chapter 2 imply that a larger number were, when interviewed, in an occupation which to some extent they had chosen. But for some people, including men on Rule 43 and others too, choice was very limited and they did not get what they really wanted out of the range of occupations for inmates at that prison.

One hundred and forty-four inmates who were doing prison work at the time of interview were asked whether, before starting their current sentence, they had any kind of occupational skill, regardless of how much it was or where they had acquired it. One hundred and fifteen said they had. We asked these people whether their skill had been used at any time, in *any* prison activity, during this sentence. Only 37 per cent had used it in some way and only 19 per cent were using it now (e.g. in kitchens or Works). Three-quarters of those whose pre-sentence skill was not currently being used said they knew of some prison activity where they thought they could have used it, though by no means all of them had asked to do so.

Altogether it seemed that while a majority of our sample of prisoners, sooner or later, had some choice of occupation and staff tried to accommodate their preferences, this was very far from being a methodical arrangement for assessing their needs and then placing them in the most appropriate way. Nor was there any system for ensuring that the range of occupations a prison provided would match the needs of the population it received. And even if it did, there was no assurance that the next prison to which those inmates might be moved had a programme which would enable them to continue their training or work experience.

These matters are in the province of sentence planning, which we discuss in Chapter 7. Certainly at the time our sample of inmates were interviewed sentence planning was in its infancy[4] and it has since developed. But as we saw in Chapter 2, in 1996 sentence planning seemed to be more concerned with getting prisoners into courses on offending behaviour than with ensuring that they were guided into suitable work. Overall it seemed in 1996, as in earlier years, that the work an inmate was given to do in prison was, for many, largely a lucky dip.

THE NATIONAL SCENE

Kinds of work

Table 1 is intended to give an idea of the bran tub. It shows the main kinds of work in prison establishments in 1996, and for each kind how many prisons provided it and roughly how many prisoners at any one time were doing it. The table does not cover a few kinds of work done at all prisons by very small numbers of inmates, such as orderlies, clerks and stores assistants, nor does it include some rarer jobs like editing a prison magazine or (at Holloway, for instance) running a charity shop. It does not include training courses or educa-tion. The table takes into account all 131 prison establishments (including remand centres and Young Offender Institutions) which were operating in 1996, apart from the four contracted out to private management. It has been compiled from several sources and the numbers of prisoners shown are only approximate.[5]

The first thing noticeable about Table 1 is that it accounts for less than half

Table 1 Main kinds of prison work in 1996

Work	No. of prisons providing it	No. of prisoners employed in it (approximate)	% of total prisoners in this table (23,950 = 100%)
(a) *PES industries*			
clothing manufacture	46	1,940	8.1
other textile products	19	700	2.9
weaving	5	150	0.6
other fabric manufacture	3	230	1.0
sewing machine repairs	4	90	0.4
contract services (light assembly, etc.)	50	1,440	6.0
laundry	44	720	3.0
engineering	17	600	2.5
woodwork	16	600	2.5
footwear and leather goods	5	200	0.8
printing and desktop publishing	13	180	0.8
plastics products	4	40	0.2
concrete products	3	30	0.1
brush making	1	40	0.2
(b) *PES farms and gardens*			
farming	42	880	3.7
gardens	128	1,150	4.8
(c) *Other*			
kitchens	123	1,870	7.8
other domestic (cleaners, servery, etc.)	131	11,700	48.9
Works (building maintenance)	131	1,390	5.8

Sources: PES, Prison Service regime monitoring statistics.
Notes:
Total number of prisons: 131. Total number of prisoners included in this table: 23,950. Total prison population: approximately 53,000, which includes (1) small numbers of prisoners employed in kinds of work not shown here, (2) prisoners occupied in ways other than work, (3) unoccupied prisoners. All the figures in this table exclude the four contracted-out prisons, whose population totalled approximately 2,300.

the prison population: the numbers of prisoners it shows as employed total 23,950 and the prison population in 1996 was well over 50,000. The gap is largely explained by several factors. Remand prisoners, who form about a quarter of the population, usually do not work. About a fifth of the population (and rather more than this among young offenders) are in education or training courses and about 4 per cent are in induction.[6] Some others are occupied in other kinds of courses and some in the kinds of work not covered by Table 1. Nevertheless regime monitoring figures suggest that substantial numbers of inmates are unemployed. The majority of them would be remand prisoners, but as we have seen (p. 39) unemployment can affect sentenced people also, despite the Service's policy that for adult sentenced inmates the emphasis should be on work.

Here it is worth remarking that the apparent lack of work for some prisoners occurs despite the efforts of Prison Enterprise Services to provide it. PES budget figures for industries for 1996–7, which contributed to part (a) of Table 1, show a total of 7,200 inmates employed but a total of 10,320 jobs ('resourced employment places') available for them, and a similar over-supply occurs with farms and gardens. The mismatch between workshop places and prisoners to fill them is a perennial problem for prison industrial managers. Among the reasons for it are the fluctuating labour supply, especially in prisons having many short-term prisoners; the preoccupation of staff (especially at overcrowded locals) with day-to-day pressures; governors' differing views on the relative priorities of industrial production versus other occupations for inmates; and the ambivalence of the Service as a whole about the proper role of prison work. (See p.12.)

However, we may take Table 1 as indicating most of the kinds of work available to most prisoners, and now look at it more closely. Certainly there is a great variety of work. But by far the most numerous jobs are for domestic workers: excluding kitchens, domestic service apparently occupies nearly half the prisoners in the Table. Here again people on remand account for a good deal of the story: remand centres (and remand wings in local prisons) often cannot provide work for many of their inmates but they do have to be cleaned, and regime monitoring figures suggest that they employ more domestics than do other prisons.[7]

After domestics, the biggest group of workers is in clothing and textiles: including weaving and other fabric manufacture (but not sewing machine repairs) Table 1 shows 3,020 or 13 per cent of the total. In 1996 sixty prisons had a workshop producing woven or knitted fabrics or articles made from them, and eighteen had at least two such workshops. In many prisons workshops making garments are known as 'the tailors' and this chapter includes a description of them. Later we will address the question of whether in the 1990s so many prisoners (especially men) should be occupied in this kind of work.

Next in frequency of inmate employment, occupying 8 per cent in Table 1, are kitchens: a service essential to morale in every prison, and the one with which we begin our detailed descriptions later in this chapter. Next is a group of workshops called contract services, employing 6 per cent. These typically do unskilled light assembly operations for outside firms, and we describe them too. (Some other prison workshops also take in contract work.) Next in frequency of employment come Works departments, employing 6 per cent of the total in Table 1, gardens at 5 per cent, farming at 4 per cent, and laundry work at 3 per cent. Of all the types of work employing at least 200 prisoners in Table 1, only engineering is not represented in our descriptions, as none of the six research prisons had an engineering production shop.[8] Among the smaller groups our descriptions include printing and leather goods (and also weaving, described separately from tailoring), as these were exemplified in the study.

A note on Prison Enterprise Services

The kinds of work shown in parts (a) and (b) of Table 1 come under the auspices of Prison Enterprise Services (formerly PSIF). Until the Woolf reforms PSIF at

HQ exercised central control and management of the industrial work in all prisons. Following Woolf (see pp. 14, 17) the role of PSIF at the centre changed to one of giving advice, oversight and support to prison governors, who gradually acquired much more freedom to find and manage their own supplies of work for prisoners if they wanted to. In 1993 PSIF (Central Services) Division stated its purpose as:

> serving and supporting prison establishments in the cost-effective provision of purposeful work and training, thereby giving prisoners the opportunity to acquire knowledge, attitudes, skills and habits which will help them to lead law-abiding and useful lives in custody and after release.[9]

A brochure addressed to governors[10] offered a 'one-stop enterprise service' including, among other things, advice and support on investment, product development, plant maintenance, production scheduling, accreditation for quality assurance (especially BS 5750) and negotiation of contracts. Governors were free to find local sources of work as well as, or instead of, accepting what PSIF provided centrally.

Involvement of the private sector was encouraged and could take several forms. Prison-made products could be marketed to outside customers. Firms could send in components for assembly in prison workshops. A prison and a private firm could form a partnership for making particular goods or services. A private company could set up business within a prison, paying rent and employing prisoners. By 1996 PSIF had changed its name to Prison Enterprise Services and was vigorously advertising its capabilities to prisons and outside bodies. In that year also, reorganisation at Prison Service HQ brought PES together with other branches concerned in developing activities for prisoners – including education, physical education, NVQs, offending behaviour programmes and inmates' pay – under the head of 'regime services'. This move was intended to promote co-operation between the various departments of a prison in shaping constructive regimes, instead of the divisions and competition for inmate labour which had formerly been common.

One function of PES was to help prisons achieve ways of paying inmates 'real' or 'enhanced' wages as part of the national framework of incentives (see pp. 22–3). The national budget for prisoners' pay allowed governors an average of £7 a week for each inmate, and any extra had to be raised by increased productivity. One way of attempting this was by selling goods to outside customers, but it was not the only method. Farms and gardens, for example, could earn more by making their produce so attractive that prison kitchens bought more of it than the minimum they were obliged to. At Kirkham, for instance, the farm raised money for enhanced earnings in this way, while the timber workshop did so by outside sales. (See p. 48.)

Making extra money was not easy. In February 1996 PES records showed that three prisons had real wages schemes: East Sutton Park, where four inmates earned £135 a week making cheese for the outside market; Hewell Grange, where four inmates earned the same amount by farm work; and Latchmere House, where seventeen inmates earned up to £80 a week by several means, chiefly through contracts for the light assembly shop and through making plastic products, some in partnership with a private firm. Thus there were just twenty-five prisoners earning realistic pay. Eighteen prisons had enhanced pay schemes, involving 1,317 inmates in total through a variety of work and marketing arrangements. These included, among others, nine prisons whose textile work-shops made some products for outside companies. The enhanced earnings received at the eighteen establishments ranged from an average of £10 a week at Ashwell and Albany to £21 a week at Coldingley (though of course some individuals earned more). The list of prisons planning enhanced earnings schemes was rapidly growing: Maidstone's, for example, started in April 1996 (pp. 55–6).

Partly in conjunction with these developments, PES was helping prisons to start new kinds of work not traditionally carried on in penal institutions. In 1996 these included, for example, desktop publishing, microfiching records, growing mushrooms, producing printed circuit boards, and upholstery. Outside commercial firms and public sector bodies were involved in many of these ventures. So far they employed only small numbers of prisoners.

Having thus surveyed the national scene of prison work, we come to our detailed descriptions of fourteen particular kinds. These draw largely on our observations and interviews at the six prisons in 1992–3, supplemented by some later information from PES, the prisons themselves and other sources. In gathering prisoners' opinions we chatted informally with workers during observations, we asked inmates in general about the popularity of various prison jobs, and we closely questioned the inmates in our main interview sample about the kinds of work they were then doing. One measurement was a 'satisfaction score' based on three factors which can contribute to a person's job satisfaction: feeling a sense of achievement, finding the work interesting, and feeling some sense of power or control over events. Inmates in the main interview sample were asked whether their current work gave them any of these things, and from their answers we compiled a score which could run from zero (no satisfaction) to a maximum of six points. The score gives some indication of how satisfying, or otherwise, the interviewees found their prison jobs.

For ten kinds of work we also describe the examples we saw in outside industry, followed by a short comment. Apart from these ten kinds being presented before the others, they are dealt with in no special order except that we have chosen to begin with the one most essential: kitchens, whose workers enable other workers to eat.

KITCHENS

In prison

Most kitchens, each preparing hundreds or thousands of meals daily for inmates, were run by prison staff with the help of inmate workers, though by 1996 nine establishments (none among our research six) had contracted out their kitchen to private caterers. Typically a prison kitchen was in the charge of officers who had been trained in catering, but civilian instructors were also employed, and there was an increasing trend towards civilian staffing. At the four kitchens we observed in 1992, the number of inmate workers ranged from about eighteen at Channings Wood (with two staff, for 1,600 meals a day) to thirty-eight at Liverpool (with twelve staff, for 3,300 meals). Equipment at that time was a large range of traditional industrial catering machinery: big ovens, steamers and boilers ('coppers'); slicers, mixers and moulders; refrigerators and food trolleys, etc. By 1996 a programme of kitchen refurbishment throughout the Service had replaced some of these items with more modern and versatile appliances like combination ovens and tilting kettles, but no prison kitchen used the cook-chill methods we saw in operation outside (see next section). Prison caterers had a budget (with a national minimum of £1.37 per inmate per day) to buy ingredients as they saw fit (with the proviso that 26 per cent had to be spent on produce from prison farms and gardens). Some prisons provided a choice of menu, but others (Liverpool, for instance) did not, except as required to cater for religious or ethnic groups.

The organisation of the kitchen work we saw differed slightly between prisons, but many of the inmates worked in small teams defined by the various tasks: e.g. cleaning, vegetable preparation, 'the coppers' (boiling stews, rice, custard), butchery, bakery, stores, and so on. Often a team of inmates was led by a 'No. 1' who acted as demonstrator and co-ordinator but had little real authority over his colleagues. Except at Holloway the instructors did most of the actual cooking, with the inmates doing mainly the less skilled tasks. Food ready for eating was put in big containers on to heated trolleys and sent to the wings for dishing up there to individual diners. Kitchen workers were under a good deal of pressure to get the meals ready on time. The atmosphere in the kitchens was generally busy, orderly and noisy, with most of the inmates working hard and the instructors in cheerful control of operations.

Working hours varied somewhat, but typically were at least fifty a week. At Highpoint inmates worked from 7.30 a.m. to 12.30 p.m. (including breakfast on duty) and 2.30 p.m. to 5.30 p.m., with just two rest afternoons weekly. At Channings Wood the earliest workers started at 6 a.m. and, like their colleagues, finished at 5 p.m. with a two-hour midday break; they worked seven days a week. Pay depended on task and skill and was in four grades, except at Holloway where all kitchen workers received the same pay. Most new recruits would start on the lowest grade as washers-up and progress, though any who already had skills, like butchers or bakers, might enter at a higher grade and remain in their speciality. At some prisons, notably Holloway, kitchen inmates tended to stay for many months or several years, making a fairly stable workforce, but at others (especially Liverpool) high turnover could cause problems for the staff.

Training for many inmates in the kitchen was limited to elementary instruction in operating the equipment, but others did acquire some cooking skills. Pressure on staff and inmates to get the meals out on time, together with (in some kitchens) high inmate turnover, militated against systematic training in cooking. Nevertheless in 1995–6, including vocational training courses as well as work in the kitchen, forty-seven prisons were offering NVQ training in catering and 182 prisoners achieved a full NVQ, the great majority at level 1.[11] Kitchen workers and some others, notably domestics serving meals in the wings, were encouraged and very often required (unless employed for only a very short time) to obtain a basic certificate in food hygiene like that of the Institute of Environmental Health Officers. This took six hours' tuition by either kitchen or education staff.

Although kitchen instructors said that many of their inmates were not really interested in the work, they wanted to give training to those who were. One officer in charge (R016), speaking in 1992 when the NVQ programme was struggling to start, said:

> I'd like to get the NVQ off the ground. Not only does it give us a little bit of satisfaction, it makes us far more efficient if the job's done properly, and it give the inmates a bit of satisfaction – you give them a little bit of paper saying that they've *passed*, then it means something to them, and it makes the job a damn sight more interesting.

Inmates in general regarded kitchens as one of the best prison jobs for three main reasons: the relatively good pay, the long working hours which helped to pass the time, and the perks, both official and unofficial. Some prisons allowed their kitchen workers to cook their own meals, and most allowed them extra food (to be eaten in the kitchen) when on duty; there was much resentment in one kitchen when the latter privilege was temporarily withdrawn. Illegitimate perks included opportunities to purloin food for trade with other inmates. ('You'd be surprised where they put it, too,' said one instructor.) A chicken would fetch half an ounce of tobacco. One kitchen worker ran a little business by smuggling left-over food back to his cell, where he made toasted sandwiches for sale (his customers paid in phone cards). Altogether, kitchen work was seen as 'a good bird killer' (i.e. helping to serve one's time). In our main inmate sample sixteen out of seventeen kitchen workers were there by their own choice, and of twenty-two others to whom we chatted informally in the kitchens sixteen said it was a definite help in getting through their sentence. Other reasons for wanting kitchen work were to use existing skills or experience (thirteen of those to whom we chatted said this was so for them), and a smaller group (seven out of twenty-two) hoped they would learn something for use on release, though some were disappointed when they found that the level of skills taught was so low.

The average job satisfaction score for the kitchen workers in our main sample was 2.25, practically the same as that for all inmate workers together (2.21). Workers scoring highly were likely to be those given some responsibility for cooking and scope for contributing to high-quality meals. For example:

> R665 has recently been promoted from the 'potwash' to the bakery team, where everyone knows what needs doing and they work together to achieve it. He is pleased when he sees a good row of loaves he has helped to produce. (But he would like the week's menu to be less predictable, instead of always buns on Monday, rock cakes Tuesday…)

> R668 specialises in cooking for vegans and vegetarians. He is keen on 'healthy eating' and enjoys putting out good food. He knows his fellow inmates like the meals because the numbers asking for them have increased.

Others, however, got less satisfaction:

> R573: 'Prison food is just stew and slops, that's all it is basically. There's not really a great deal to do. It's all just bunged in the copper, stirring it round, a few bits and pieces added to it, and that's it.'

> R514: 'I know they're down to a budget, but at the end of the day…if you've got a bit of meat, you could do a lot more with it than they do.'

> R515: 'When I do mash I like to take all the black bits out of the potatoes, but there isn't enough time to do that.…They put onions or curry powder into everything.'

Other negative comments referred to the heat, the early start, and the rush at meal times.

Holloway's kitchen appeared to give workers rather more scope for creativity than some others did. It employed numbers of foreign inmates who were allowed, within the limitations of the kitchen budget and the ingredients available, to try recipes from their home countries. If the results were successful the staff promoted such meals throughout the prison.

At Highpoint in 1996 we were told that North prison now had a new kitchen. Not only had the equipment been upgraded (and cash catering introduced) but the staff now were all civilians and some were women. This, said our informant, had achieved a more pleasant working atmosphere and better presentation of the food.

A note on the officers' mess

At each prison the staff restaurant ('officers' mess') employed a few inmates, and this was usually a coveted prison job. Typically the mess kitchen, though still equipped for industrial catering, was much smaller than the main prison kitchen and was run quite separately, with different menus and its own supplies of food coming in from outside. A prison officer was in charge, but civilian staff might also be employed, and inmates helped with almost every aspect of the catering.

Because the mess was usually outside the prison walls, inmates working there were very carefully selected as low security risks, and they had to be presentable and trustworthy. Most enjoyed the work and their privileged position. R680, for instance, said: 'Yes, great satisfaction....I like helping with the cooking, presenting the food....I enjoy feeding people really.' R609 particularly liked helping prepare a buffet for staff functions at weekends: 'On a busy Saturday, when we're getting it ready, that's a good buzz....We set up the big table, it looks terrific when it's laid out.' And R548, recalling his time in a mess, said:

> I was getting better food, food from outside, and the officers were paying for it so I felt even better. The officers were more friendly with me because I was handling their food. They'd get matey with me so I'd give them bigger portions. It was nice to be on the other side for a change.

Outside example

This was an NHS hospital catering service comprising two parts: a kitchen which prepared approximately 4,000 'cook-chill' meals daily for sale to four hospitals; and the catering department of one of them, which fed 400 patients and 150 staff by buying meals from this kitchen, together with other food (like fresh sandwiches and fruit).

In the kitchen 4,000 meals were produced daily by eight workers: two supervising chefs, two other chefs and four catering assistants. There were also three porters and two clerks, and the whole kitchen was run by a manager and his deputy. The production staff worked a 39-hour week in straight shifts spread between 7 a.m. and 8 p.m., with occasional very small amounts of overtime.

The kitchen actually comprised a large number of rooms all at different controlled temperatures, and was full of modern machinery and highly automated. Equipment included, for example, a cook tank (which had cost £30,000), two cryogenic chillers, heat-sealing machines, special storage racks for the cold rooms, and much else. Raw materials were bought in ready-prepared (e.g. frozen foods, peeled potatoes) and assembled by the assistants or made up by the chefs according to recipes. When cooked, the food was portioned out into plastic containers, heat sealed, chilled and stored ready for distribution to the purchasing hospitals. For supplying the hospital we visited, which was on the same site, the kitchen had a conveyor belt and food trolleys. Patients' orders were all made up within two hours of receipt.

The operations were closely and smoothly regulated, with steady flows of work and no rush periods. The manager said he could not imagine making a steak and kidney pie without a computer telling him what to buy and the processes to get the timing right. Each worker had their own duties, with little interchange of jobs (to prevent cross-contamination) and little need for one person to help another (because of the strict allocation of space in ovens and chillers). The whole kitchen appeared very sanitised and orderly, with constant cleaning going on.

All production staff had a City and Guilds qualification (C&G 706/1 for assistants, 706/2 for chefs).[12] Hygiene was strongly emphasised. Workers who did not already have the basic food-handling certificate were being trained to acquire it, and all received refresher courses. Pay for catering assistants and porters was £14,000 and for chefs £16,000; rates were enhanced by an attendance allowance, and bonuses for high-quality products and for working at low temperatures. The manager thought his workers' main sources of job satisfaction were the pay and good working conditions. The automated processes allowed little scope for individual creativity, and there were no official perks. (Meals on duty had to be paid for. It was suggested that staff occasionally contrived unofficial perks by negotiating cash-on-delivery deals with outside suppliers of food.)

The hospital catering department (which bought these meals and other food) employed twenty-six catering assistants and two supervisors, besides the manager and her deputy. The assistants worked a 35-hour week in shifts between 8 a.m. and 8 p.m. They were divided into four groups: for plating-up meals, serving in the restaurant, tending the vending machines, and taking trolleys to the wards for service to patients there. Team work was encouraged. The plating team had two hours to get meals plated and out, and although there were rush periods in the restaurant the workers altogether did not appear to be under great pressure.

Qualifications were not necessary, though a few of the workers had C&G 706/1. Hygiene was strongly emphasised, and all assistants received ongoing (uncertificated) training in hygiene and 'customer care'. The assistants' work was largely routine, but they were encouraged to contribute ideas when, for example, new menus or special functions were being planned. Staff were allowed one meal on duty (and some probably took more).

Both the kitchen and the hospital catering department had very few discipline problems, and the workforces were extremely stable, the kitchens having lost only one worker in the previous three years and the catering department none. There was thus very little scope for promotion or need for recruitment. Any vacancies would be advertised internally, at the jobcentre and in the local press, and applicants with experience of catering and an understanding of hygiene would be sought. Asked whether they would consider employing ex-prisoners, the kitchen manager appeared very doubtful, but the catering manager said it would depend on the nature of the offence (e.g. a conviction for theft or fraud would be frowned on), whether the applicant had catering experience, and whether they showed willingness to be law-abiding and to work hard.

Comments

The most obvious differences between the hospital kitchen and the prison ones (apart from the pay) were that the prison kitchens used more workers, working longer hours, to produce a similar number of meals. The hospital kitchen ran by modern technology, whereas the prison kitchens used traditional industrial equipment. The hospital kitchen ran quietly and smoothly, without the noise, heat and rush of the prisons. Although the prison kitchens generally looked clean, the hospital kitchen was cleaner and the quality of its meals higher than some of those we saw in prisons. Of course not all outside catering organisations use such automated 'hi-tech' methods, though the trend is growing.

GARDENS

In prison

Almost all prisons had gardens, and some of them regularly won prizes. In our research sample the Category C and D prisons (Channings Wood, Highpoint and Kirkham) had plenty of space, and besides ornamental flower beds and lawns there were sportsfields, greenhouses and vegetable gardens. Kirkham, for example, sold produce on the open market as well as supplying food and bedding plants to other prisons. In 1992 Kirkham had 4 acres of glasshouses and 150 polytunnels producing tomatoes and many kinds of salads, while its open fields grew several varieties of root and green vegetables in addition to potatoes. By 1996 the acreage under glass and polythene had increased to seven and a half, and there was a new cold store for keeping fresh produce until it could fetch the best price.

Prisoners helped with nearly all the gardens work (except the use of chemicals) under the supervision of civilian instructors. About twice as many inmates were employed in summer as in winter, but the daily working hours were the same throughout the year, with few inmates working at weekends. Pay was in four grades. Tools and machinery were modern and in good supply; for instance, inmates drove tractors, mowers and cultivators, and used a variety of hand tools as required. In the ornamental gardens it was common for individual prisoners to have their own bed or small section to look after; others, such as vegetable pickers, worked in teams. At Channings Wood inmates of the VPU had their own separate garden but other inmates were occasionally sent over to help them. In warmer weather much of the gardens work appeared pleasant and relaxed, with some people working steadily and others less so. In winter there was naturally far less outdoor activity, though prisoners had to shovel snow when necessary and there was still work in the greenhouses.

Gardens instructors often found that inmates sent to them by the labour board were a very mixed lot, with many having no experience and no interest in the work, at any rate initially. 'They're as green as grass,' said R035, while R036 said, 'Normally we get the ones that nobody else wants.' The presence of unwilling workers made difficulties for the staff, who had to spend much time organising them while leaving others to get on with tasks under less supervision than was desirable.

Nonetheless there were ways of generating enthusiasm. Highpoint staff had transformed the motivation of reluctant recruits who had arrived with the attitude 'we're builders, we don't want to dig gardens' by inviting them to design and build raised beds (with brick walls) and then choose plants with which to stock them (certain plants, of course, not being permitted). Training in horticulture was given to workers who showed interest, especially the minority of inmates who stayed two years or longer. By 1995–6 twenty-five prisons were offering NVQ training in amenity horticulture and three were offering it in commercial horticulture, and in that year seventy-two prisoners achieved a full certificate, nearly all at level 1.

However, in spring 1996 budget cuts had reduced some training prospects. Kirkham was no longer giving certificated training, and its ratio of inmates per member of staff had risen from about twelve to twenty-five.[13] Highpoint had bought no seeds for three months, so production in the polytunnels was interrupted. At Highpoint also, it was planned that after the present gardens manager retired his post would be downgraded to that of foreman to save money, and that the thirteen inmates now working in 'market gardens' would instead be employed on general grounds maintenance.

Prisoners in general viewed gardens work in summer as one of the best prison jobs because it offered fresh air and sunshine together with a sense of relative freedom. This was especially so for Category D inmates who could work outside the gate, though by 1996 the new security rules had reduced their number. Perks in the form of garden produce seemed fairly unimportant, though salad pickers might supplement their diets, and a greenhouse instructor said that if a small ornamental plant disappeared to decorate someone's cell while his back was turned, 'Well, my back's turned.' In 1992 there were opportunities at Kirkham to collect parcels left at the boundary by outsiders, but by 1996 the new fourteen-foot fence had put a stop to that.

Though a few found field work and picking tomatoes boring, most garden workers to whom we spoke liked their jobs, especially when they had some responsibility for their own patch. They enjoyed the exercise, using the equipment and helping plants to grow. Of seven to whom we chatted informally, none had any previous skill in gardening but four thought it could be useful after release, for 'do-it-yourself' (DIY) rather than employment. Of the nine garden workers in our main inmate sample eight had asked for gardens, and for those nine the average job satisfaction score was 4.11, well above the average of 2.21 for all workers. For example:

R687 had acquired some skills in a garden training scheme before coming to prison and is now learning more, including the care of trees and shrubs (though Holloway has no certificated training). She digs, plants and weeds, rejoicing in the vigorous manual work. She likes to go out in the morning and see that the plants she put in a short time before have taken root: knowing that they will thrive is 'a boost to my ego'. She also enjoys the friendship of the prison's cat, which regularly visits her while she is working.

R513 works on his own outside the gate, collecting his tools each day and feeling like 'more or less my own boss'. He is proud of the very attractive flower beds he helped to make. 'They definitely make me feel good. Even when I am gone from this place they'll still be there.'

A note on Kirkham's packing shed

In 1992 Kirkham had a large packing shed where about twenty inmates worked peeling vegetables, packing them and loading them for transport to other prisons. It had a big potato peeling machine, other machines, water troughs, plastic sacks, pallets and other equipment, but some of the work had to be done by hand and most of it was very routine. The room was noisy (with machines and radios on) and the workers looked busy but not cheerful. The packing shed was then one of the prison's most unpopular jobs, and farm or garden workers who misbehaved were liable to be sent for a spell there.

By 1996 this place had been transformed. Upgraded equipment included a potato processor which washed and bagged as well as peeling, and a tomato grader which sorted the fruits by size and colour and packed them into cartons. Inmates drove forklift trucks and loaded refrigerated lorries which took the produce to twenty-two other prisons. Now paying enhanced wages, the 'veg prep' was a sought-after job, and a manager said that productivity had increased by three or four times.

Outside examples

We visited two employers for comparison: a vegetable grower and a nursery producing ornamental plants.

Vegetable grower

This firm supplied tomatoes and salads under contract for a high-class supermarket chain. It was one of several sites owned by one company, and our interviewees were the firm's glasshouse director and two of his site managers. The site described here had eight and a half acres under glass in two sections: one cultivating only tomatoes between December and October, and the other growing tomatoes from February to September and then lettuces during the winter. At the end of each tomato season the houses were completely cleared out and sterilised and the soil and growbags prepared for planting the next crop. Plants were bought in from an outside propagator.

Staff comprised three at supervisor level, and basic workers who fell into two distinct groups: about fifteen full-timers who worked all year round, and about twenty-four part-timers who were engaged for the main tomato harvesting season from May to September. Each full-time worker had a negotiated contract to care for an agreed number (several thousand) of tomato plants as his own 'patch'. Those who undertook the most worked up to seventy hours a week, earning about £400 in the height of the season, and then dropped back to thirty-nine hours for about £150 a week between September and February, the lowest grade of pay being set at the Agricultural Wages Board (AWB) rate. Their most skilled task was managing the growing plants to produce exactly the required standard of fruit, and in this they worked as individuals; in the autumn clear-out before the new planting they worked in teams on the less skilled labouring tasks. Many of these full-time workers had been with the firm at least five years, and but for the recession might have had the opportunity of promotion to supervisor or assistant manager.

The part-timers were casual workers engaged afresh each season, though many came year after year. They worked from 7 a.m. to 11 a.m., adults working Monday to Friday and schoolchildren coming in on Saturdays. All were paid piece rates (with the AWB as a floor) and an average worker could earn £4 to £5 an hour. These people picked the tomatoes directly into trays for supermarkets, according to strict criteria of size, shape and colour and under very close supervision.

Training was given to both groups of workers in short sessions as required, on matters like safe lifting and harvesting. The full-time workers, but not the casuals, did a basic health and hygiene certificate, and any sprayers who did not have a certificate would be sent on a course to get one. As well as the basic workers who received these kinds of training, the garden had one person doing a three-year apprenticeship in horticulture, who was expected eventually to achieve NVQ level 3 when the syllabus had been finalised.

As well as seasonal peaks and troughs there were daily deadlines during tomato harvesting, and hourly deadlines for cutting lettuces. The atmosphere was strict and businesslike, with insistence on very high quality. The director said, 'We are working at the top end of the customer spectrum...the company is not interested in mass production of things anybody can do.' Full-time employees clocked in, and any who were more than three minutes late had fifteen minutes' pay deducted. There was no scope for individuality in the way the work was done, except that full-timers could decide how long to work to fulfil their tomato contracts, and there was friendly rivalry between them over the yield and appearance of their patches. Unauthorised removal of anything from the site brought instant dismissal, but staff were given vegetables on bank holidays and a hamper at Christmas.

The part-timers were recruited each season principally by word of mouth and a vacancy board at the gate, and also by local press advertisements. The director said he would give preference to applicants who came knocking at the door 'because at least they've had the nous to actually come out looking for work, as opposed to sitting back and waiting to see [if there was a press advertisement]'. Previous experience was an advantage but not essential. If any full-time vacancies occurred they would be advertised similarly and in the trade press, and applicants with experience in a tomato garden would be preferred. The company did not ask applicants for basic grade positions whether they had criminal records. The two site managers made it clear that they just looked for willingness and ability to do the work, and in fact one of them at that time had two ex-prisoners in his workforce.

Nursery

This was a large business supplying ornamental plants wholesale to garden centres, and our main informant was the managing director. On two sites, the nursery produced over a million plants a year in huge variety. The propagation site had four acres of glasshouses and the growing-on site occupied twenty acres, with glasshouses, polytunnels, open spaces and a packing shed. Besides managers and supervisors, the employees numbered about a hundred during the busiest period (March to May), and gradually reduced by September to about fifty for the winter months. Thus, as at the vegetable grower's, the nursery staff divided into permanent and casual workers, but unlike the vegetable workers the nursery people when employed all worked full-time, a forty-hour week Monday to Friday with little overtime. There were several grades of pay depending on task and ability, with the AWB rates as minimum.

Plants were all grown in pots from seeds or cuttings. The nursery was like a big factory with a great variety of manual operations, many of them fairly simple. We saw a team of women (preferred for their dexterity) who rooted cuttings into little pots; another team operated a simple potting machine; other people moved loaded trolleys to where their colleagues set out pots; others were responsible for watering and spraying. In the packing shed the pots brought in on trailers from the garden areas were sorted, labelled and packed for transport by lorry to the firm's customers. The nursery manager ran the production schedule and his supervisors had a good deal of responsibility for care of the plants (which all appeared in excellent condition), but the basic workers had little scope for initiative. The working atmosphere seemed busy and purposeful.

Most training of basic workers took place on the job as required, and some could learn a variety of operations to broaden their skills. The director emphasised practical training and was a little sceptical of paper qualifications, though some staff were sent away for courses to qualify in skills such as spraying, forklift driving or first-aid. Students wanting work experience were gladly taken on during the busy season. Seasonal workers, initially unskilled, were recruited each spring through the jobcentre and local press. For permanent jobs, applicants with training or experience in nursery work would be welcome, but because of the recession there had been no vacancy in the last four years. Most of the present supervisors had risen through the ranks. The director said all job applicants were asked to declare any unspent convictions, but a person with a criminal record would be considered on merit, and experience or training in nursery work would count in their favour.

Comments

Compared with the vegetable grower and plant nursery we saw, prison gardens at Channings Wood, Highpoint and Kirkham offered more variety, more scope for initiative and in some respects more training (at least until 1996) to basic-grade workers who were interested and willing. Although the quality of prison produce was high, that of the vegetable grower was much higher, achieved in conditions of close supervision, strict discipline and great pressure of time schedules. High standards and orderliness were obvious at the nursery too, though there seemed to be slightly less pressure, and the nursery was more like the prison gardens than was the vegetable grower in its arrangements for varying the size of the labour force according to seasons. The prison gardens with their sportsfields, lawns, flower beds and food production covered a greater variety of work than either of the two employers, and inmates who wanted (and whose stay was long enough) to train for NVQ level 2 (when available) might have good opportunities, except for some operations like spraying. But they would have to work a good deal harder for an outside employer than did most of the leisurely garden workers we saw in the prisons.

FARMS

In prison

Kirkham Prison's farm, typical in many ways of others, had over 500 acres devoted to dairying, cattle rearing, pigs and arable crops. The 150-strong dairy herd supplied milk to prisons and the open market, the annual yield per cow averaging 6,300 litres in 1996. Calves were reared as replacement stock and for sale, and 1,200 pigs (from eighty breeding sows) supplied bacon and pork, mainly to other prisons. Two rare breeds – longhorn cattle and British Lop pigs – were reared for showing and sale, and frequently won prizes. The fields grew grass for animal feed and a variety of vegetables for human consumption.

About twenty-eight prisoners shared the farm work with civilian staff, who in 1992 numbered five. Because the farm was about twenty miles from the prison the inmate workers were transported there each morning, and in 1992 there were two shifts, an early one from 5.30 a.m. and a later one from 9 a.m., both finishing at 4 p.m. By 1996 this had changed to one inmate shift from 8 a.m. to 5 p.m. and the number of staff had increased to seven, the staff having taken over the early milking. Inmates' pay was graded according to task and skill, and in 1996 the farm paid enhanced wages.

To the visitor the working atmosphere was orderly and businesslike. The indoor rearing pens for calves and pigs were clean and well-equipped, and the milking parlour and adjacent pasteurising plant were shining and full of modern technology. Cows grazed in the fields and the prize pigs lived free-range. Prisoners helped with all the work, usually in teams under a staff member and with a No. 1. The most skilled work was in the dairy unit and caring for the young stock, with daily deadlines for milking, cleaning and feeding. A new inmate would usually start in the 'labour gang' whose tasks included fencing, digging, lifting potatoes and so on, all with appropriate machinery, and from there a capable man could work his way up to a more responsible job such as the No. 1 in charge of farrowing, building stone walls or tractor driving.

Of Kirkham inmates assigned to the farms and gardens department, the farm received the most willing and reliable men, though they included a wide range of ability and some recruits had no idea of what farming work involved. The staff placed strong and continual emphasis on health and safety: as one instructor said, 'If there was a finger or something going missing we'd be hung out to dry.' Some men proved capable but others needed repeatedly to be told and shown what to do. Only inmates over 40, with a full clean driving licence, were allowed to drive tractors.

At the time of our first research visit in 1992, five inmates were training for NVQ level 1 in agricultural skills, but four years later Kirkham offered no NVQs, though nationally seven other prisons did so and in 1995–6 fifteen prisoners gained a full certificate (five at level 1 and ten at level 2). Kirkham farm workers were taught on the job according to ability, but the only qualification available in 1996 was the basic food hygiene certificate, compulsory for those handling food.

Staff said inmates either loved the farm work or hated it. Only a few Kirkham inmates interviewed thought the farm one of the best jobs (mentioning freedom, fresh air and the opportunity to drive tractors) but not all of them had been there, and the early start in all weathers (in 1992) would have put many of them off. But for farm workers who did 'stick it out' the work could be very satisfying: vigorous outdoor labour, learning new skills and caring for animals. Exhibiting at agricultural shows could sometimes provide a welcome break of three or four days and nights away from the prison. Of the three farm workers who turned up in our main interview sample two were thoroughly enjoying it:

> R533: A middle-aged city-dweller, he has never done anything like it before, but now it feels just like a holiday. He feeds stock, drives a tractor, mends fences and walls, and is left largely on his own to do what he sees is needed. He has enjoyed learning to handle cows. 'Cows can be bloody-minded.'

> R532 has learned to care for pigs. 'It's like a hobby – I'm enjoying it. It's a long day, but it's a good day.'

And then there were the illicit perks. One inmate who had worked on a prison farm hinted at 'arranging days out', but probably more frequent was 'the drop' – caches of contraband (drugs, alcohol, tobacco) left by members of the public, walking through the farm, for inmates to carry back to prison. One staff member said, 'We try and catch as much as we can, but you could chase yourself silly....What we catch is probably the tip of the iceberg.' Just before our updating visit two Kirkham farm workers had been demoted after being caught bringing back binliners full of drink which had been left for them.

Outside example

The farm we visited to compare with Kirkham's was a property of 1,200 acres, divided like the prison farm between dairy, pigs and arable. The dairy herd included 320 cows producing an annual average of 6,700 litres of milk per cow, and replacement calves were reared. The pig unit, with 240 breeding sows, was wholly for producing meat. The fields grew grass and cereals (chiefly wheat, oats and oilseed rape) for animal and human foodstuffs.

Besides the farm manager and his office staff, the farm was run by a permanent workforce of three foremen (dairy, pigs and arable), seven other full-time workers and two part-timers, plus six to eight temporary workers brought in at harvest time. The dairy men worked a ten-hour day (excluding meal breaks) starting at 4.45 a.m., eleven days a fortnight, and the pig workers (who included one woman employed especially to care for the farrowing sows and their newborns) did an eight-hour day twelve days a fortnight. Pay was based on AWB rates plus an additional bonus: a basic-grade permanent worker received between £11,000 and £12,000 a year. Staff perks comprised free milk, a nominal rent for the six who lived in farm houses, and having their council tax paid by the farm.

In many respects the work was similar to what went on at Kirkham, and with great emphasis on high quality. The dairy unit did not pasteurise, but sent its cooled milk away to market every day in tankers. High yield was achieved by very close attention to the feeding of each cow. In the pig unit the sows' breeding pens were similar to Kirkham's, but after weaning the piglets were intensively reared in 'piggieboxes': mobile structures comprising several tiers of cages each holding about eight piglets, with slatted floors, automatic feeding and temperature controls, and all kept extremely clean. However, this intensive system was gradually being changed (in response to public opinion, said the manager) to one rearing the pigs at ground level in ventilated sheds which would give them more room. The arable unit differed from Kirkham's in concentrating on cereals and engaging casual labour for harvesting.

Each of the foremen told us of his satisfaction with the work. They said all their workers knew what had to be done in the daily rhythm of tasks, they solved any problems themselves and just got on with it. Enjoyment was derived from the variety of work, from growing things and from pride in good results. The dairyman said, 'The cows are one big family. We've bred three generations of them, we know all the cows as individuals, we knew their parents and grandparents.' Two factors appearing to contribute much to the farm's success were the strong team spirit among the staff of each unit, and the constant exchange of information between management and workers.

All the permanent staff were highly skilled and three had been apprentices there, though there were no apprentices now. Most had been employed by the farm for many years, and the last vacancy had occurred two years ago. The manager said that he would fill any by making his own enquiries of colleagues and family friends for a person with the right skills or experience, and would check references very carefully. He recruited the casual labourers in the same way, by word of mouth and recommendation, not by advertising. He said he would almost certainly not consider an ex-prisoner, out of concern for the security of the estate and the safety of families living on it.

Comments

The satisfactions of farm work, to willing workers, were obvious at both this farm and Kirkham. The main contrast between the two, apart from size and the differences in product already mentioned, was in the number of workers employed, the prison having far more and producing much less. This was due not to mechanisation – the equipment and materials at both farms were broadly similar – but to the inmate workforce at Kirkham being far less skilled, less stable and more in need of supervision.

TEXTILES AND CLOTHING

As Table 1 has shown, textiles and clothing manufacture occupied in 1995–6 the second largest group of prison workers, with nearly a half of all prisons having at least one such workshop. The 'needle trades' have been a traditional form of prison work for well over a century, although machines long ago replaced sewing by hand. Sewing machines take up less space and are cheaper to install than much other industrial equipment, and the products can supply many of the requirements of prisons for garments and bedding as well as making goods for sale outside. A PES leaflet in 1996 showed a turnover of £14 million a year in this sector and listed a great variety of products, including work garments, shirts, underwear, casual wear, bedlinen and blankets. Fabrics made included denim, shirting, sheeting and interlock. Several prisons provided a cutting service and one (Blundeston) specialised in design.

The clothing and textile industry in prisons was one of the first to offer NVQ training to inmates, and in 1995–6 thirty-three establishments were doing so. One hundred and thirty-five prisoners achieved a full certificate, the great majority in production machine sewing at level 2. Garment production workshops in men's prisons are commonly called 'the tailors' and we saw three of them as well as the sewing room at Holloway. These are described, and compared with an outside clothing factory, in the first section below. The following section describes the weaving workshops we saw at Kirkham, together with an outside comparison.

Machine sewing in prison

The tailors' workshops we saw in 1992–3 were making white cotton coats (for servery workers) at Channings Wood, denim jeans at Highpoint and pyjama jackets at Liverpool, while the sewing room at Holloway was making kitchen workers' white caps as well as hemming sheets and towels. The inmate workers numbered about thirty at Holloway and sixty to eighty at the men's prisons, under civilian instructors who at Liverpool and Highpoint included both men and women.

The equipment comprised small industrial sewing machines – flatbed machines, overlockers, buttonholers, etc. – and a range of hand tools. The larger workshops had a Hoffman press, and Channings Wood and Liverpool had a cutting section. The machinists mostly worked as individuals, on just one opera-tion at a time repeatedly: sewing seams, attaching pockets or inserting zips, and so on. At Channings Wood and Liverpool the machines were arranged in lines, and at Highpoint in groups of six. At Holloway some were in pairs facing each other so that friends could chat while working. Some inmates worked as demon-strators or quality checkers, or 'ran the line' by collecting and distributing work; these arrangements varied somewhat between the four workshops. Cutting was the most skilled job, and the finished garments were of very high quality.

Except at Holloway most workers were paid piece rates, so that a prisoner's earnings depended on his output, with a ceiling; at Holloway pay was in several grades depending on quality and the worker's length of service. The working atmosphere was noisy (with the machines and radio on) and generally busy. In 1992 production runs could be very long: an order from PSIF HQ for jeans or boxer shorts might occupy a workshop for up to a year. By 1996 things had changed so that orders were for only three months at a time. This could give workers a little more variety (unless an order was immediately repeated), though one manager said that production was now harder to plan smoothly and he preferred the old system.

Initial training for a new recruit in operating a sewing machine needed a few days at Holloway, and usually several weeks for the men. Thereafter a worker would be assigned to a task according to his or her ability. Those who stayed long enough could learn several machines: at Highpoint a demonstrator, for example, could do eight operations. NVQs to level 2 were available at Channings Wood and Highpoint, and the instructors at these prisons regarded NVQ training, for the minority of inmates who were interested, as the most positive aspect of their work. Holloway sewing workers were encouraged to attend the education department's class in textiles (and occasionally given time off work to do so), though the skills learned there were unlikely to be used in the workshop.

Among the majority of male inmates generally 'the tailors' was one of the most unpopular jobs, mainly because they felt it was boring and of little rele-vance to them. Several said it was 'women's work'. Ethnic minority inmates tended to see it differently and we met several, like R625 below, who thought it might be useful experience for the future. A few others also found they liked it, despite their initial dismay when first confronted with a sewing machine, and the roles of quality inspector and (for one man who had been an engineer) machine maintenance were relatively responsible. At Highpoint the majority's dislike of the work was somewhat softened by the pleasant working atmosphere engendered by the female instructors, and Liverpool men usually stayed only a few weeks anyway before transfer to other prisons.

At Channings Wood in 1992 'the tailors' was the most hated job in the prison, and this made life difficult for the instructors. They had to accept all comers, most of their recruits were not there by choice, and a prison manager freely admitted that the tailors' shop was used to contain disaffected inmates who could not be occupied anywhere else. Production was hindered by the presence of the 'scallywags', who the instructors felt sometimes numbered nearly half their work-force, and almost the only 'carrot' they could offer was to promise an inmate that if he stuck it out and worked well for three months they would recommend him to the labour board for transfer to work more to his liking.

Four years later, however, several factors at Channings Wood had combined to ease matters. Under the new incentive scheme the basic regime had replaced the tailors as a 'sin bin', and the new light assembly shop absorbed inmates with the shortest sentences so that the tailors' workforce was a little more stable. And one instructor now gave a special induction to new arrivals who had been assigned to 'primary labour': he showed them over both the wood assembly and the tailors' shops, gave them a talk on health and safety, and tried to make them feel welcome. Quite often, we were told, men given a choice between these two shops now opted for the tailors.

In the Holloway sewing room in 1993 the atmosphere was very different from those of the male tailors' shops. Most of the women in the sewing room had asked to work there and wanted to stay, and the two instructors had a high repu-tation for giving them personal interest and care. Here too there was a very popular incentive scheme: if the workers completed the week's production quota by Friday lunchtime they could have Friday afternoons to sew whatever they wanted from a special store of materials (sent in by well-wishers), or to learn extra dressmaking skills from the instructors.

Of twenty sewing workers to whom we chatted informally, nine said the work was related in some way to their previous experience, eleven thought it a definite help in getting through their sentence and six thought it would be useful after release. The majority of these positive answers came from Holloway. Our main inmate sample included eighteen sewing workers, twelve of whom had had no choice about doing it. Sixteen of this group were scored for job satisfaction and their average score was 1.0, nearly the lowest of all the main groups of workers scored. The following examples illustrate a range of views.

> R625, serving a long sentence in Maidstone, has been in the tailors' shop there for two years by his own choice. He has learned all the operations including cutting and is now a quality checker. An unskilled labourer before his sentence, R, who is Asian, sees this as an opportunity to learn a trade for his release. 'I'm doing what I think is good for me.' His wife can sew too, he says, so perhaps eventually they can set up in business together.

R583 is also a quality checker and feels that in the tailors' shop he has some responsibility. But he works there only to kill time. On the outside his trade is industrial painting, and 'inspecting a pair of jeans won't get me a good job'.

R505, a former computer operator, has been in the tailors for five months. He is machining collars on to white servery jackets. 'They're just, like, forcing you to do the same job over and over again. It gets pretty boring after a while....There's no colour out there – it's just straight white jackets. Even if they put green ones in front of you that would be a change, something different to look at.'

R504: 'It's back to the old way of punishment....You're just sat there...you're treated completely different. They say here's your material, this is what you have to do to get your pay, and get on with it.'

Perks available in the tailors could be fairly important. Holloway sewing workers were allowed to mend and iron their own clothes on Friday afternoons, and in the male prisons instructors might turn a blind eye to such things. But some men went further. Prison garments could be altered to give a bit of individuality: trousers shortened, collars narrowed, sleeves cut off to make T-shirts. 'It makes your wardrobe a bit bigger, don't it, 'cos if you was to wear the clothes they give you here, like one pair of jeans a week, you know' (R567). And such things could be done for friends in return for other favours.

Outside example

We visited a small factory making skirts on a 'cut, make and trim' basis (i.e. batch production with pattern and fabric supplied by the customer). It made about a thousand skirts a week, and our informants were the workroom supervisor and the representative of a garment manufacturers' association who had arranged our visit.

The workroom was smaller than any of the prison tailors' workshops, and was equipped with very similar machines and one or two others (including a vacuum shaver for removing threads instead of snipping them off by hand as prisoners did). Eleven people worked there: the supervisor (a woman), a cutter and presser (men), and eight women machinists. The firm also employed about half a dozen machinists who worked at home.

The room was fairly quiet and extremely busy, with the machinists whizzing through their work. Most did just one or two operations, but they could change round for variety if they wished. The most skilled worker was the supervisor who could operate all the machines and make up demonstration samples. The firm made only skirts, but production runs were short: we saw three styles being made, and every week or so would bring a fresh order with a different fabric and style. The supervisor said, 'It's better to change, it's better psychologically. The change relaxes your mind, you have more energy.' There was a forty-hour working week and most people were on piece rates, earning between £100 and £150 weekly.

Very little time was given to training because of the need for production to compete with rival manufacturers: the supervisor said, 'It's all rush, rush, rush.' Recruits (who usually came by word of mouth) were expected to be skilled already, and we were told there was a good deal of poaching between firms. But if a machinist showed real interest and talent the supervisor would give her experience on all the machines to train her as a 'sample sewer' (as she was herself), who were hard to come by. None of the workers had formal qualifications, and job applicants would be expected simply to show that they could do the work. Questions about a criminal record would not be asked.

In a discussion on the industry our informants said that cutters and pressers were nearly all men, but machinists (unless they were immigrants) were nearly all women. But the supervisor said that if a man applied who was a versatile machinist she would be pleased to take him. 'I think men have more stamina.'

Comments

This small factory was in London, which is not a centre of the clothing trade, and we were told that in other parts of the country there was more interest in training and the development of NVQs. The contrast between the training available in prison workshops (to those few inmates who were keen) and the absence of it at the firm we visited was interesting. Another difference was that, although in both places the work was largely de-skilled, the factory had smaller runs and could provide its workers with more variety as relief from boredom. The biggest contrast was in the ratio of the sexes: outside prisons sewing machinists are mostly women, but inside they are perforce mostly men, of whom few have any real interest in the work.

Weaving in prison

Like its outside counterpart in prosperous times, the prison weaving industry was concentrated in the north-west of England, and we saw it in operation at Kirkham in 1992. Here in a large weaving shed about thirty prisoners and several civilian instructors were producing plain coloured cotton cloth, while nearby in a smaller building, the warp preparation shed, a workforce of half that size prepared the yarn for the weavers.

In the weaving shed inmates ran Northrop looms and other machines for winding, knotting, plaiting and other operations, while a few worked as quality inspectors or cleaners. The 'warp prep' was equipped with a sizing machine, high-speed beamers, winders and knotters. Both workshops were extremely noisy when the machines were running; conversation was impossible, and all workers had to wear ear protectors. At the time of our visit the weaving shed was also very dusty, with a fine cloud in the upper air, and we were told that some of the overhead water sprayers were faulty. The looms were forty years old and outmoded, and a manager said that to comply with current health and safety legislation the equipment needed to be replaced. (In 1993 it was, as discussed later in this section.)

All the inmates seemed to be working hard, some as individuals and others in pairs or small teams, and the cloth appeared of good quality. The working week was thirty-three hours, and pay, which included an environment allowance, was graded according to skill and the number of machines operated. An inmate running six looms in the weaving shed could earn the highest prison pay at Kirkham. Basic training was given on each machine as required and, especially in the 'warp prep', staff offered capable workers systematic training on a variety of machines. Those who stayed about six months could gain a certificate of competence in the machines they had used, issued by the local college of further education. In 1996, however, no qualifications were available.

Kirkham inmates in general in 1992 regarded 'the weavers' as one of the worst prison jobs because of the noise and dust. One of the instructors said, 'We never get volunteers. A lot of people go white the first time they come up here.' Nevertheless it was recognised as a good 'bird killer': all nine inmates to whom we chatted briefly said it helped them to get through their sentence, and three had had some previous experience in the textile industry, though most of the nine would not be seeking such work after release. Only four weavers in our main inmate sample could be scored for job satisfaction, but all scored at least three points and two scored the maximum of six. They spoke of pleasure at seeing the results of their work, the interest of learning new skills, and the responsibility of running the machines, where they could set their own pace.

> R531, in 'warp prep', said: 'What I make as the end result goes on to these machines...for making materials for our shirts and things like that....It's a job where it's up to you how much work you can contribute in a day.' He felt there was a good spirit among his workmates, and looked forward to work each morning.

> R529, however, had a somewhat different point of view. After complaining mildly that weavers were not allowed to sit down while working and that the ten-minute rest breaks were too short, he said the work was useful because the noise of the looms sent him into a trance which helped him to forget he was in prison. But then he added, quite cheerfully, that the rhythm of the looms was 'You never get out, you never get out' (!)

Opportunities for perks were not obvious but an astute inmate could find some. R527's job was to check the finished cloth for flaws, and on his actions the pay of other weavers partly depended. If he passed their work they might earn the highest grade, £6.90 a week, but if he sent their cloth back for correction they would earn no more than £4.20. R arranged with some of his colleagues that he would pass their faulty work if they paid him a weekly Mars bar, and as a

Mars bar cost 25p both parties benefited, said R. But he declined to supply this service to inmates he regarded as mere 'skivers' in the weaving shed.

Between 1993 and 1996 the weaving industries at Kirkham and other prisons were overhauled and modernised at a cost of approximately half a million pounds. Up-to-date machinery was put in, there was far less dust (though still much noise), and weavers were no longer paid a special allowance. We were told at Kirkham in 1996 that although new inmates at first still had an unfavourable perception of the weavers, with time and experience they found the work satisfying and production had increased.

Outside example

Our comparison visit was made in mid-1993 to a mill producing high-class dress and suit fabrics, where we saw the operations and interviewed two managers. We also had a discussion with the manager of another mill.

The one visited had several sheds for warp preparation and weaving, together with a small laboratory for design and development. Weaving was done on Sulzer looms, two-colour and four-colour, and all the machinery was very modern, some having electronic controls. Compared with what we had seen at Kirkham the previous year there was more space between the machines and they made less dust and noise, though ear protectors were still needed. Production was continuous, twenty-four hours a day in three shifts, and each shift employed ten weavers, two or three overlookers (who repaired any faults) and a shift manager. Weavers were paid at a flat rate of £130 a week plus a production bonus of up to £100 weekly, which brought their total pay to above average rates. The manager said that although the flat rate was low it was policy to reward the workforce well for good quality.

The firm was a family business and most of the workers were in families too, with spouses and two or three generations present. Three-quarters were women, and most had been with the firm for many years. Apart from overlookers, who were sent to Switzerland for short courses on the Sulzer machines, the company did very little training. The manager said they had no time to train people from scratch and that if a vacancy occurred he could easily recruit weavers from other mills which had closed down. This would probably be done by word of mouth; he would use the jobcentre for unskilled workers such as cleaners. He said applicants for weaving jobs would not necessarily be refused because of a criminal record: he would consider them on their merits and would look for good training and references.

All our informants emphasised the severe and continuing decline over the last forty years in the British weaving industry. The mill we visited had survived by installing 'Rolls Royce' equipment. The manager of the second mill said his workforce had been reduced from 120 to 70 in the last few years, and that he still had a few Northrop machines (such as we had seen at Kirkham) but was about to export them to Third World countries, which were practically the only places using them nowadays.

Comments

The contrast between Kirkham in 1992 and the outside mills spoke for itself. Though the Kirkham inmates worked hard, produced good quality and derived some satisfaction from their labour, their working conditions were poor and the machinery then in use was very out of date. The collapse of the British weaving industry raises the question of whether prisons should continue to do such work, and this will be addressed in Chapter 7. We may note here, however, that the decision to renew the prisons' weaving industry from 1993 was made by PSIF at a time when it still had central control of prison workshops. In 1996 we discussed the matter with four people in Lancashire: a senior prison manager, a senior probation officer specialising in vocational guidance and employment issues, and a staff member from each of the two Lancashire TECs. None thought the decision had been sensible.

WORKS

In prison

Maintenance of prison buildings, and sometimes special jobs like installing integral sanitation (in 1992, at Maidstone for example) were carried out by each prison's Works department. The Works manager and his deputies were prison officers and most of the work was done by civilian tradesmen, such as plumbers, carpenters and electricians, but some of these would have one or two inmates working with them, while inmate painters under supervision might form a larger team. At most of the prisons, Works inmates usually did the normal prison working day, but at Liverpool they worked longer (seven hours instead of five). A few Works inmates had special roles: Maidstone had a glazier and Liverpool a drains-clearer, who could be called out at any time. Works inmates were generally paid a flat rate.

Inmates for the Works were usually hand-picked by Works officers, who looked for people with genuine trade skills, or at least aptitude, among those inmates who applied. Long-termers were preferred if possible. Highpoint (North) had a deliberate policy of recruiting Works inmates by word of mouth, similar to an outside building site: a man wanting to join had to make his interest known through other people who could recommend him, and one new to the prison had to build up his reputation in other ways first, perhaps by voluntarily helping the painting gang.

Works inmates were unlikely to receive systematic training on the job, though they might pick up some skills depending on their enthusiasm and the inclination of the tradesman they were helping. As one Works officer, R027, said:

> We are here for the purpose of maintaining maintenance. Inmates are there to help us carry out that work; they are not here for any other reason on the Works department. They're not here to gain knowledge, they're not here to

gain experience. If they do then that's great, I'm happy with that and I suppose most people are, but officially there is nothing laid down.

In 1992 Works departments also ran the construction industry training courses which later offered NVQs and are discussed in Chapter 5. But it was not common for trainees to move on to Works jobs except at Highpoint (North) where several had done so. One supervisor said, 'You would have thought it would be a follow-on process.' Security rules often prevented even skilled inmates from being given much responsibility or carrying tools, apart from painters with their pots and brushes. An officer explained that if Works inmates were allowed tools others would put pressure on them or steal tools to try to escape. 'At the end of the day the overriding factor is that you cannot give inmates tools because they'll be through the wire with them.' This consideration actually seemed more in evidence at Highpoint, a Category C prison with mesh fences, than at the higher-security prisons of Liverpool and Maidstone which were enclosed by thick walls, and where, exceptionally, the drains-clearer and the glazier (respectively) were allowed their own limited tool kits and had some responsibility for arranging their own work.

Most Works inmates had a clearly subordinate role to that of the staff tradesmen: as one of the latter said, 'If a barrow wants pushing, they push it, I walk alongside it....They know I don't carry cans of paint....They know they carry.' Many of the civilian staff were middle-aged men who worked at a fairly leisurely pace, a fact remarked on by both prison officers and inmates. (One inmate who had been a building site foreman spoke scathingly of 'council yards' and 'elderly gentlemen that are due to retire and take a relaxed view of life'.) Nevertheless inmates in the Works could derive benefits. The less formal relationship between a staff tradesman and his 'mate' could help to steady an unsettled prisoner and reduce peer pressure, and a senior staff member at Holloway, where female inmates helped on the Works, said that some formerly difficult women had 'blossomed' through working in men's company. There were some opportunities to use trade skills, and a few inmates made real gains: for example, we met an electrician who as well as practising in the Works was allowed out to college one day a week to learn the latest wiring regulations.

Inmates in general did not regard Works as one of the best prison jobs, but those who had chosen it generally stayed. Of eleven Works men to whom we chatted informally, seven said it was a definite help in getting through their sentence, and among six who turned up in our main inmate sample the average satisfaction score was 3.33, above the average of 2.21 for all inmate workers. Painters especially could get a sense of achievement: R613 said, 'When you paint the wing out and it's looking nice and clean...you have a little high.' Another example of satisfaction was the following.

R640 is helping to install pipes in cells as part of the integral sanitation programme. He has not done such work before, though he has enjoyed the prison's evening classes in welding. He picked up the necessary skills quickly, feels trusted by the staff to use them, and looks with pleasure at the results. Also he likes being active; his previous prison job was sedentary, but now he is constantly moving about and feels much fitter.

Perks for some Works helpers included frequent cups of tea with the civilian tradesmen, and relative freedom of movement around the prison which could give opportunities for illicit trading. And R640 said that sometimes he could put up shelves for other inmates in their cells, in return for favours from them.

Outside example

A visit was made to a building site where the erection of two four-storey blocks of accommodation for students was in progress. When completed the buildings would contain over 400 bedrooms, other residential facilities and a conference centre, and they were about half finished at the time of our visit. They were being built to the customer's requirements by a large 'design and build' construction company and its sub-contractors, and our interviewees were the customer's clerk of works and the company's site agent.

Practically all building trades, and over a thousand workers, would be involved at some stage, and at present there were about 120 men on site, including drainlayers, scaffolders, crane operators, bricklayers, electricians, plumbers, steel fixers, carpenters and plasterers. Besides these tradesmen there were labourers digging, carrying and mixing. Roofers, painters, carpet layers and furniture fitters would arrive later. The contracted hours of work were nine a day with four on Saturday mornings. A tradesman might earn about £50 a day and a labourer £30, but had it not been for the recession these rates might have been doubled. The working atmosphere was brisk and purposeful; the contract included a tight completion deadline and a performance bond. Tradesmen were expected to know their job, supervise their assistants and get on with it. There could be competition between, for example, teams of electricians wiring adjacent sets of rooms, and bonus payments for good fast work.

The sub-contractors hired their own employees, but the company might also engage some workers, mainly unskilled, directly. Vacancies would be advertised in the local press and jobcentre, and many applicants might also come through word of mouth and asking at the site. Except where safety regulations required it, tradesmen would not necessarily be expected to have paper qualifications, but they would have to show on the first day that they could do the job. Both informants said that, apart from the company's permanent professional staff, job applicants would not be asked about criminal records, and sub-contractors would not be expected to ask them either.

Comments

Apart from the usual ones of hours and pay, the most obvious differences between the building site workers and inmates in prison Works departments were the variety of work, the level of skill, the degree of responsibility and the brisk working pace. Prison labour seemed slow and childish by comparison.

LAUNDRY

In prison

In many prisons inmates could use small wing launderettes in their own time, but also one in three establishments had a large laundry which employed some prisoners in washing clothes and linen, often for a group of prisons and sometimes for outside customers too. Kirkham, for example, supplied a service to local hotels. At Channings Wood, Maidstone and Liverpool the laundry was one of the occupations reserved for vulnerable prisoners, and each had a workforce of between twenty and thirty inmates in the charge of an officer instructor and other staff.

The equipment was that of a commercial laundry: big automatic washing machines, water extractors and tumble dryers, calender presses and other ironing machines. Channings Wood had a special press for officers' shirts. (There were no facilities for dry cleaning.) Inmate workers sorted the incoming items and fed them through every stage of washing, drying, pressing and folding, and finally packed and loaded the clean laundry on to lorries ready for taking away. There was a strong emphasis on safety, and only the staff operated switches for the main supplies of power and water. The working atmosphere was orderly and busy.

Daily working hours were those usual for the prison, and pay was graded according to task and effort. Some inmates worked in pairs and others in bigger teams according to the machine they attended. Channings Wood had a No. 1 as demonstrator for each operation. The instructors gave training as required for the work, recruits being put on unskilled tasks at first, and if a man stayed at least three months, as many did, he might learn two types of machine. No qualifications were available in 1992, but by 1995–6 Channings Wood was one of thirteen prisons nationally which were offering NVQs, and in that year a total of fifty-five inmates gained a full certificate, including two at level 3.

Once learned the laundry work was fairly routine, but there were valued perks. Inmates were allowed to wash their own clothes but illicit benefits went further: washing could be done for friends in return for favours and extra garments could be added to one's wardrobe or taken out to trade round the prison. Apart from mentioning such things, inmates in general had no strong views about the laundry as a prison job, and our interviewees included only a handful of people with prison laundry experience. Two examples illustrate the range of views:

> R635, formerly a painter and decorator with his own business, has been in the laundry two months. His job is to shake out the dried items, put them

through the calender roller and fold them. 'I'll be brain dead by the time I leave the laundry.' He would like more variety and has asked to be put on another machine, but has been told there is no vacancy.

R649, a shirt presser, feels he is learning a skill and is quick at it. He sets personal targets and tries to beat them: 'I get a buzz out of it if I can do more than my normal day.' He finds it interesting: 'Looking at the stuff that comes in: we wash things for the hospital – theatre gowns, football kit, everything.' And as a No. 1 he controls others' access to perks: 'Somebody has got to ask me first of all if he can take a shirt. Can't just pick them up and take one.'

Outside example

This was a commercial laundry whose services included contracts for twenty-eight hospitals. It also did dry cleaning and had a small amount of custom from the general public. Altogether a broad range of linen and garments was processed, and in the laundry the firm employed over fifty assistants working under eight supervisors and a manageress. Our informant was the firm's general manager.

The laundry processes were very similar to what we had seen in prison, and so were the machines, though there were more of them. The place was extremely busy, with hourly deadlines to fulfil the hospital contracts, and the assistants worked under constant supervision. Basic pay was £3.07 an hour rising to £3.90 for the more skilled workers, with a small productivity bonus and also some limited overtime above the 39-hour normal week. Staff could have their own laundry and dry cleaning done at half price.

When vacancies occurred the firm recruited unskilled people and trained them on the job. It was policy that all assistants should know all the operations so as to cover for absences when necessary, but otherwise training was not structured and there were no qualifications. The manager said that recently business had improved and he had just engaged three new workers (through the jobcentre), the first recruitment for over two years. Applicants would not be asked about criminal records.

Comments

Apart from being bigger and including dry cleaning, this commercial laundry appeared to be very like the prison ones. The machinery was similar, and both employed unskilled workers who learned on the job. Pay for the firm's workers was low; pay for prisoners was of course very much lower, but some of the inmate laundry workers found compensation in other ways. At the time of our visits no qualifications were available in the laundry industry but two years later NVQs became established, and then it seemed that training in a prison laundry might well equip an interested worker for similar employment outside.

WOODWORK

In prison

Woodwork shops employed prisoners in making a variety of products, including cell furniture for prisons and articles for sale on the open market. Kirkham's wares in 1996 included bird tables, garden sheds and self-assembly stables in flat packs, produced in the timber shop where inmates could earn up to £60 a week in enhanced wages. Our observations of woodwork took place in 1992 at Channings Wood and Liverpool, whose arrangements were similar to each other in some ways and different in others.

Channings Wood had two separate workshops, with separate workforces, for cutting (machining) and assembly. The machine shop was reserved for inmates of the VPU and employed about twenty-four, under four civilian instructors, in cutting and shaping wood ready for assembly. They used high-quality machines including bandsaws, routers, moulders and drills to produce stacks of the required components. Most men worked in pairs at a machine, one feeding and his colleague taking off, while two were 'inspectors' and there were a few general labourers who fetched and carried. The room was well organised and busy, though noisy, and staff said the workforce was well motivated and stable, inmates' average stay being about a year.

In the assembly shop next door over forty inmates under four instructors assembled the pieces using mainly hand tools like screwdrivers. Most worked as individuals on just one or two operations at a time, in de-skilled production-line style, rather than working on complete articles. One or two men were packers, and the most responsible roles were those of quality inspector and 'pieceport' who issued and collected pieces as required for any one job. The products were mainly simple cell furniture like small tables and cupboards, but the shop also had an outside contract for making television speaker cabinets, and from time to time there were contracts for hospital furniture. Some inmates in the assembly shop looked busy but others did not; the average stay was only two or three months and the staff found some men hard to motivate.

Instructors in both workshops would put a new inmate on unskilled tasks at first and then train him as required for the work and according to his ability, rotating tasks for those who wanted to learn. In the machine shop a man who stayed a year would learn several machines, though only at the level of machine minder, not tradesman. In the assembly shop a man who stayed six months could learn most operations, and if capable could be promoted to the speaker cabinet section where the work included spray painting. No qualifications were then available, but the instructors liked training inmates and looked forward to the national introduction of NVQs in the furniture industry. Two years later these were in place and in 1995–6 five prisons (including Channings Wood) were offering them, nine prisoners achieving a full certificate (all at level 2) in that year.

Liverpool also had two separate workshops, each about half the size of those at Channings Wood. The machine shop was very similar except that it did not employ vulnerable prisoners and the average stay was much shorter. The assembly shop, however, differed from that at Channings Wood in having smaller production runs and making a greater variety of articles: we saw, for example, TV cabinets, louvred doors, dog-training hurdles, greenhouse platforms and much else. It was really a jobbing carpentry shop and inmates could learn a variety of skills, though not spray painting. At that time (1992) one woodwork instructor also taught evening classes in the education department and an inmate from the machine shop attended them, though later those classes stopped. No qualifications were available. At Kirkham inmates in the woodwork shop had been able to gain a local college certificate for the machines they had learned to operate, but by 1996 Kirkham did no certificated training.

Liverpool and Kirkham inmates in general had no strong views about the woodwork shops, and among our few interviewees with experience of them opinions were mainly favourable, especially at Liverpool where one example was the following.

R559, a former salesman, is making prison furniture in the carpentry shop. He has not done this sort of work before but he likes it, and in the seven weeks he has been here he has learned frame assembly, sanding, staining, painting and varnishing. It gives him a sense of achievement: 'You're seeing something that you've created, you're watching it grow, and it'll be there when you leave. It's one of the best workshops in this prison.' R also makes matchstick jewellery boxes in his cell as a hobby, and is looking forward to joining the woodwork evening class when there is a vacancy.

At Channings Wood, however, the wood assembly shop in 1992 had a different reputation. It was then second only to the tailors in being the most unpopular job in the prison, mainly because (inmates said) it was boring and the workers were cooped up inside all day. Most interviewees who had actually worked there endorsed this opinion, complaining about the de-skilled repetitive nature of the operations, and several also thought the staff were bossy and petty. For example:

R510, a former bricklayer, has been in the assembly shop for a month, screwing and gluing panels which are parts of cell wardrobes. He finds the pace too slow. 'Just fiddling around with bits of screws....Before you do the job they come and tell you where to put the screws, but it's obvious, you can see where. It just feels like they're taking the mickey out of you. It's insulting your intelligence as far as I'm concerned.' He would get more satisfaction if allowed to start from scratch and make the complete article. 'Then you've achieved something when it's all come together, instead of just putting the screws in.'

Of seventeen woodworkers to whom we chatted informally, six said the work was related in some way to their previous experience and seven said it was a definite help in getting through their sentence, though ten thought it would not help them on release. In our main interview sample there were twelve woodworkers, most of them at Channings Wood. The average job satisfaction score for those twelve was 1.42, well below the average for all workers of 2.21. One of the few high scorers was a paint sprayer, and another was R559, quoted above.

Illicit perks did not seem to feature greatly in the woodwork shops. R510, an experienced prisoner, said, 'If there are any I haven't found them out. I normally find them out straight away.' Opportunities did occur, when an instructor's back was turned, to take small pieces of materials or to use glue or sanders for hobby articles. And more than one Channings Wood interviewee said he had devised ways of avoiding work.

Outside example

We visited a medium-sized furniture factory making two types of product: high-quality upholstered sofas and armchairs to customers' individual orders (from a range of styles), and bulk quantities of plainer items like small tables, chairs and benches under contract for schools and other institutions. Altogether the firm made about 7,000 articles a year, and our interviewee was the managing director.

Most comparable to what we had seen in prison were the machine and assembly workshops (not the upholstery), which together employed eight tradesmen and a manager. In the machine shop one worker cut timber into basic pieces and then others shaped and smoothed them into curved arms, backs and so on for the frames for the upholstered items, or table tops, legs, chair seats and backs for the contract articles. Each man specialised in a certain type of machine (such as benchsaw, spindle moulder, sander) and ran his own small group of them. The two assembly workshops had piles of components neatly arranged on shelves and four men steadily assembling them as required. Normally each assembler (chairworker) would make one complete frame or table except for the final stage of rubbing and varnishing, which was carried out by a polisher. The chairworker would identify his own work by signing the frame as he completed it. Sometimes small teams of chairworkers would work together to produce a batch, but even in this case the assembly work was not as de-skilled as at Channings Wood. To a visitor the machine and assembly workshops seemed surprisingly small considering the volume of production, but they were tidy and busy. Basic working hours were thirty-nine a week, with overtime if orders piled up. The top rate of pay for skilled workers was £7 an hour.

The machines were very similar to those in the prisons. Our interviewee commented that they were typical for a small or medium-sized factory like his, and that machinists trained on them would be welcome if he had a vacancy. A large firm making cabinets (e.g. for kitchens or shopfittings) would have automated multi-link machines. None of his were computer-controlled, but he hoped when the present recession lifted to replace some by more modern ones, which could be.

The firm always trained apprentices (for a term of between two and four years) and had two at present (in the upholstery shop). It had participated in developing NVQs for the furniture industry and our interviewee looked forward to their introduction. Most of his skilled machinists and chairworkers had been there many years and there were no vacancies at present: if recruitment were necessary he would use word of mouth and the local press. He would not ask applicants about criminal records (except for a driver, who needed a clean licence) and had in fact employed a few such people, who had done well.

Comments

The machine and assembly workshops at this firm had a good deal in common with prison woodworking shops in the equipment and the main operations. Some of their products were more interesting than the prison ones and were finished to a higher standard. There was a similar emphasis on the importance of training, though the firm's employees reached much greater levels of skill. A major difference was that the assembly work was less de-skilled than that at Channings Wood, thus affording more opportunities for job satisfaction. Also there were far fewer workers, and they worked more steadily. But it seemed that the prison workshops had the potential to give willing workers skills relevant to the industry outside.

PRINTING

In prison

Thirteen prisons in 1996 had workshops doing machine printing, desktop publishing or both. Desktop publishing was a fairly recent development (in prisons as elsewhere) but machine printing had been established for many years. By the 1990s prison products included multi-coloured illustrated brochures, booklets and reports, as well as plainer stationery items for government departments, and computer-aided design was coming into the workshops.

One of the largest printing shops was at Maidstone, where in 1992 we saw up to sixty inmates, under six civilian instructors, producing stationery, leaflets and booklets for the Prison Service. The equipment included both outdated and modern tools: on the one hand old typecasting and letterpress machines, and on the other hand up-to-date litho printers, a camera and an Applemac computer. By 1996 a second Applemac and a scanner (for reproducing photographs) had been added. The finishing department had modern machines for drilling, stitching and cutting, though there was only one folding machine and large quantities of leaflets were folded by hand. Equipment in the bookbinding section included machines for sewing, gluing and gold blocking.

Inmates operated most of the printing machines, and though some of their work was skilled much was routine and repetitive. Others sat at a table manually folding and packing leaflets. The bookbinding section had more interesting work and in 1992 was relatively quiet, in contrast to the main printing room which was very noisy; later the bookbinders were absorbed into the main room. Most of the workers were busy but did not appear to be under pressure. Training was given on the job as required for any one operation, and a keen worker who stayed several months could learn a variety. The staff would have liked to do more training than they felt the demands of production allowed time for, but no qualifications were available. (NVQs were not established in the machine printing industry until 1996.)

Some inmates liked the print shop, but others said it was the worst in the prison because it was noisy and boring (and dirty because of the ink). While Maidstone inmates had a good deal of occupational choice they had to go somewhere, and the print shop in 1992 had, in the words of one Maidstone manager, 'a residue of inmates who won't be accepted anywhere else'. Others were more motivated and would have liked better training in printing skills. Only three men with experience of the Maidstone print shop occurred in our main inmate sample. R539, who was making plates from photographic negatives, felt this was a fairly low-level skill and that the print shop was 'just occupational therapy, most of the time'. R638, whose work was folding cut card to make file covers, said (when asked if his job helped him forget the 'pains of imprisonment'):

> I think it makes me worse. If the work was interesting it might take my mind off it, but to me the work isn't interesting so I have more time to think. Too much thinking isn't good for you....The print shop winds me up.

R621, a former businessman, thought the working pace was slow and that materials were wasted. But he had appreciated the staff's help in his preparations for release. He was applying to a funding body for a grant to help restart his company, and the print shop manager had allowed him to use the binding and gold-blocking machines to make his supporting documents into an attractive booklet. Apart from this instance we heard of no perks, legitimate or other, available to inmates in the printing shop.

Outside example

This was a firm of high-class colour printers whose main products were brochures and other publicity material for an established range of clients such as financial institutions. It had a graphic design studio employing four artists and a spacious printing workshop with about twenty people, where craftsmen and their assistants operated the presses and skilled finishers transformed big colour-printed sheets into the final product. The firm did not do bookbinding. Basic salaries were £6,000–£8,000 for machine assistants and £15,000–£20,000 for skilled printers; most employees had been with the firm at least four years and some for much longer. Our informant was one of the departmental managers.

The equipment was very modern and included some machines we had seen at Maidstone, notably Heidelberg litho printers, a range of finishing machines and Applemac computers. The firm had recently bought a press which would print more than four colours at once, and for reproducing photographs they used computer scanners. The printed products we saw were of extremely high quality. Apprentices were no longer trained because of the pressure for production, but a recruit skilled in some kind of printing could be taken on (if there was a vacancy) and trained on the firm's machines. The firm received a lot of speculative applications and would also recruit through word of mouth, not advertising. Unskilled people could be engaged as machine assistants or warehouse workers. An applicant's criminal record would not be asked about or considered relevant, said our informant; what mattered was ability to do the job and to fit in with the good working relations of the existing team.

Comments

In some ways this printing company was not comparable to the Maidstone workshop in 1992 because of the big difference in product; a 'high street' jobbing printer might have been a nearer comparator. But since then prison printing shops have become more sophisticated, and even in 1992 the one we saw had, as well as some very outdated equipment, modern machines like some of those at the company. It seemed that if prisoners were systematically trained on them they might be well placed to apply later for printing jobs, if there were any, with outside firms, at least as machine assistants to begin with and perhaps looking further. The other striking point was the level of job satisfaction which the company's printers must have gained from the results of their work (as well as their pay), compared with the boredom suffered by inmates manually folding paper at Maidstone.

LEATHER GOODS

In prison

None of the four prisons making footwear was among our research six, but we looked briefly at Liverpool's workshop making small leather goods, the only one of its kind in prisons. The products were items like industrial gloves, pouches of various kinds, dog leads and belts. Most were fairly plain and destined for prison use, but some belts were sold outside, and the quality looked good. Gloves for builders and welders were the main articles being made at the time of our visit.

The leather shop was reserved as occupation mainly for long-sentence prisoners deemed to be high security risks, and the ratio of staff to inmates was consequently greater than we had seen elsewhere. About twenty inmates worked on production, with three instructors helping and three prison officers watching. (By 1996 the number of places for inmates had increased to forty.) The atmosphere was businesslike with inmates working hard, but they also had opportunities to chat. They worked as individuals using a variety of equipment: power tools included flatbed sewing machines, a clicker press, a shaver, cutters, irons and riveters, while among the hand tools were markers, shears, knives, hammers and punches. Inmates were trained on the equipment as necessary but no qualifications were available.

Until 1992 this workshop had been devoted to mailbags, and senior prison staff said that the change to leather goods had greatly increased the motivation of its inmates. This might change when the present workforce moved on and was replaced by people without memories of the mailbags, but at present it was functioning well. Only one leather worker turned up in our main interview sample:

> R552, who outside prison supports himself in summer by gardening and in winter by theft and burglary, is serving his fifth sentence. His previous prison jobs have included weaving and mailbag sewing. Now in Liverpool, he has been put into the leather shop, where he cuts piles of leather into shapes and then machine stitches them to make welders' mitts. He found this slightly interesting at first but not later when he had got used to it, though the occupation is fairly helpful for getting through his sentence. 'I'm not going to be making gloves when I go out.'

Outside example

Our main comparison visit was to a fairly large leather goods manufacturer making three types of product: 'small goods' like wallets and gift items, 'strap goods' like belts and dog leads, and soft luggage. The first two were most comparable with what we had seen in the prison. The firm produced plain and fancy goods of very high quality for well-known brand names, and our main informant was the production director. We also visited a training centre for leather workers, where a senior tutor supplied further information.

At its busiest time of year (three months before Christmas) the factory employed about 130 bench workers, of whom 80 per cent were women; cutters and some of the others were men. The lowest rate of pay was £2.50 an hour, and a skilled worker might average £150 a week. Staff could buy goods at discount prices, and take scraps of leather for their own use. In the small goods workshop most of the tools we had seen in prison were in use, the main exception being that the factory had cylinder arm sewing machines rather than flatbed ones, and had other equipment like embossers. Allowing for the fact that some products were more elaborate than the prison goods, the various operations were the same. The working atmosphere was orderly, good-humoured, fairly noisy and very busy.

Most of the operatives specialised in just one type of work (such as preparing, machining or riveting) and the director said there was a trend to de-skill the production process, though at the same time people would be moved about so as to learn several operations. About thirty of his workforce, including several Youth Trainees, were working for NVQs, for which level 2 had recently been developed in the leather industry. Turnover among the staff was very low, and all the present supervisors had come up from the shop floor. The director said that if he were recruiting he would use mainly word of mouth and would hope to get people already skilled, though they would need to be trained in the firm's ways. A person with, say, six months' experience of leather cutting, shaving or machining would be very welcome to apply. Applicants were not asked about criminal records and people with one would not be barred from consideration, but the firm would want references for assurance that they had the required skill.

Comments

As far as we could tell, the work processes and equipment in the prison workshop were very like most of those at the factory, though the latter produced higher-class goods and did more training. It seemed that training in the Liverpool workshop could equip a man for such work outside, if he were sufficiently interested and *if* there were jobs available.

LIGHT ASSEMBLY (CONTRACT SERVICES)

Many prisons, including four of the research six, had workshops doing light assembly work, occasionally for the Prison Service but usually on contract for outside companies. Typically the tasks were simple, unskilled and repetitive: assembling fishing lines, decorating party hats, stuffing envelopes, cutting bundles of string for mop heads, assembling electric plugs, and so on. They were done mostly by hand, using simple tools which, with the materials, were supplied by the contracting company, while the prison supplied the space and supervised the inmate labour. In pre-recession days some contracts had been won for more interesting work, such as the complete assembly of table lamps or infants' pushchairs, but in the 1990s the work was, in the words of one prison manager, 'usually boring, mundane, tedious and low-priced'.

In the four prisons in 1992 the light assembly shops provided work for somewhat different types of inmates, depending on whether the prison treated its vulnerable prisoners separately from others. At Maidstone, which did, the light assembly shop was for most Rule 43 men the only alternative work to the laundry. Liverpool at that time had two assembly shops, one for Rule 43s and the other for inmates regarded as 'inadequate' and those withdrawing from drugs; later these arrangements changed when a third assembly shop was added. At Kirkham in 1992 inmates graded medically unfit for heavier work went into the light assembly. At Highpoint in that year it seemed that the light assembly shop was used to contain the disaffected and those for whom no other work was available, but later it was used more as temporary occupation for men waiting for a course vacancy. By 1996 Channings Wood also had an assembly shop, taking prisoners who arrived with only a few weeks left to serve. Generally speaking, the light assembly was seen by managers as 'pick up and put down' work for prisoners who, for various reasons, could not be assigned to anything more demanding. Most workshops occupied about fifty inmates, but Liverpool's largest one was double that size. Staff were a mixture of prison officers and civilians.

Training was confined to health and safety and instruction in the simple operations required. Workers wanting variety could request a change of task. Some worked individually and others in small teams, and the Rule 43 shops at Maidstone and Liverpool gave some inmates more responsible roles like demonstrator, checker or team leader ('No. 1'). Rule 43 inmates were said to be a more stable and well motivated workforce than most others in the light assembly shops, and certainly the atmosphere in the big Liverpool shop when we visited it was cheerful and very busy, with workers apparently taking pride in the quality of their products.

Inmates interviewed for the research had sometimes worked in light assembly shops at other prisons though they were not in the light assembly now, and from all with such experience we gathered a range of views. Some people said the work helped pass the time though they were not learning anything useful. Some gained social benefits, like R653 who found it better than lying all day on his bed in his cell: 'I've started talking to people again...it gets you friendly.' Some compensated for the monotony by trying to beat their own targets or by finding other sources of interest, like R550 who amused himself by observing awkward characters among his colleagues. Several people said they liked the work better when it was done for charities, as occasionally happened.

But the general opinion of the light assembly shops among inmates may be gathered from the various names they used for them, some of which were also used by prison staff: the Noddy/chicken/monkey/Muppet/cabbage/fraggle shop.[14] R649, a former roadbuilder, described the assembly work as 'messing about with little doodly things'. R519, a qualified marine engineer, on arrival at Kirkham was offered the assembly shop because of his age (50) but refused to go. 'There's no way I'm going to sit on a chair and play with bits of string....I'm a reasonably educated person, you're not going to treat me like some lunatic.' (He was eventually assigned to the weavers.)

For the eleven light assembly workers in our main inmate sample, the average satisfaction score was 0.73, the lowest for any group having at least five members. The views of R643 and R636 were fairly typical.

R643, a former bricklayer, has been in the assembly shop for seven months, tightening screws in shelf fittings and assembling fishing lines. It gives him no satisfaction at all. 'Putting in screws, day in, day out, you end up having nightmares about screws...or about crab lines.'

R636, who has certificates in management and mechanical engineering, has been in the light assembly shop ('the brain-dead department') for six months, and his present task is wiring and assembling ceiling roses. He attends education classes for half of each day and works in the assembly shop for the other half. Of the latter he says: 'The only way I can explain the chicken shop: it's like having a good meal with your friends and family, and you have to do the washing up, like it or not....The instructors themselves realise how demoralising the job is.'

We were unable to find a comparable outside factory to visit, because in the 1990s they were increasingly scarce. The real comparators would have been either sheltered workshops for the mentally handicapped or the large number of people employed doing unskilled assembly work at home. In 1996 Huws,[15] reviewing studies of such homework, found that typically it was insecure, very badly paid, and carried out in conditions which exploited the worker in several ways. It must be seriously doubted how far prisoners benefit by being occupied in work which in the outside world is like that.

DOMESTIC WORK

All prisons employed some inmates on domestic chores, and Table 1 shows that over the system as a whole such work was by far the most common kind. As with kitchens, the Works and some industries, prisoners' labour was used on domestic tasks in order to help keep establishments running. A large proportion of all domestics were cleaners and servery workers.

Cleaners and servery workers

Here we describe mainly the work of those whose duties were to clean the wings, dining areas or other communal parts of the prison, and to serve inmates' meals from the food trolleys sent through from the kitchen. Wing cleaners and servers were usually chosen by wing officers from those among their inmates who had applied for these jobs and whom they judged to be clean, reliable and responsible, though cleaning parties could also be 'padded' on occasion by absorbing some inmates who might otherwise be unemployed. The six research prisons all had slightly different arrangements, and we learned most at Channings Wood, Highpoint and Holloway.

Channings Wood wing cleaners started work at 7.30 a.m. by fetching the trolleys and serving breakfast, then tidied up, and then cleaned the wing using machines (such as vacuum cleaners and polishers) and hand tools. Later in the day they had to serve the other meals and clean up. Those who worked well were given time off during the day to go to the gym, and staff arranged rotas so that, in turn, cleaners could have weekend evenings out of their cells when most other inmates were locked up. An officer said, 'We make the job as attractive as possible', and they expected prisoners' co-operation in return. Certainly the wings, at the time of research, looked clean. All the cleaners did the kitchen staff's short training course for a health and hygiene certificate, and there was good liaison with the vocational training course in industrial cleaning (see p. 136). Inmates in general at Channings Wood regarded the cleaners as having one of the best prison jobs because of the free time and opportunities at the servery to get extra food. They recognised that cleaners were likely to be long-sentence and co-operative prisoners, and some described successful applicants as 'crawlers'.

Highpoint wing cleaners and servery workers were separate groups. The servers worked at every mealtime and cleaned the dining areas afterwards, but for wing cleaners at the time of our first visit it was 'task and finish': the cleaner could do his 'patch' and then have the rest of the day free for gym or (weather permitting) sunbathing. One in North prison (where inmates were allowed more freedom than in South) told us he worked for only an hour a day (seven days a week) and then planned the rest of his day as he liked. At that time there seemed to be a great many cleaners, and a prison manager said that wing and office cleaning was 'just filling in time for the inmate because we don't know of anything better that we can get him to do'. It was also said that the wing recesses (showers and toilets) were filthy and that the cleaners did not get enough supervision. Later in 1992 inmate cleaners at Highpoint were put 'under contract' to work longer and better for their pay, which caused some resentment, and at our updating visit we were told that the system had been further tightened up, with all cleaners (like most other Highpoint workers by then) having job descriptions. Among the Highpoint inmates we interviewed, not many mentioned cleaning as one of the best jobs, and several thought that cleaning recesses was one of the worst.

Cleaning work at Holloway presented in some ways a rather different picture from that at the male prisons. In each wing three inmates worked as a team, choosing one of their members as leader, and their duties included cleaning the wing, serving food, sorting laundry, and organising supplies and stores under supervision. Cleaning standards at that time (1993) were high: for example, skirting boards had to be scrubbed by hand as well as floors being scrubbed and polished by machine. The cleaners were out of their cells from 7.30 a.m. to 8 p.m., working when required. Compared with most other inmates they had a fair degree of responsibility and the wing staff largely left them to get on with it. One member of Holloway's staff described the role of the cleaners as liaison between the wing officers and the other inmates: 'They're a very important part of the running of each unit [wing].' However, all five inmates (including two cleaners) who were asked in interview about the popularity of the cleaners' job said it was one of the worst in the prison. Cleaners, they said, had to clear up the mess made by other inmates, some of whom were demanding and abusive.

At Maidstone cleaners and servers were separate groups, and servers trained for the health and hygiene certificate. Inmates in general had no strong views about the desirability of these jobs. At Liverpool cleaners and servers did not have the freedom of those at the lower security prisons to go off duty, but they had more time unlocked than most of their fellow inmates, they could shower every day and get extra food. These advantages made cleaning a popular job, and not the least important of the perks was mobility in the prison; as R653 said, 'It gives you freedom to run round and do – prison politics, you know, do what you've got to do, wheeling and dealing.'

A few cleaners' posts entailed extra responsibility, privileges or sources of interest, being in some ways more akin to orderlies' jobs (see p. 102). R666, for instance, a hospital cleaner, was trusted to arrange his own work schedule; he could make tea and toast for himself when he liked, and keep jam in the fridge. He felt his work was useful in preventing the spread of infection. 'Don't want people walking in there and coming out with German measles or something.' R534 had been the cleaner in the governor's office and used to make tea for visitors. 'That was interesting because I was mixing with people, I wasn't just a number.'

For many inmates, however, the perceived benefits of cleaning and servery jobs lay not in the work itself but in the opportunities for getting time off and for trading extra food, or other goods, around the prison. On a different note, an aspect of cleaning work as integral to prison life was pointed out by R572, a wing cleaner. Asked whether his job ever helped him to forget he was a prisoner, he said that on the contrary it reminded him. 'You think of any sort of TV thing that shows you a prison, it shows you a cleaner mopping the landing, mop and bucket, in his vest, doing the landing. So it brings it home that you're in prison.'

Our main inmate sample (over all six prisons) included nineteen cleaners and servery workers, and for sixteen of them we were able to assign a job satisfaction score. The average was 1.56, rather below the average for all workers of 2.21. While a few interviewees spoke positively of liking responsibility for their own areas and seeing nice clean floors, most felt that cleaning was a thankless task and that their rewards came in other ways.

A note on litter picking

Tidying rubbish from the prison grounds, a job known variously as 'the GM party' (grounds maintenance), 'wombling' or 'the bomb squad', was much less popular than other cleaning work. Advantages were fresh air, short hours and mobility (with, at some prisons, a little cart that might carry other things too), but most inmates saw it as an unpleasant job because of the nature of some of the rubbish, and the smell.

ORDERLIES AND CLERKS

Inmates who helped, albeit in a lowly role, with the administration of the prison were in a rather different position from most inmate workers. Though there were grades of orderly they generally had more freedom and responsibility, and enjoyed closer personal relationships with the staff with whom they worked. One manager described them as 'pets', and an orderly serving staff might sometimes receive extra rewards like small amounts of tobacco. Officers selected as orderlies those inmates whom they judged to be reliable, discreet and (especially for those coming into contact with the public) smart and well-spoken.

Orderlies were generally seen as having 'plum' jobs, and so to a lesser extent were workshop office clerks, some of whom were former businessmen and adopted a rather superior attitude to their fellows on the shop floor. One of the most envied was the reception orderly who had access to information about new arrivals and to items they might bring in from outside. An orderly working in the induction wing or at the labour board might be able to 'put in a word' for an inmate who wanted a certain job. Inmates chosen as orderlies and clerks were seen by a good many others in such terms as 'arselickers', 'pen pushers', 'the money men – fraudsters and that…creeping to the officers'. R530, a lower-grade orderly, described the 'pecking order' among orderlies and clerks themselves, saying, 'The [higher-grade] orderlies will look down on us – the grey trousers and shirts brigade. To us it's like, we're from the council estate and they're from the suburbs.'

Certain orderlies, besides working closely with staff, had special responsibility in regard to the activities of other inmates – more responsibility than a workshop No. 1. One education orderly, for instance, helped to induct new trainees on a computer course and was sometimes left in charge of them. The prime example was the position of gym orderly which, especially in male prisons, was said to be a top job. The gym orderly might have to do cleaning duties ('scummy shower mats' said R634) and hump equipment about, but he also enjoyed the freedom of the apparatus on which to keep fit, and he could show off his muscles to inmates at the physical education sessions where he acted as assistant to the instructor. He might have considerable influence with other inmates. (One officer remarked that at his establishment the man appointed as gym orderly was likely to be 'the biggest gangster in the prison'.) However R685, who had been gym orderly at a prison which offered its facilities to outside community groups, had taken pleasure in helping pensioners and disabled children to use the swimming pool.

Thus the perks and satisfactions of orderlies' work were varied. Our main inmate sample included ten orderlies and clerks of whom eight were scored for job satisfaction. Their average score was only 3.13, less than might perhaps have been expected. The low figure resulted partly from people who felt that routine clerical tasks were beneath their abilities, and partly from some who felt that despite their privileged role they had little real power and were not really trusted by the staff. R535 expressed this ambivalence clearly:

> R535 is an orderly in the gardens office. He keeps the labour records accurately, he makes tea for the staff, and he also has to clean the toilets. But he would like the staff to trust him more than he feels they do. He has a long previous record for burglary but is now an elderly man (which is why he was put into the gardens office) and he has his principles: most of his victims were commercial firms, he says, he would never do things like picking pockets or cheating on bus fares. In the gardens office, 'if anything's

knocking around that belongs to one of them, I go out of my way to make sure it's all right. But it don't seem as if I've got their confidence.' ('They still don't trust you, because of your burglary record?') 'Correct, yes. And I find that very hard, you know, to cope with....At times I feel I'm one of the group [the gardens staff] but I realise I'm on my own....I'd rather be, sort of, classed as one of them, from the point of view of protecting what's theirs....[But] I'm still on the inmate side of the fence.'

STORES ASSISTANTS

Stores work was popular, particularly the clothing exchange store (CES) where inmates received clean prison clothes and bedlinen and handed in dirty ones for sending to the laundry. There were valued opportunities for CES workers to get the best garments for themselves or for trade. But as well as such perks, several interviewees with CES experience at different prisons said they liked the work: it was varied and useful, they had some responsibility for their own section, and the instructor in charge promoted a good team spirit.

R664, who at one prison had experienced both the tailors' workshop and the CES, drew an interesting contrast between them. In the tailors, he said, there was constant pressure for production ('It's just one big turnaround'), the piles of jeans to be stitched seemed never-ending, and if he took a break he would lose pay because of being on piece rates. But in the CES there was a finite set of tasks to be done each day and at the end of it he could sit down and think, 'That's the day's work done.' And whereas the products of the tailors were all sent away to other prisons, in the CES R felt his work benefited himself and his fellows: he felt some identification with it.

A NOTE ON LESS COMMON KINDS OF WORK

In prison

There were several other kinds of work, done by only a few prisoners, which offered above-average responsibility, sense of usefulness, contact with staff or creativity. For example: producing the prison magazine; working in the craft shop or charity shop (at Holloway); the barber; Braille transcription for the blind; pottery technician or bookbinder in the education department, and so on. The group of seven inmates in our main sample who did such jobs had a much higher average satisfaction score (4.86) than most other prison workers.

Outside community work

At most of the prisons a few inmates near their release dates were allowed to go out daily to do voluntary work (with prison pay) in the local community, though by 1996 fewer were doing so because of tighter security rules. Examples of such work were gardening for disabled people, painting a playgroup's hall, and helping handicapped children. Usually such jobs lasted only a few days or weeks, and next time other eligible prisoners would have a turn. A governor spoke for many staff in describing the benefits of community work: it got inmates out of the prison into normal life, the work was evidently useful, it touched their consciences, and it 'added to the ethos of the prison'.

Prisoners interviewed were enthusiastic and would have liked more. R606, a gardener, said working outside for others in his free time gave him self-respect. R537 mentioned with pleasure that his community work had been praised on local radio. R561, recalling his time in a Works party sent to restore a church, said:

> I really loved it. It wasn't, like, thinking about prison, coming back to prison at night. The outside world, with proper civilians out there, everyone's so friendly out there, they don't treat you like an animal, they treat you with respect.

GENERAL COMMENTS

In this chapter we have tried to take the reader inside prison, so to speak, to look at what prisoners engaged in various kinds of work were actually doing and how they felt about it. Our verbal pictures were drawn against the background provided by national statistics, which revealed that despite the efforts of PES to facilitate a variety of industries large numbers of inmates were occupied in domestic and other tasks needing little skill.

Altogether the various occupations were something of a patchwork, having grown up in different ways and for different reasons. Prisoners were employed in kitchens, in gardens, as cleaners and in Works departments so that their labour could help keep the prisons running, as had been the case for well over a century. Traditional in origin, too, were workshops like the tailors and the light assembly, which could be set up fairly cheaply and occupy large numbers of inmates under close supervision in tasks needing relatively little training. Their products, like those of the farm, gardens, laundry and woodwork shops, helped the system towards self-sufficiency and could also bring in money to subsidise its costs. Newer industries like desktop publishing could share the latter aims. In recent years, as periodically in earlier times (see pp. 6, 7) prison industries had been re-equipped and modernised, and there was now a drive for high quality and – for some prisoners – good training. Some other kinds of prison work were done for charity. In the next chapter we address more systematically the aims and purposes of prison work; at the moment we simply observe that the different kinds formed a diverse picture, and that for many incoming prisoners their assignment to a prison job largely resembled a lucky dip.

Ten kinds of prison work were compared with examples of their counterparts in outside industry. These outside firms were a haphazard sample, but overall the comparisons suggested a number of themes and issues. In actual content much prison work was like what went on outside: the equipment and processes were similar and the products were of comparable quality. Often the organisation of the workplace was similar. But a big difference was that the prison employed many more workers to produce the same amount; in general prisoners worked more slowly (except in kitchens), their hours were shorter (except in kitchens and at Kirkham), they had less skill and responsibility, and they needed more supervision.

On the other hand it seemed that the training available, or potentially available, in prisons was greater than that offered their workers by the majority of outside companies we visited. Most of these employers said that *if* recruiting they would look for people who had had some training already. It was interesting that seven said job applicants would not be questioned about criminal records, and three others were cautiously willing to consider ex-offenders on their merits. (We do not know how typical the firms were in this respect.) Chapter 5 addresses the subject of vocational training, but from the evidence presented so far it seemed that people trained in prisons to the level of NVQ 2 in catering, horticulture, machine sewing, weaving, laundry work, wood machining, printing or leather goods would be well placed to apply for semi-skilled jobs in those industries *if* there were any (and if they could keep up with the speed of production).

But most of the twelve employers we visited were not recruiting, and some had not done so for years. Informants emphasised the collapse of the weaving industry and the decline in agriculture, and the others too were (in 1993) still affected by the recession. The extent to which the kinds of work done in prisons actually match the pattern of likely employment opportunities outside is one of the major topics to be addressed in Chapter 7. Meanwhile we now come in Chapter 4 to a closer examination of some aspects of prison work in general, including the fundamental question of what prison work is *for*.

4 General features of prison work

INTRODUCTION

The last chapter portrayed different kinds of prison work one by one. Now we draw together evidence from all the kinds of work studied to look at salient features of prison work in general. These features largely correspond to several of those which the Prison Service in 1992 listed in its first criterion for judging prison work,[1] as follows:

> Is the work experience realistic compared with that likely to be found outside, in terms of: acceptance of responsibility; hours of attendance; production processes/technology; interaction with others (supervisors, work-mates); incentives for good work/penalties for poor performance; chances of the inmate getting that kind of job outside; the pace of work?

In this chapter we examine how the instructors organised and managed their workforces, the amounts of responsibility given to prisoners, questions of productivity, and aspects of prisoners' job satisfaction. We enquire whether instructors tried to help their workers move towards outside employment, and what their aims as prison instructors actually were. We note the views of staff and prisoners on the benefits inmates can derive from prison work, and on the ways in which it does and does not resemble work outside. Eventually, having built up an overall picture of the nature of prison work, we present the results of an assessment by staff and prisoners as to what it is all *for*: what are the purposes of prison work, and what *should* they be?

ORGANISATION OF THE WORKPLACE

Except in the case of a Works helper or a wing cleaner, work instructors often knew little about a fresh recruit until he or she arrived, because they had usually played no part in the selection. After brief initial training, including health and safety, the newcomer was set to work. Where possible existing skills (if any) would be taken into account in allocating tasks, but generally this did not happen. People were usually given the least skilled tasks at first and later moved round, for training or for variety, and the best instructors organised the work with an eye to motivation and morale. R023, for instance, in charge of a laundry, took care to plan finite loads so that workers could complete a load and then have a tea break; otherwise, he said, with a continuous flow like an assembly line 'they just plod'.

Some inmates worked as individuals and others in pairs or teams, depending on the task and the instructor's style of management. Although occasionally group feeling among a knot of prisoners could be counter-productive, instructors generally tried to encourage co-operation and team spirit. R037, a gardens instructor, described how he would use peer pressure to influence a lazy team member: 'If he is not pulling his weight you make it known to all of them that "he is letting your job down".' R549, an experienced prisoner, had liked making army camouflage nets in an assembly shop where the instructor arranged the men in teams of eight, each team round a table fastening patches on one net, and held competitions between the teams with praise for the winners.

Fluctuating numbers due to prisoners being transferred in or out, especially at a local prison like Liverpool, could cause problems for the staff. In some workplaces the amount of work could be adjusted to suit, but a shortage of workers in the kitchen or laundry could put essential services (and tempers in the prison generally) at risk. Workshop production was lost when numbers fell. At other times some instructors were given more workers than they needed because of management's wish to keep inmates occupied. One instructor (R038) said:

> In here [i.e. prison] you're tied down with that many bodies under your feet. Outside you'd just go on and get it done, or you'd get a machine to do it. I think the biggest thing, for somebody to take a job in here, is to find that you've got all those people to utilise all day.

This raises the question of whether the main purpose of employing inmates was to get the work done or to keep them busy, which will be taken up later.

WORKING ATMOSPHERE AND RELATIONSHIPS

At the workplaces we observed the atmosphere was generally good-humoured, orderly and businesslike. Instructors who were prison officers had of course received training in managing prisoners, and so had most of the civilian instructors though some of them would have liked more. Asked how they managed their workforce, instructors stressed good personal relationships: fairness, praise for good work, personal interest and consideration. R023 said he looked for opportunities of giving his men dignity: for example, he would consult a former lorry driver about the correct weights for loading the van, or a former electrician about the motors of the shop's machines. Prisoners indicated that they had more respect for instructors who participated in the work than for those who merely supervised. R649, for instance, said of the two in his workplace:

Basically they're quite good....They watch the work progress...and do their best to help you. They'll not sit about in a chair with a cup in their hand all day, they're always active...they'll give you a hand.

Several instructors said that they would help their workers with personal problems and could sometimes resolve them more quickly than officers on the wings. The importance to prisoners of work instructors' sensitivity was clearly expressed by R512:

Outside you haven't got the pressures you have in prison. For example you might not get a letter, you might not get a visit, you might get a bad letter. And you take it to work, you've got to, because here you're in a closed environment.

R033, in charge of a workshop, well understood this:

You've got to have feelings for them, praise them and try to listen if they're not happy – a personal touch....I act like a boss and a father – I have a quiet word with any who's not acting normally.

Several prisoners recounted instances where instructors had helped with personal matters by advice, by allowing telephone calls or by intervening to speed up some procedure in the prison.

Male prisoners appreciated the presence of women among the instructors. R545 said, 'Not being around females for so long you look up to them, you admire them for being females.' R581 in the tailors' shop at Highpoint said the four women instructors there had better control than the male ones, while R567 in the same shop said:

When I was in the Ville [Pentonville] there's women teachers, but...if you go up to talk to one of them, outside the education [department], one of the screws would rush up thinking you was going to do something, you know. They was very iffy about it. But here you just get on nice with them...they don't hassle you...it makes it happier as well, makes it feel like you're on the out, not just men all over the place.

Altogether it seemed that relationships between work instructors and inmate workers were generally fairly harmonious: out of 129 prisoners interviewed 53 per cent said their relations with staff at work were 'good' and 40 per cent that they were 'usually OK'.

But there was another side to it. When we asked inmates how they would wish to be treated by supervisors in a prison workplace, a common theme was the desire above all to be treated with respect: as individuals and as adults, 'like normal people', 'not like prisoners or robots or children'; and some evidence suggested that this did not always happen. Several instructors in describing their methods spoke of 'kidology' and 'kidding along the line'. One in a workshop unpopular with inmates said, 'You gee them along by fair means or foul.' Some prisoners' answers implied that they felt they were treated like children in a schoolroom, and R653, working in a light assembly shop, expressed this directly:

> We're treated like little children....For example, before we come back to the wing we have to sit at our tables, and the tables have to be clean, and he only does one table at a time....It reminds me of when I was at primary school....It's degrading....Some people don't mind it, but I do.

R673 said, 'You meet a lot of people in prison who behave like kids because they're made to behave like kids, people talk to them like kids.' This raises the question of giving inmate workers responsibility, which we discuss in the next section.

Relationships between workmates seemed on the whole to be amicable. Of 116 inmates asked, 28 per cent said they worked alone and most of those preferred to do so. Among the rest 89 per cent said that relationships were 'good' or 'OK'. Several spoke of 'a good bunch of lads', and only five admitted to having problems in getting on with their colleagues. But No. 1s were not always popular, as we mention in the next section, while staff pointed out that prisoners could not get away from those whom they disliked at the end of the working day.

RESPONSIBLE ROLES FOR PRISONERS

The amount of responsibility given to an inmate worker depended on the type of work, the type of prison, security considerations and the instructor's style of management (as well as, naturally, on the individual concerned). Some roles had implications for the holder's relationships with fellow-inmates and with prison staff, as will be seen.

At Kirkham, an open prison, some of the most responsible jobs were on the farm. The prisoner in charge of the farrowing house, for instance, or a tractor driver who could be anywhere within the boundary, were left alone for hours at a time to get on with their work as they saw fit. The staff were ultimately in charge, of course, but they trusted the inmate specialists to use their skills without constant supervision. Another prisoner ran the farm's produce shop, handling stock and money and dealing with customers including the public. By contrast, most Works assistants in closed prisons had very little responsibility, as was described on p. 86. Even those with trade skills were unlikely to be entrusted with tools, and instead they acted more as 'bag carriers' to the staff tradesmen because of the prison's concern about security.

In closed workshops, especially where operations were de-skilled, most workers had only a low level of responsibility. A little more was given to those appointed as demonstrator, quality checker or No. 1 at the head of a team. But the No. 1s were not always popular: two interviewees in an assembly shop said that the No. 1 there was lazy and just watched while others did the work. And the role of the No. 1, while giving somewhat more scope for a sense of control and power to make decisions, could also cause discomfort through divided loyalties. On the one hand, the instructor expected more of the No. 1 and would back him or her up. (R023 said, 'If an inmate comes to me with a question about the work, I'll say, "Ask the No. 1."') On the other hand, resentment could arise among other inmates who felt their erstwhile colleague was identifying with 'the system'. In this respect a No. 1's position was like that of an orderly, and R535 (pp. 102–3) was an example of one who felt uncomfortable about which side he was on. An orderly at Holloway expressed the dilemma very clearly:

> R686 is sometimes left in charge of the room (a small workplace) when the staff are elsewhere. She feels trusted and in control. But other inmates 'can get stroppy...some say, "D'you think you're staff, then? Where's your keys, who do you think you are?"' She feels she has responsibility but no real authority, and she also feels 'like everyone's servant because I wash the cups'. But she regards her situation as a challenge, as good experience in developing her social skills.

Some instructors felt strongly that prisoners could not be put in charge of other prisoners. R012, a kitchen instructor, designated several of his key workers like the butcher and baker as No. 1s, but these men worked alone on skilled tasks, not as team leaders. Asked whether there was more scope for inmates to exercise power or responsibility he said, 'None whatsoever, because that would be the tail wagging the dog. It's not possible because of the constraints.'

In our interviews with prisoners one question was as follows:

> In your present job, are there any aspects of it you can decide for yourself, like what to do next, where to go, how to arrange things? Does it give you any feeling that you have some power, some control over things, you can decide what will happen?

Possible answers were 'yes, definitely', 'maybe a little', 'no, not really' or 'don't know'. Of 126 workers 30 per cent said 'yes' and 15 per cent 'maybe a little'. Thus fewer than half felt their prison job gave them any sense of responsibility as thus defined. Personal responsibility is an important aspect of preparation for outside employment, but the research found that many prison workers got very little of it and that some staff felt that because they were prisoners they could not have more.

PRISONERS' PAY

Another aspect of personal responsibility is for people to manage their own money: to earn their keep and pay their way. As was seen on pp. 59 and 64, even in 1996 the 'wages' paid to prisoners for their work were in nearly all cases still at the level of children's pocket money, averaging £7 a week, while the prison supplied the basic necessities of life whether the prisoner worked or not.

The issues surrounding prisoners' pay have been aired for many decades and will not be rehearsed at length here. They were thoroughly examined by Woolf,[2] who said, 'A realistic wage would be a way of ensuring that the prisoner takes greater responsibility for himself in prison and outside.' Similar views were held by many of the senior prison staff interviewed in our research, who felt that paying inmate workers wages approaching those in outside industry would enable them to pay for their prison board and lodging, save money against their release, contribute to their families' upkeep, and send some compensation to their victims. This would give them more incentive to work in prison and would increase their sense of responsibility and self-esteem. One governor (R096) said:

> If we were able to actually pay realistic wages or salaries, then in some ways that could begin to address some of the other sorts of social issues about making people more responsible for themselves, their families and so on...they [could] actually feel they're giving something back as opposed to constantly taking.

A very similar sentiment was expressed by R539, an inmate serving six years and working in the print shop at Maidstone. He thought enabling a prisoner to support his family would give him self-respect, and then said:

> If a man's come into prison for crime, and he's got no real values or anything anyway, how can you teach him values, teach him the lessons of life, if you devalue him while he's here? It just doesn't make sense.

Staff criticised the facility whereby inmates could have 'private cash' sent in (if they had funds outside prison or if their families could afford it). One instructor said, 'It creates a two-tier system. Those who haven't got their own are more disadvantaged still, while others have lost the incentive to work.' In 1996 this problem was partly addressed by the new framework for incentive schemes which restricted prisoners' access to private cash (see p. 23) though not eliminating their reliance on it.

Work instructors interviewed, along with other staff, believed that 'getting a little bit of money' was prisoners' most important reason for taking part in work, though prisoners themselves said otherwise (see p. 124). In fact inmates' views on how much prison workers should be paid, and why, were surprisingly varied. Out of 127 workers 36 per cent suggested amounts not exceeding £10 a week and 21 per cent suggested between £11 and £20, while at the other end of the scale only 6 per cent suggested more than £50. A quarter of the prisoners asked did not specify an amount, though 17 per cent of the whole sample said that prison pay should be comparable to outside wages. Thus the majority suggested very modest sums.

Many inmates offered more than one reason for the amount they proposed. The commonest reason (given by 55 per cent) was that prison pay should enable them to buy goods at the prison shop (tobacco, phone cards, toiletries, food supplements, etc.) without having to borrow from their fellows. But among the other reasons, 21 per cent of people mentioned saving for release, 13 per cent sending money to their families and 7 per cent paying board. Also, 17 per cent said prison pay should not be as much as outside because after all they were in prison; and while 14 per cent said the pay should reward inmates fairly for their work a handful (4 per cent) said it must take account of what the prison (or workshop) could afford.

Thus altogether there was a variety of views among prisoners. The figures given in the preceding two paragraphs do not represent a complete survey of inmates' views on prison pay (because interview time did not allow it), but they have interesting implications. They suggest that as long as prison supplied the necessities of life many inmates saw prison pay as simply weekly pocket money and would accept a modest amount, provided it enabled them to buy what they wanted at the shop without getting into debt. But when they looked beyond their immediate needs prisoners wanted to earn money for more 'adult' purposes, especially savings to tide them over on release and also to help their families. (These results are consistent with the National Prison Survey, which found that 93 per cent of prisoners, when asked, wanted to be paid more in order to save, and 76 per cent wanted to send money to their families.)[3] At the same time, though the idea of pay comparable to outside was naturally attractive, not all thought it would be justified in prison.

Those interviews took place in 1992–3. Since then the Prison Service has been trying to move towards enabling prisoners to take greater financial responsibility in money matters. Incentives and enhanced earnings schemes have been introduced and in 1996 the Prisoners' Earnings Act was passed, enabling prisons to deduct from inmates' enhanced earnings (if sufficient) sums towards their prison board, dependants, victim support or crime prevention, and compulsory savings. But in 1998 the Act had not yet been put into practice in prisons,[4] and as we have seen (p. 64), even under the enhanced earnings schemes average pay in 1996 was less than £20 a week, while the number of prisoners receiving 'real wages' was minuscule. Clearly there was a long way to go to reach the position favoured by Woolf.

QUALITY AND QUANTITY; WORKING PACE AND HOURS

In the early 1990s the Prison Service made a drive for high quality in its products. Farm operations complied with Ministry of Agriculture standards and

European Union guidelines, and by the end of 1996 15 per cent of PES work-shops had achieved BS 5750. At the other main kinds of workplace – kitchens, Works and domestic – our observations suggested that quality could vary. But work instructors in general tried hard to instil high standards and good practices into their workforces, and on the whole they felt that good quality was achieved despite limited budgets and prisoners' limited skills. Our comparisons with outside industry tended to bear this out.

Productivity was a different matter. As was noted in Chapter 3, in many work-places far more workers were employed than would have been if the work were outside prison, and the working pace (except in kitchens) was generally slower. Turnover of workers was often high, as those with short sentences came and went while others were granted a 'change of labour', and, for many, dislike of the work militated against high motivation.

Prisoners' short working hours were a long-standing problem. Those at the six research prisons were typical: generally twenty-five hours a week or less, except in kitchens and at Kirkham. At most establishments the daily routine meant that the inmates' working day was fitted inside the prison officers' working day, so that prisoners typically began work later than 8 a.m., stopped earlier than 12 noon when they were returned to their wings for lunch and a roll check and the officers had their lunch, restarted later than 1.30 p.m. and finished some time after 4 p.m. when they went back to the wings for a roll check and the evening meal. Efforts made by particular prisons from time to time to increase the inmates' working day were difficult to sustain. At Coldingley 'industrial' prison, for example, hours had fluctuated (p. 11), and at the rebuilt prison at Manchester, where the original agreement for the new regime had included a working day of seven hours, the Inspectors found in late 1995 that it was only six.[5] And at work there were continual interruptions: for individuals, because of official and private visits, medical appointments, sessions with probation, exercise, canteen (shop) and so on; and for whole workplaces because of other prison priorities like searches or staff training, or the absence of instructors for any reason (no substi-tutes being provided).

All these things – the slow pace, high turnover, low motivation among many workers, the short working hours and interruptions – combined to depress the amount of work done. One manager said that although the workshop produc-tivity standard was officially set at 30 per cent to allow for interruptions, in practice it was actually sometimes as low as 8 per cent.

Prisoners interviewed were asked how they felt about the pace and hours of prison work and what they thought working pace and hours would be like in jobs outside. Most interviewees felt the prison working pace was satisfactory: of 116 asked 69 per cent said the pace was 'OK', and the others were evenly divided between those saying 'too fast' and 'too slow'. But 71 per cent said that if they were in an outside job they would have to work faster. Asked how they felt about the hours of prison work, half said they were 'OK'. Most of the rest wanted to work longer hours to relieve boredom, to get through the day more easily, or to have longer intervals between meals. Reasons for wanting shorter hours included dislike of the work, wanting more time in the gym and wanting a better place in the queue at mealtimes.

The great majority of inmates asked (85 per cent of ninety-eight) said that if they were in an outside job the hours would be longer, and nearly two-thirds of that group said they would *want* to work longer hours, or would not mind doing so. The main reasons were that they would be earning good money and doing work they enjoyed. The following case illustrates several interesting points:

> R572, a bricklayer by trade, is working in prison as a wing cleaner, an hour or so a day seven days a week. He works at his own pace and the hours suit him in the prison context, but outside he would be working much harder, from choice. 'I'm dying to lay a brick.' And he thinks it will be hard to adjust: 'I think, when I get out, I'm going to find it hard for a little while…to drop back into the round of work, the speed, and the fact of doing it eight hours or more a day. I think I'll find that difficult for the first week or two because [here] it's so lax…it's going to be hard, when I get out, to do a day's work.…I'll get over it, but I know it's going to be a struggle.'

These findings on pace and hours suggest that inmates felt a clear distinction: prison work was one thing, 'proper work' outside was something else. They largely accepted the prison working pace and hours as facts of their sentence to which they had to adapt, but they knew that the 'real world' of work outside was different, and many looked forward to rejoining it, or trying to.

PRISONERS' JOB SATISFACTION: ACHIEVEMENT, INTEREST AND POWER

The six-point job satisfaction score quoted in Chapter 3 for different kinds of prison work rested on three elements: a sense of achievement, feeling some interest in the work, and feeling some sense of power or control over events (see p. 110). Inmates were asked in some detail whether their current prison work offered any of these. To each question over half answered 'no' or 'don't know', one in seven answered 'maybe a little', and up to one-third answered with a definite 'yes'. These answers were scored at zero, one and two points respectively, so that the maximum score obtainable by a prisoner who said 'yes, definitely' to all three questions was six points. For 121 workers doing a great variety of work the average score was only 2.21 points. This implies that inmates did not get much of these kinds of satisfaction from prison work, though some types of work were more satisfying than others, as was seen in Chapter 3. The low average score of 2.21 contrasted with the average of 4.36 points for twenty-five inmates interviewed who were attending training courses or general education. The essential difference between them and the workers was that those in training or education had asked for that prison occupation and saw it as something personally useful for their future, whereas few of the workers did, as will be seen on p. 120.

Inmate workers who said 'no' or 'maybe a little' to any of the three questions were asked whether they had ever had a job outside prison that gave them more, and their answers were unhesitating. Eighty-seven per cent (out of ninety-two) had worked outside in a job which, compared with their prison work, gave them more sense of achievement, interest or power (or two or all three of these things). Four examples follow.

R567 in tailors: Outside, was a removals van helper. He enjoyed achieving a set task in a day, working hard with a mate and getting it all done. It was interesting travelling around, seeing different places, sometimes staying overnight.

R512 in woodwork: Outside, was a machine fitter. That gave him a sense of power 'because if the machine was broke they'd have to wait for me to come and fix it'.

R565 in kitchen: Outside, had worked as a disc jockey in pubs, which gave him all three kinds of satisfaction: he likes music, a DJ's job is to make people happy and enable them to dance.

R506 in wood assembly: Outside, had worked tarmacking roads. It gave him a sense of achievement: 'The money was good, the hours were all right like, and the work was hard but it was satisfying....You're doing good, you know what I mean, making roads.'

Perhaps these prisoners were taking a rose-tinted view of their lives outside. But that does not alter the fact that they and many others felt they got little satisfaction from their jobs in prison. When asked how the work might be improved to give them more, two-fifths made positive suggestions of which the most frequent were: give more variety of tasks; make a greater variety of products (in kitchen, tailors, woodwork, light assembly); arrange the work so that inmates make complete articles instead of doing just a few de-skilled operations; have better communication between staff and inmates; give inmates more trust and responsibility in their work; and provide more training leading to qualifications. Vocational training of prisoners is examined in the next chapter.

THE ROLES OF THE WORK INSTRUCTORS

Much of this chapter so far has examined aspects of the prisoners' situation at work. Now we turn to the work instructors and look at two topics: the extent of their contacts with work outside prison, especially in regard to helping their inmate workers prepare for release; and the important question of what, as prison work instructors, they were actually trying to do.

Looking to the outside world and prisoners' future

The great majority of work instructors interviewed (twenty-seven out of thirty) had trade qualifications and had worked in the same industry outside prison, though not all of them recently. We asked them whether they tried to help their inmate workers by advising them about employment and job hunting, or by contacting potential employers or giving references for any who were interested. Half said they did chat with their workers about the outside world and their future prospects, and would give advice if asked. But very few instructors would contact possible employers or give references. (Out of seventeen asked, only three said they ever did so.)

There seemed to be two main explanations for this reluctance to offer specific help. The first was that many of the instructors we interviewed felt largely out of touch with their industries outside prison; they read trade journals, but only a few thought they were adequately informed about current developments. Out of thirty instructors eight were satisfied with official provision for enabling them to keep up to date; sixteen were not and wanted more; and the other six supplemented what they were given by making private contacts. Several said that HQ was reluctant to pay for attendance at industrial exhibitions, and that the former practice of allowing instructors a 'refresher' week with an outside firm every five years or so had lapsed, though the Service ran internal courses. One prison manager said that nowadays the Service placed less emphasis than before on expert trade knowledge and more on instructors' ability to manage large numbers of prisoners. Two groups of instructors seemed better placed than others for making outside contacts: farm staff, who met other farmers at shows where the prison exhibited its prize animals; and instructors in light assembly shops, who would visit an outside employer when negotiating a prison contract. Ironically, the latter type of work was one offering prisoners least in the way of skills training or future job prospects.

The second factor was a belief that prison staff were not permitted to give references or to keep in contact with ex-inmates. Several instructors specifically mentioned this, some with regret. They would have liked to help former workers if occasion arose and they would have liked feedback about their progress in the outside world. R023 felt there was not enough 'shared working' on throughcare. He would have liked to accompany a released inmate to see a prospective employer and give information on the spot, but he could not. 'The Probation Service have it all wrong.' Only four out of sixteen instructors said they had ever been in touch with ex-inmates after release.

This question of instructors, and indeed other staff, being allowed to help in prisoners' plans for release and then keep in touch with them after they left was discussed with several senior managers in the Service. The general feeling was that transition to release was the business of the Probation Service, and that contact between prison staff and ex-prisoners was to be discouraged, if not actually forbidden. In practice, it was said, there might sometimes be informal contact with potential employers by telephone, and staff might occasionally hear of ex-prisoners' progress. Opinion was divided on whether this was desirable. Some staff felt they would have liked feedback, like R054, a prison manager who said:

> If we are able to spend that amount of time and effort on Jones, and here we are three months down the road, and Jones is in employment and has not actually re-offended, then that is job satisfaction. But if you don't know you have achieved any result it is a bit like walking down a dark street.

Others felt that the boundary between prison and the outside world was proper and should not be crossed. A principal officer involved in assigning inmates to prison jobs expressed it thus: 'Ours is a people business. People in prison are our product. Once the product has left the factory, that's our job done.'

Some work instructors shared the latter view, feeling that their job was simply to get the work done with prisoners' labour, and that what happened to the prisoners later was not their concern. But other instructors would have liked to help more than they felt they were allowed to. Altogether it seemed that to a large extent prison isolated not only prisoners but also work instructors from the world outside, and that instructors' interest in inmates and potential for preparing them for employment was not being fully used. Instructors often knew 'their' prisoners better than officers on the wings: they watched their progress at work and took a personal interest in their welfare. They ought to have been invited to participate in sentence planning for their charges and in arrangements for helping them into employment outside. But that very rarely happened.

Work instructors' aims

In view of all this, we asked work instructors what their aims were in their daily work with prisoners. Each of thirty-one interviewed was asked: 'In your work with inmates, how much emphasis do you give to each of the following?' and offered a list of nine items to be rated for importance. These included, for example, 'producing high quality goods or services', 'training inmates in vocational skills', 'teaching inmates to respect good honest work'. The details of this exercise are given in Appendix 1, and the results showed several things. First, the instructors on average thought all nine aims were important. Second, as a group they had clear priorities: top priority was given to producing goods or services of high quality, and next came training inmates in good work habits. By contrast, training inmates in vocational skills received nearly the lowest priority, but at the same time this aim was the one whose importance evoked most disagreement among the instructors, some rating it very high and others very low. This suggests a need for the Prison Service to have a clear policy about the emphasis to be given to training as one of the functions of prison work. Later in the book, after reviewing findings from the follow-up study of released prisoners, we will set out the case for arguing that training should have high priority.

GENERAL BENEFITS OF PRISON WORK TO INMATES

Staff and prisoners were asked, in different ways, for their views about the benefits to inmates of working in prison. The staff views are presented first.

Staff views

Work instructors, as has just been seen, did not give their prime attention to vocational training, and they mostly thought their inmate workers would at best acquire only low levels of trade skills. But they did emphasise training in good work habits which could help with seeking employment after release and with life generally. One workshop instructor (R005) said somewhat cynically, 'It's a therapy because it gets them out of bed, gets them in here and teaches them that sometimes they have to do something they don't like. That's a very good therapy.' But, more positively, there was broad agreement among instructors that prison work could impart good habits such as punctuality (especially at prisons like Channings Wood where inmates had to get themselves to work rather than be escorted), a steady working pace, attention to quality, co-operation and discipline – in short, the common requirements of a structured workplace, from which inmates, especially those who had had very little experience of regular employment outside, could gain stability and confidence.

Other prison staff spoke of the value of work in occupying inmates out of their cells and helping them get through their sentence. They also largely agreed with the work instructors about the benefits of good work habits, though some were slightly cooler about the extent to which these were actually achieved. The utility of boring prison work as preparation for a job outside (even though that might be boring too) was sometimes doubted. And it was recognised that in prison the abnormal conditions of work did not favour good habits. One industrial manager, referring to the way in which workshop interruptions led to loss of motivation and concentration, said in tones of some exasperation, 'What would do these inmates a hell of a lot of good is to *work* them, work them hard. But that doesn't happen here.'

We carried out a short exercise to try to measure the extent to which staff other than work instructors thought prison work benefited inmates. In each of the six prisons ratings were made by three or four people whose roles gave them familiarity with at least some types of work: altogether there were twenty-one raters including heads of inmate activities, industrial managers and uniformed officers with particular knowledge. They were asked to rate the kinds of work they knew best on two criteria: (a) the value of the work for helping prisoners to serve their sentence calmly, without causing trouble or getting into trouble during it, and (b) the value of the work for increasing prisoners' chances of getting or keeping a job after their release. At least nine raters rated eight kinds of work: cleaners and servery, gardens, kitchen, laundry, light assembly, orderly, tailors, and Works.

The results showed that for helping inmates to serve their sentence all eight kinds of work except the tailors were thought useful by a majority of raters (and the tailors was thought useful by nearly half). The kinds with top ratings were Works and kitchen. For helping ex-inmates' job prospects, however, all kinds of work except the laundry were thought less useful. Top ratings were given to Works and laundry; kitchen and gardens were thought useful by at least half; but light assembly, orderly and tailors were thought useful by only a small minority, and cleaning and servery work by none at all. This was a small exercise but it suggests that these prison staff thought the value of most kinds of prison work for helping inmates after release, as opposed to helping them during their confinement, was fairly low. This opinion largely accorded with that of the inmates, as will now be seen.

Prisoners' views

These were gathered in two stages. In the first stage inmate workers were asked three questions about the value of their current job in helping them to cope with imprisonment. The first question was: 'Does it ever help you to forget you're in prison?' to which 47 per cent (of 117) answered yes. (When invited to mention other things that helped them forget they produced a wide range, in which the most frequent were drugs, the gym and sports events, and reading.) The second question was: 'Does it ever give you a feeling of self-respect?' to which 44 per cent answered yes. (Among other things giving self-respect the gym was the most often mentioned.) The third question was: 'How useful is it in helping you to get through your sentence without getting into trouble?' to which 56 per cent answered that their work was 'very' or 'fairly' helpful. (Other helpful things included the gym and sports, reading and cell hobbies.) Thus around half the inmate workers interviewed felt that their job was helping them to cope with being in prison. (By contrast, a positive answer to each of the three questions was given by at least two-thirds of interviewees who were taking training courses or education.) The numbers doing particular kinds of work were too small for proper comparisons, but the most apparently helpful jobs included Works, kitchen, weavers and gardens.

The second stage of enquiry was that seventy-seven inmate workers who were within three months of release were asked about the value of their work as preparation for outside employment, and this time the question referred to all prison work done during the current sentence. The interviewee was shown a list of six statements about skills and work habits, and invited to indicate for each one (a) whether it was true for him or her, and (b) if it was true, whether that might help in finding or keeping a job after release. The only one of the six which was endorsed as true by at least half the sample was 'I did good quality work'; this is consistent with the work instructors' emphasis on high quality that has already been seen. But only a quarter of the inmates thought that that experience might help them to get a job on release. The other five statements referred to learning new work skills, keeping up existing skills, working regular hours, accepting orders from the boss, and co-operating with workmates. Up to 44 per cent agreed that they had done those things in the course of prison work. But each was endorsed by fewer than 30 per cent as possibly useful for employment on release. In regard to skills, only 22 per cent thought they might be helped by having learned new work skills and only 9 per cent said their prison work had enabled them to keep up skills they already had that might be useful. When we recall (p. 59) that 60 per cent of inmates had wanted a prison occupation which would give them a skill, maintain an existing one or at least use their previous experience, it is clear that many must have been disappointed.

Altogether, this second stage revealed that on average only about 20 per cent of the inmate workers interviewed felt that they had gained from prison advantages in skills or work habits which might help them in getting employment on release. A very similar result was found in the National Prison Survey.[6] Twenty per cent is less than half the proportion who felt that prison work helped them to cope with their sentence, as described in the first stage. This difference in views was thus in line with that of the prison staff in the exercise mentioned on pp. 118–19.

We end this section on a wry note by quoting one inmate's suggestion of another benefit of prison work. Inmates may have been disappointed with skills training and sceptical about the acquisition of work habits, but R601, who was dismissed from his prison kitchen job when his 'fiddles' became too blatant, said:

> All the staff know you get perks....Prison is one big trading post...always full of trading. It's important because it keeps your mind active. If you didn't have trade in prison you'd have people coming out of prison in pretty poor mental health....It keeps your mind sharp.

IS PRISON WORK LIKE OUTSIDE WORK?

Staff and inmates interviewed were invited to discuss this question and their responses are summarised here.

Staff views

Staff pointed out obvious similarities between some kinds of prison work and outside employment: the content of the work, the equipment used, organisation at the workplace (such as production lines) and the emphasis on high quality. Other common features mentioned were the sheer facts of regularly going to work, and fitting in with workplace routine and discipline.

But the list of differences was far greater. Staff cited the following, while recognising that some might vary with the type of prison job:

- Working conditions. Obviously pay, and (in most prisons) working hours. Prisoners do not get annual holidays, pensions or trade union rights.

- Much prison work is low-skilled, labour-intensive, menial and dull. Workers have few initial skills, they receive minimal training, only low achievements are expected of them.
- Prison work gives little real sense of progression. There is no career structure, workers cannot aspire to responsible jobs. Instead they may ask for a 'change of labour' every three months or so.
- Social contacts. Inmates have to live with their colleagues, who may or may not be congenial, instead of going home at the end of the day. Workplace friendships, said one staff member, are 'institutional friendships'.
- Slower pace. Several staff felt prison workshops were not really under the same commercial pressures as outside despite Home Office assertions.
- Compulsion and restrictions. Inmate workers have little choice, often they are locked in workshops, they cannot go out for lunch or to a canteen, they are watched and not trusted with tools.
- Despite what has just been said, prison jobs have less real discipline. 'The sack' does not mean so much. Inmates who misbehave at work are treated like naughty children instead of responsible adults.
- Motivations are different. Inmates do not see prison work as relevant to their lives, they have less commitment and interest in it. They are not working to support themselves or their families; their basic needs are supplied whether they work or not.

R078, a thoughtful prison officer, summed up much of the above when he said:

> There's a great deal of difference....In prison it's very artificial. Outside, you're earning a salary, you're living a full life, in prison you're living part of a life. A lot of your life is very controlled, where it wouldn't be outside, you'd make more decisions outside....This is a half-life. Things stop once you come into prison.

Prisoners' views

Inmates comparing prison work with work outside had very similar views to those of staff. Of ninety-eight workers asked, only one third saw *any* resemblances between inside and outside jobs. Differences most frequently mentioned were the pay, the compulsion and lack of choice, and the close supervision and lack of responsibility. Other items covered almost the same range as those cited by staff. R572 described the lack of motivation in the following way:

> Nobody wants to do it. Most of it is 'Well, sod 'em, I'm not doing their work, I'm not, you know, I'll do it just to get them off my back and I'll just do enough.' A lot of the excuse is the measly wages, and the other thing is 'Why should I work in prison, they're punishing me, why should I do anything for them?'...It's not set up the same. People haven't got the attitude towards work. Working in the outside, people go to work because it's

their job, they go and do their job hopefully to the best they can, they take their wages at the end of the week and they try to sort out their bills with what they've got. In prison if you don't work you still get much the same, you're going to live much the same life in prison whether you work or whether you don't. There's no matter of like, 'well, if I work hard I'm going to do better'. There's no incentive in prison.

Thus both staff and inmates largely agreed that prison work and outside work were very different. In the last two quotations (R078 and R572) we see again the theme of inmates' lack of responsibility and the state of dependence that prison life, including prison work, induces.

Those interviews took place before the introduction in 1995–6 of the national framework of incentive schemes whose official aims were, among other things, to encourage prisoners to behave responsibly, work hard, take part in other constructive activity, and progress through the prison system (p. 23). Our research did not include any evaluation of the new schemes, which at the time of our updating visits had just begun in four of the six prisons. It seemed likely, from what we were told, that the prospect of promotion and demotion between the 'differential regimes' might well encourage inmates to behave acceptably as prisoners and to avail themselves of activities that were offered. But one of the 'key earnable privileges', eligibility to work for enhanced wages, was as yet open to only a small minority and even most of them were unlikely to earn enough to pay their way. It seemed doubtful whether the incentive schemes would radically change the overall pattern of differences between prison work and outside work that has been depicted in the last two pages, or transform the way in which prisoners looked towards their futures. And one of the most imaginative schemes, that at Maidstone (p. 55), was said quite frankly by a senior manager to have the basic purpose of control within the prison.

PERCEPTIONS OF THE AIMS AND PURPOSES OF PRISON WORK

This chapter has examined some general features of prison work as exemplified at the six research prisons. We have looked at aspects of workplace organisation, and at relationships between inmates and their supervisors, noting that despite the latter's personal interest in their workers and a generally harmonious atmosphere some prisoners felt they were treated like children. Most inmates had little real opportunity for responsibility, a situation reinforced by their low levels of pay. The slow pace and short hours at many workplaces were largely accepted as facts of prison life, but inmates were well aware that the world of work outside was more demanding and many looked forward to eventual participation in it. The majority had had at least one outside job which they felt gave them more interest, sense of achievement, or power to make decisions than they experienced in their prison work.

As for the work instructors, it seemed that they too were largely isolated by the prison walls, often having only limited opportunities to keep up with their industries outside and being discouraged from making contacts which might help their inmates into employment. Instructors gave top priority in their work to achieving high quality, but disagreed on the importance of teaching prisoners vocational skills. Ratings by other staff of the value of prison work to inmates showed that they felt most kinds of work were more useful in helping people to get through their sentence than in preparing them for jobs on release, and ratings by inmates largely agreed with this view. Comparing prison work with outside work, staff pointed out obvious similarities but also produced a long list of differences, while only one in three inmates could perceive any similarities.

Now in this section we look through the eyes of staff and prisoners at two basic questions: what is prison work *for*? and what *should* it be for? We wanted to explore people's perceptions of the aims and purposes of prison work, so at the end of each interview the respondent was invited to complete a set of forms which, with explanations, asked in effect the following questions:

To ninety-seven staff:

1   Why do you think the Prison Service provides work for prison inmates?
2   What do you think would be good reasons for providing it?
3   Why do you think inmates do it?

To 134 inmates with experience of prison work:

1   Why do you think the authorities provide work for prison inmates?
2   Why do you do the work?

The forms offered lists of more than a dozen possible reasons and respondents were asked to rate the importance of each one. The results of this exercise are reported in Appendix 2, and the main findings were as follows.

The staff group as a whole perceived the Prison Service as providing work for inmates primarily for the purpose of managing and controlling the prison on a day-to-day basis: the reasons ranked highest were 'to give inmates time out of cell, something to do' and 'to keep them busy, stop them causing trouble'. (These were endorsed as important to Prison Service HQ by 88 per cent and 86 per cent respectively of the staff raters.) But also, and nearly as important (to HQ, said staff) were the aims of improving inmates' prospects of future employment by giving them skills and work habits. Using inmate labour to help keep the prison running came next. Somewhat lower down, but still endorsed as important by more than half the staff raters, were the aims of commercial enterprise, enabling inmates to earn money, and improving inmates' characters (e.g. by teaching them to respect the work ethic and contribute to the community). At the bottom end of the scale only 6 per cent of staff thought that prison work was provided as punishment.

Staff themselves thought that preparing inmates for employment after release would be the *best* justification for prison work: imparting skills and work habits were endorsed as good reasons by 94 per cent. Next came giving inmates time out of cell, inculcating the work ethic, and enabling them to earn money. The list of items was practically the same as that in the preceding paragraph, and for any one reason there was little difference between the proportion of staff perceiving it as important to HQ and the proportion thinking it a good reason. But overall there was a distinct difference in emphasis. Reasons having to do with treating inmates as people, rather than with the maintenance of the system, were all rated more highly as good reasons for inmates to work than they were as perceived reasons for official practice. By contrast, reasons to do with managing the system were all rated lower as good reasons than as perceived reasons for practice.

Inmates as a group, rating their own reasons for working, placed highest 'to get through my sentence without trouble, as soon as possible', which was endorsed by 94 per cent. Next came passing the time and getting out of cell. These three items together, expressing the aim of getting through one's sentence, can be seen as the counterpart of the official aim of managing the prison and keeping it ticking over. 'To get a little bit of money' came fourth at 73 per cent, followed by 'interesting activity, helps to take my mind off prison' at 69 per cent. Other reasons rated as important by more than half the inmates included the opportunity to mix with people, using up mental energy, the feeling that one ought to work, compliance with prison regulations, and learning or using skills for future employment. Reasons endorsed by fewer than half included getting perks, work habits for future employment, the hope of parole, and compulsion ('I only work because the authorities make me', endorsed by 29 per cent). Ranked lowest was working in order to relieve guilt, which only 10 per cent of inmates said was important to them.

A comparison of inmates' own reasons with what staff perceived as inmates' reasons put most items into two groups: those where staff and inmates broadly agreed and those where they did not. Staff perceptions were largely accurate about the importance inmates attached to getting through their sentence, the smaller weight given to work as an interesting activity, the still smaller weights given to acquiring skills and work habits, and the unimportance of relieving guilt. But on other items, including money, perks, the hope of parole, and compulsion, staff perceptions of inmates' motives for working were unduly negative. (In fact staff thought inmates' highest motivation was money, which according to inmates was not so.)

Inmates' perceptions of the authorities' reasons for providing prison work placed highest 'to keep them busy, stop them causing trouble' (endorsed as important by 80 per cent), followed by helping to keep the prison running and giving time out of cell. Thus inmates, like staff, believed that the authorities gave first priority to managing the prison. Just over half felt the authorities used inmates as cheap labour. At the bottom of the scale 29 per cent of inmates felt that prison work was intended as punishment: the minority holding this opinion was much greater among inmates than it was among staff.

Roughly half the inmates credited the authorities with wanting to give them useful skills and work habits. This reflects much the same weight as inmates themselves gave to these items as reasons for working, but considerably less than the credit staff gave to official intentions, which prompts the following comment. When they came into prison the majority of inmates had hoped for a prison occupation which would use their existing skills (if any) or give them new ones (p. 59), but by the time they got near the end of their sentence many felt this had not happened (p. 120). It is therefore not surprising that despite the official intentions (as perceived by staff) that prison work should help equip inmates for the future, and despite staff's own desires to do this, only half our sample of inmates, when asked in this exercise, answered that learning skills and work habits was an important reason for them to work in prison.

The items which this exercise invited staff and inmates to consider included most of those which, as Chapter 1 relates (p. 12), have been advanced over the last two centuries, at one time or another, as purposes of prison work. (The main exception was deterrence, which our lists did not include.) The rating exercise showed most of these purposes to be still salient in the minds of staff, inmates or both, though some were expressed in more modern terms. Work as redemption from sin or relief from guilt had nearly dropped out of the picture, and work as punishment was given very little credence by staff, though more than a quarter of the inmates believed it to be so intended. But most of the other purposes – aiding discipline, maintaining the system, offsetting costs, lightening the pains of imprisonment, imparting the work ethic, teaching trade skills, improving character, providing occupation – were still very much to the fore. We saw in Chapter 1 that the relative emphases given to these aims have shifted back and forth over time with the changing currents of penal philosophy. Now the results of the rating exercise prompt the following observation.

Over half the staff sample rated the great majority of reasons as important, both as official reasons and as good ones. The items covered a wide range, and one interpretation could simply be that prison staff see prisoners' work as a multi-purpose activity. But the reasons are hardly all in the same direction, and it could be argued that some are at odds with one another. For example, merely giving inmates 'something to do' is not the same as improving their characters; and training them in work skills for release may be incompatible with running workshops as a commercial enterprise to offset costs. These divergences suggest a second interpretation: that prison staff are confused about what the main purpose of prison work is or ought to be. And the inmates' ratings of reasons they perceived as important to the authorities also covered a wide range of divergent items, which could suggest either that inmates perceive the authorities to be confused or that they themselves are confused about why prisoners are required to work.

The confusion needs to be resolved. There are some indications that it may exist not only among staff who have to manage prisons and instruct inmate workers, but also at higher levels. First, as we noted on p. 17, in 1991 the Home Office statement of the purposes of prison work (in *Custody, Care and Justice*) gave first mention to maintaining the system and last mention to preparing prisoners for jobs on release, whereas two years later PSIF implied that the relative priorities of these two purposes were the other way round. Second, we note the history of Coldingley (pp. 10–11), whose shifting purposes over nearly thirty years well illustrate the Inspectors' 1988 remark (p. 12) about official ambivalence towards prison work, and which the Prison Service in 1997 was once again trying to develop as an industrial prison.

SOME POINTS OF COMPARISON WITH DAWSON'S 1972 STUDY OF PRISON WORKSHOPS

Before leaving this chapter it is appropriate to mention a piece of research on prison work carried out by Sandra Dawson[7, 8] twenty years before the Brunel study. It was an investigation of industrial workshops in three English training prisons (none of them among our research six); as in our study, Dawson observed work processes, attended meetings, examined records and interviewed inmates, work instructors and prison managers. This was at a time when Prison Service HQ were still optimistic about the rehabilitative value of prison work, Coldingley industrial prison (which was not in Dawson's sample) had recently been established, and prison industries, typically working a 35-hour week in training prisons, were showing signs of profit (see p. 8). Also, in the world of work outside prisons there was relatively full employment and few indications of the severe changes which were soon to come and which we outline in Chapter 7 (pp. 185–7).

Several of Dawson's findings may usefully be compared with our own. Although three-quarters of the inmate workers she interviewed said they would like to learn a trade or skill while in prison (and most when outside had had unstable employment, often in unskilled jobs), 86 per cent were engaged in the workshops in only routine semi-skilled or unskilled tasks. Eighty-four per cent thought that the purpose of prison industry was either to make money for the prison by exploiting inmate labour or to keep prisoners occupied. Nearly 80 per cent saw no resemblance between prison work and outside work (the biggest difference being lack of freedom and choice), and nearly three-quarters felt that their prison work experience would have no effect on their attitudes towards working when released. All these results are quite close to some of the Brunel findings and suggest that, then as later, prisoners saw prison work as having little relevance to their outside working lives, though many would have wished it otherwise.

Work instructors whom Dawson questioned about their role gave responses which suggest some of the confusion that we felt was discernible from the Brunel results. When asked what were their main responsibilities, they (as a group) gave first priority to producing goods to the required standards, followed by instructing inmates in the operations needed for that. When asked about objectives they might conceivably pursue, they gave first place to encouraging inmates in regular work habits, followed by teaching them skills; production and profit came lower down the list. Eighty-six per cent agreed that prison work ought to help inmates learn skills useful for outside but only 11 per cent thought that it did. Eighty-three per cent agreed that instructors always faced a conflict between aiming at efficient production and contributing to prisoners' rehabilitation. Only 23 per cent thought prison work actually helped inmates to acquire regular work habits, while 71 per cent felt it just kept them occupied. Again, the general similarity between these responses and those of staff in the Brunel study is noteworthy.

From our observations in 1992–3, some of the features of prison workshops which Dawson had described twenty years earlier were still present: the slow pace, lack of real pressure and low motivation among many inmates. Other aspects had improved: the drive for high quality, and the cheerful and purposeful atmosphere which instructors worked hard to engender. Dawson discussed the results of her study in terms of power relationships, finding (among other things) that workshop instructors had little power, both in relation to other staff groups (custodial officers, treatment specialists and administrators) and in relation to motivating their inmate workers for production. Although by the early 1990s the organisational structure of prisons had changed, it seemed that the isolation of the work instructors largely persisted (see p. 117). One could hope for it to be lessened by further changes that were taking place: the growth of NVQs (see Chapter 5) and the bringing together at HQ of prison industries with other departments concerned in developing activities for prisoners (p. 63). But in Chapter 7 we will suggest ways in which a great deal more could be done to enable instructors to use their potential for helping inmates and to play a full part in the life of the prison.

The similarities between the Brunel findings and those of Dawson cited above – prisoners' feeling that prison work was irrelevant to life outside, and work instructors' uncertainties about their role – should be viewed in the context of the multifarious purposes for prison work which have been put forward over very many years, and the Prison Service's continued ambivalence towards them. In Chapter 7 we will set out a detailed argument that the primary purpose of prison work should be to fit prisoners for employment on release. We will explore the issues involved in realising that purpose, and our discussion will be founded on much of what has been said in the last two chapters together with material yet to be presented. Particularly important will be the analyses (to come in Chapter 6) of released prisoners' experiences of seeking work. But first, in Chapter 5, we look at prisons' provision for inmates' vocational training.

5   Vocational training in prisons

INTRODUCTION

Our descriptions of the six research prisons in Chapter 2 included mention of their training courses, and Chapter 3 touched on the training which inmates doing various kinds of prison work received on the job. Now we look more closely at prisoners' opportunities for vocational training and especially, though not only, at full-time courses. First we look at some data indicating the national scene, and then draw on material from the six prisons, and from a comparison with some outside training courses, to examine various aspects of training.

THE NATIONAL SCENE

In 1995–6, according to regime monitoring statistics, approximately 3,000 inmates, on average, in all Prison Service establishments (including those for young offenders) were occupied during the day in vocational training courses.[1] This figure was approximately 7 per cent of the total monitored prison population, a proportion which had stayed fairly constant since 1992. The proportion was higher in establishments for young offenders (14 per cent) than in those for adults (6 per cent). As well as people engaged in these courses, which usually ran for several months, some other inmates would have been learning vocational skills in their prison jobs, in other education classes or in gym sessions with physical education (PE) instructors, but the numbers training in these ways were not recorded.

National Vocational Qualifications

From 1990 the Prison Service mounted a drive to enable prisoners to train for NVQs, which in the UK were gradually being developed in many occupations to complement or replace older familiar certificates like those issued by City and Guilds (C&G) or local colleges of further education. In January 1991 the Director General wrote:[2]

The National Vocational Qualification system has become a recognised benchmark for all employment training....It will provide far better opportunities for training and employment for prisoners on their release...indeed, without NVQs they will be at a serious disadvantage in the job market.

The policy was to provide NVQ training and assessment 'as soon as practicable' in kitchens, industrial workshops, farms, Works departments, vocational training courses, education and PE departments. Prison Service HQ set up liaison with TECs and with the 'lead bodies' which decided NVQ standards for each industry, and prison staff were to receive the training and accreditation necessary to help inmates work towards the new certificates. A major advantage of NVQs, compared with some of the qualifications they superseded, was that each comprised a number of units to be achieved at the trainee's own pace. Thus a person whose training was interrupted for any reason (including, in the case of a prisoner, transfer to another prison or release) could be credited with units already achieved and then, in theory, continue the training elsewhere in order to complete the full certificate at NVQ level 1, 2 or higher.

Establishing NVQs in prisons was a slow and difficult business for the first few years, and at the time of our main research in 1992–3 they were in a state of flux. Nationally NVQs were not yet available for all the main kinds of prison work and training; for some that were, the syllabuses kept changing; there were delays over registration; and sometimes departments in prisons disputed whose budget should pay. Work instructors and trainers who had been keen to participate felt thwarted and disappointed, prison managers too felt frustrated by the stop–go progress, and some prisoners who had started training in the expectation of a certificate did not receive one.

But by 1994 the situation had greatly improved, with prisons offering NVQs in forty-eight different trades and occupations (compared with twenty-four two years previously). In 1994–5 3,543 inmates were registered as candidates, 13,470 units were awarded and 1,264 full NVQs attained, the last figure being more than double that for 1993–4. A Prison Service development officer described progress in 1994–5 as 'an explosion of achievement'.[3] In 1995–6 the figures were 3,156 inmates registered, 17,309 units awarded and 1,837 full NVQs attained (1,164 at level 1, 665 at level 2, and 8 at level 3). These statistics are discussed on p. 141. However, in spring 1996 there were signs that budget cuts might jeopardise progress. NVQ training was being offered in fewer subjects and by fewer prisons than a year earlier, and several establishments were saying that after 1 April they would give up their NVQ certification to save money. (Among the six research prisons Kirkham did so.)

Other qualifications

Before NVQs came in, one of the commonest qualifications in prisons was the C&G skills certificate, available in a variety of trades, especially those in the construction industry. Others which could lead to C&G certificates included, for example, motor mechanics, welding, industrial cleaning, catering, printing and information technology. Office skills could be recognised by RSA or Pitman certificates, and a number of local colleges awarded certificates in subjects like textile technology or business start-up.

The full-time courses leading to these qualifications occupied prisoners for the same, or nearly the same, daytime hours as others were occupied in prison work.[4] Typically a course lasted four to six months, though by no means all the trainees stayed to complete it, as will be discussed below. Other inmates could study over a longer period for some of the same qualifications during daytime education or in evening classes, some of which were held in vocational subjects. Some inmates working in farms and gardens could achieve National Proficiency Test certificates with the help of their instructors. Also, at some prisons a very few carefully selected inmates were allowed out on day-release to attend a local college, though the numbers doing so were much smaller after the tightening of security rules in 1995.

Prisoners could also train for other certificates which normally required less time than those just mentioned but which might help in future job applications. PE departments encouraged inmates to work for certificates like the Community Sports Leader Award, and some ran first-aid courses. Many kitchen and servery workers acquired the basic food hygiene certificate, which needed six hours' training.

All the courses and qualifications mentioned above are examples, not an exhaustive list, of the vocational training offered by prisons to some inmates in the early 1990s and later. Apart from NVQs no central records were kept of how many people gained certificates. The levels of training reached by inmates in our research sample will be described later in this chapter.

TRAINING COURSES AT THE SIX PRISONS

At the time of our main research fieldwork in 1992–3 the six prisons were between them running thirty-eight full-time vocational courses in twenty-one subjects. Each had at least one construction industry (CIT) course run by Works staff (Holloway taught painting and decorating, the same as at male prisons); Highpoint had most, with five. The other courses, run by education departments, included subjects as diverse as, for example, industrial cleaning, engineering skills, hairdressing and computers. Four prisons ran business start-up courses for people wanting to be self-employed. Most courses lasted at least four months except at Kirkham, where apart from a CIT course in building operations they were very short ones of only two weeks. Pay for inmates on courses (and for those in other daytime education) was at a standard rate somewhat less than the rate for nearly all grades of inmate workers. (Typically it was £3.30 a week before December 1992 and £5 afterwards; and see p. 59.) Trainees could aim for various qualifications, most commonly (at that time) C&G skills tests.

By the time of our updating visits in 1996 there had been some changes, which for each prison were noted in Chapter 2. The biggest, of course, was the move to NVQs, and at some prisons, notably Highpoint, one result was more flexibility in the length of training. There, we were told, a trainee would be allowed to stay in his course (other things being equal) until he reached NVQ level 1, taking six months if necessary, but after that only the most keen and able would be kept on to aim for level 2. At Maidstone, with its stable population, all trainees could aspire to level 2 and some would go further. At Liverpool, with its high turnover, level 1 was the aim.

Kirkham in 1996 was offering less training than before (and no NVQs), while training at Holloway had almost collapsed (p. 44). But the other four prisons were holding their own despite fears for the future. There had been some minor changes in the mix of courses offered, and some other alterations which are taken into account below. In other respects our updating visits gave no reason to think that vocational training was substantially different from what we had found in 1992–3. At that time we gathered information about seventeen courses by interviewing the instructors in all of them, observing eleven of them in action, and collecting other data. The seventeen covered the following subjects: painting and decorating, building operatives, bricklaying, plumbing, industrial cleaning, catering, welding and sheetmetal, engineering, hairdressing, motor mechanics, business start-up and office skills. We also obtained some data from interviewing inmates who had attended other courses, including similar ones at other prisons.

Typically a course had twelve places and was taught by one instructor. In the rest of this chapter we refer to instructors of training courses as trainers to distinguish them from instructors who supervised inmates at work (without in the least implying that the work instructors did no training).

ACCESS AND SELECTION

At the three prisons with a VPU – Channings Wood, Liverpool and Maidstone – most full-time courses were in the main prison so VPU inmates could not go to them, but the VPU's own education programme offered some vocational subjects, including a computer course at Channings Wood and Maidstone. Most of the prisons' incentive schemes (running from 1995–6) did not greatly affect inmates' access to training except for the few demoted to the basic regime. At Highpoint a man wanting one of the CIT courses in North prison, with its lower security, would have to wait for promotion to the 'standard-plus' regime, but we were told he would have a 70 per cent chance of getting it eventually. At Liverpool inmates wanting courses or education classes had to have security clearance, and we were told in 1992 that this restricted the numbers eligible, but by 1996, when the education department under its new contractor was more proactive, it seemed that security was much less of a hindrance. However, at all the prisons most courses had waiting lists, some of them several months long.

For all courses inmates were selected by the trainer, usually after an interview, from among those who applied, and the move had to be ratified by the labour board. Trainers when considering applicants looked for keenness almost above all else. One with a long waiting list said he deliberately chose 'the cream' and that the competition kept his students on their toes. Another selected from his list those who repeatedly came to ask him how near they were to the top of it. In contrast, a third used his list in strict order, and when a vacancy occurred he took the initiative in checking whether the applicant next in the queue was still interested.

One test of motivation was whether the inmate was willing to accept the low rate of pay, compared with what he or she might have earned in a prison job. Trainer R040, describing his selection procedure, said, 'The first question is: can they survive on the wage? Those who smoke a lot or have to phone can't usually manage.' Apart from high motivation, the majority of trainers looked for at least basic literacy and (for some trades) numeracy, and sometimes applicants otherwise suitable were sent to the education department for a 'brush up' before being accepted.

In many cases one of the important selection criteria was the length of sentence an applicant still had to serve before his or her expected date of release. In 1992 six trainers interviewed said they would normally not accept anyone who had less time available than the length of the course (four months or more). Apart from applicants who approached the trainer direct and were told this, it is likely that other would-be trainees were discouraged by the labour board, or by fellow-inmates, from applying for this reason. So the length of a trainer's waiting list probably often underestimated the degree of potential interest by inmates in that course. Five other trainers said they might take a keen applicant with only a few weeks available and impart what skills they could during that period. In later years the NVQ framework with its provision for the accumulation of units should have allowed more flexibility, but with so many applicants waiting it would be understandable if trainers still preferred those who could stay for a reasonable length of time. (We did not re-interview trainers in 1996.)

Subject to these considerations, the majority of trainers ran their courses on a roll-on, roll-off basis, admitting a new trainee at almost any time if there was a vacancy. Some, however, would take in a new recruit only during the first month of a course, so an applicant whose turn came up later would have to wait until the course started again. Most courses ran throughout the year except when the trainer was on leave or away for any other reason. But in 1992–3 when the trainer was absent the course had to be suspended because the prison's budget allowed no money to engage a substitute, and we heard of several 'current' courses, including three of the five then provided at Holloway, where this had happened and trainees were being deprived of their tuition, in some cases for months. A similar problem could occur if the trainer was supplied by a local college which insisted that prisoners should be taught for only thirty-six weeks a year like its other students. Such gaps and interruptions demotivated inmates who had been keen to learn, and must have resulted in some not finishing their courses. However, in later years when prison education and training were contracted out these problems should have diminished, as contracts could specify the number of hours of tuition the contractor had to provide.

IN THE TRAINING WORKSHOPS

Facilities

Practical courses which we saw were run in well-equipped workshops. Each inmate learning painting and decorating, for example, had a little 'room' with a door and windows in which to practise the various skills. Metalwork trainees in Maidstone's welding and sheetmetal workshop had made an impressive range of articles. The trainees' hairdressing salon at Holloway was just like a high-street one. But in some courses security or other considerations prevented trainees from getting realistic experience. Liverpool bricklaying trainees could not work at a proper building site nor experience varied weather, their workshop being all indoors. Business skills trainees could do only simulated exercises, though they were encouraged to develop their own plans. And the engineering teacher at Liverpool could teach only theory in a classroom, without any facilities for practical demonstrations, in contrast to the engineering skills workshop at Highpoint where equipment included lathes, grinders, drills and a milling machine, and where one trainee had made a working model of a steam engine.

Atmosphere and relationships

In the workshops we observed the atmosphere was cheerful, quiet and busy. Trainees worked at their own pace, with a good deal of individual attention from the trainer, on projects and exercises designed to build up their skills. Some helped one another and a few had more responsible roles like demonstrator or storekeeper. Where tools were used (as in the engineering course at Highpoint or the welding course at Maidstone) it seemed that trainees were trusted with them far more than many inmates in prison jobs.

First names were often used both ways, but it was clear that most inmates respected their trainers. Trainers interviewed stressed the value of treating their students as individuals and sustaining motivation by drawing out their interests and talents. R044, for example, said, 'Discipline staff call them scumbags. To teach them we can't treat them like that,' while R042 said, 'I think everyone's worth a chance,' and R047 said he would help his trainees with welfare problems concerning other parts of the prison.

All trainers emphasised the importance of aiming at high quality in everything their students did. R039, in painting and decorating, said he tried to teach 'as tip-top as they can get. They can always lower their standards afterwards. But if you don't know how to do it properly you can never higher your standards.' As well as trade skills they taught health and safety and tidy working habits. They had wider aims too: ten trainers, when asked what other benefits inmates might derive from their courses, spoke of increased social skills, self-esteem and confidence. R046, teaching catering, said he tried to help his trainees overcome their feelings of isolation and distrust of people, while R048, in business studies, said he tried to foster self-sufficiency.

Most of the thirty-seven trainees (over nine kinds of course) to whom we chatted in their workshops appeared to be well motivated and on good terms with the staff. Of the thirteen trainees who were included in our main interview sample, ten said their relationship with the trainer was good and one that it was 'OK'. The other two, who said there were problems, felt they were not treated with sufficient respect (and one of them also wanted more help and guidance from his trainer). Like inmate workers (p. 108), the trainees wanted to be treated as fellow-humans rather than prisoners, and as adults who were willing to learn, and the majority apparently felt they were. R570, for example, said that when he first started his engineering course the trainer had said: 'While you're here you're not in a prison, as far as I'm concerned, you're in a workshop, you come to work.' That was good, said R, it put him at ease straight away.

Trainees' satisfaction

Of the thirty-seven trainees with whom we chatted informally twenty-eight said they had chosen the training in order to gain or improve skills, and seven said it was for enjoyment. For twenty-two the course was a new experience, and for fourteen it built on some knowledge they had already. Thirty said it was a definite help in getting through their sentence, and thirty-four hoped it would help them after release, in the majority of cases for jobhunting, though ten (most of whom were learning painting or building operations) said it would be mainly useful for DIY. The thirteen trainees in our main interview sample were scored for satisfaction in the same way as inmate workers (see p. 114) and their average score was 4.08, significantly higher than the average of 2.21 for workers.[5] The following were examples of high scorers:

> R575, in bricklaying, gets a sense of achievement: 'to see something that you've done, looking finished and presentable'. It's interesting, because he is learning various techniques and the proper way to build. He feels a sense of power through interpreting drawings on his own, with help from the trainer later to correct any faults in his construction.

> R611, in business studies, was self-employed before his sentence. 'It's certainly put a lot of stuff together for me that I didn't know, about running my own business, like how to do tax...how to do it legally' [R smiles] 'and how to do it properly, goals and all that....I didn't realise what decisions I was making till I did the business studies course. It's put everything together for me.'

R603, in computers, had always wanted to learn about computers and had no opportunity at school. The course definitely gives him a sense of power. 'The first time you switch on the computer you realise how much power you've got under your fingers, and you think: "Wow! This is something else! How the hell did I ever live without one of these things?"'

THE TRAINERS

All the trainers interviewed, who were civilians, were well qualified in their speciality (to at least craftsman level or equivalent) and the majority had a teaching qualification too, though they had not necessarily been trained to deal with prisoners. Those employed by a local college were mainly satisfied with their opportunities for contacts outside the prison, and some others had links through trade associations. Trainers felt more able than work instructors to give their inmates specific advice for the future: twelve out of thirteen trainers who were asked about it said they discussed work prospects with their trainees, advised them what employers looked for and gave tips on jobhunting. Eight out of twelve sometimes contacted employers or gave references, and eight occasionally heard from ex-trainees who had been released. But trainers, like work instructors, believed that the Prison Service frowned on such activities and on contacts between staff and ex-inmates. They would have liked more feedback about their former students, and two said the only way they could seek it was through the college which employed them, not through the prison. R045, regretting his lack of contact with employers, said, 'It's a very disappointing part of the job....I know some of them have settled down, but I've never had a progress report. I think it would be a good thing actually.' R108, teaching business studies, was in a different position because he ran his own consultancy outside the prison. He offered an advisory back-up service to his ex-students who were trying to become self-employed and who after release could approach him independently. A condition he insisted on was that in dealings with third parties (like bank managers) they should be honest about their prison record.[6]

CONTINUITY OF TRAINING

Links between training courses and prison jobs

Inmates who returned to prison work after completing a training course might have been able to gain more skill, or at least to consolidate what they had learned, if there had been planned links between the training courses and related prison jobs. But it seemed from our discussions with staff and inmates that such links were patchy. An obvious possible one would have been for CIT trainees to move on into the Works department, but on the whole not many did. The numbers of trainees emerging from the courses did not match the Works vacancies, which were fewer, and generally the Works preferred to recruit tradesmen with fairly long sentences for a stable workforce: Works' aims were to maintain the prison, not train inmates. Even CIT trainees who did go into Works might find themselves working at a lower level of skill than they had acquired on the course, and Works reserved some kinds of jobs for their own staff. Other examples were the courses in office and business skills whose trainees rarely got prison clerical jobs, these being given more often to other kinds of prisoners (see p. 102).

Nevertheless, throughout the six prisons links did occur. Some painting and decorating trainees did site work, and at Liverpool we met two who had had planned spells in the Works painting team, which they particularly appreciated because, they said, the course taught home decorating skills but the Works did industrial painting which added to their experience. Welding trainees had welded steel staircases at Maidstone and mended horticultural machinery at Channings Wood. At several prisons people in desktop publishing classes could do in-house printing jobs. At Highpoint in 1996 trainees in the new PE course studied in the morning and then in the afternoon they helped the PE instructors teach other inmates.

At Channings Wood some catering trainees went to work in the officers' mess and some from the industrial cleaning course became wing or departmental cleaners. A good example of the latter was the following:

> R503, aged 27, had no qualifications and was mainly unemployed during the year before he was sentenced to twelve months for burglary. At Channings Wood he was determined to make the best use of his time there. He asked for a training course and the only vacancy was in industrial cleaning, so he took that. He obtained his C&G skills certificate and was then employed as a cleaner in the education department, responsible for his own area. He saw this as good training which he hoped to use on release. 'I feel good about it, I've benefited out of the system instead of letting the system take it all out of me.'

In some cases a trainer and his or her course members as a body offered the prison a specialist service. The Channings Wood cleaning course, for instance, had spring-cleaned the visits room (for £179, whereas an outside contractor had quoted £3,000 for the job), while at Holloway staff and inmates in general could patronise the trainees' hairdressing salon. At Kirkham the building operatives' course had obtained a contract to build a prison perimeter road, which would involve them in four NVQ units.

But out of ten inmates who were in a training course when we interviewed them only two expected on completing it to move into a prison job which would use their new skill. In interviewing inmate workers we found thirty-three who said they had learned, or begun to learn, a new skill during their current sentence but before the prison job they were now doing; only five of them were using that skill in their current job, though eighteen others knew of jobs which they thought could have used it. Altogether it seemed in 1992–3 that only a small proportion of course trainees had opportunities to practise and consolidate their skill in prison jobs, and although in 1996 staff gave us other examples we felt that the prisons had potential for much more linkage.

Transfer of inmates between prisons

This was a frequent cause of interruption to training, though we could not gather any statistics on it (nor did the Service systematically keep any). Prisoners are moved from one establishment to another for all sorts of reasons, including their security category (normally expected to decrease during sentence), offence history, the estimated actual time they will serve, control and discipline, further requirements to attend court, availability of special facilities (such as the sex offender treatment programme), and – an increasing consideration with the pressure of rising numbers – the sheer need to find space somewhere or other within the system. Even in 1992 R058, a senior prison probation officer, expressed the last point thus:

> It is about filling places quickly and conveniently, about where is the coach from this reception prison going and how many seats are on it and what is the category. They have been pretty quick changing the category when it suits them.

It seemed from our discussions with staff and prisoners that preserving the continuity of an inmate's training often received little consideration when a transfer was decided, though it did happen and people with long sentences might fare best. Two such examples were the following, both with sentences of over four years:

> R636, formerly a production manager, had begun his sentence in a high-security prison where he embarked on training in computers and business studies, with a plan that he would eventually aim at a degree in technology. When interviewed he was continuing his studies in Maidstone, where he appreciated the support he received from the education staff.

> R641 before going to prison had done one and a half years of a building trades apprenticeship. During his sentence he started on a bricks CIT course in one prison, but before he could finish it he was transferred to Maidstone, where he worked in the tailors for three months while waiting for a vacancy on the bricks course. At the time of interview he had resumed bricks training and was hoping to progress to NVQ level 3.

On the other hand, someone with a long sentence, having served the early years of it in a Category A or Category B prison with good training (and we met several such inmates at Maidstone), might find on 'promotion' to a prison with lower security that the training could not continue. An example was R616:

> R616 started his sentence in a high-security prison where he did two years of a three-year course in engineering, which he enjoyed. But on transfer to Channings Wood he could not continue because there was no such course there. R had been a master builder outside and asked if he could work on the maintenance of prison staff houses, but was told that was now all done by private contractors. He was put in the tailors' shop at first and later became an orderly. He felt the transfer to Channings Wood had been a bad move for him.

Prisoners with shorter sentences were more liable to have their training interrupted by transfers, if indeed they started training at all. R580 and R555 were instances.

> R580 began his eighteen-months sentence in Norwich Prison, where he had spent seven months on remand without any work. Norwich had a CIT course in carpentry, and some weeks after being sentenced R was allowed to start on it. But after three weeks in it he was transferred to Highpoint. He asked for the carpentry course there but it was not available to inmates in South, where R was put, and also he now had barely four months till his expected date of release. He was sent to the tailors' shop and did no further training.

> R555, aged 21 when interviewed, had begun his twenty-one-months sentence in a Young Offender Institution. There he started on a painting and decorating course which was cut short by his transfer to Liverpool Prison at age 21. He would have liked to do either of the CIT courses there to get a qualification, or alternatively to do kitchen work, of which he had had some previous experience and felt he would like to learn more. But at Liverpool he got into trouble over debts to other inmates and asked for Rule 43 for his own protection. Training courses were not available in the VPU and he ended up in the light assembly shop.

Such cases raise the major issue of sentence planning, which will be addressed in Chapter 7.

Other points about continuity

Sometimes an inmate could take one course in trade skills and another in business start-up with a view to self-employment on release, and there were several instances at Channings Wood including one trainee we met in the Options For Learning scheme (see p. 145). But other people had their training interrupted, sometimes for months, because of the kinds of administrative problems described on p. 132. And some dropped out of courses for reasons of their own.

HOW MUCH TRAINING DID PRISONERS GET?

Answers from training staff

Work instructors and trainers interviewed at the six prisons were asked what level of skill their inmates reached and how many would be employable outside if there were jobs in that industry. Except for light assembly and cleaning (which were seen as unskilled), work instructors' answers amounted generally to the following: that inmates could acquire some skill if they were sufficiently interested and motivated, which the majority were not, and if they stayed long enough in that prison job; and that then, in most cases, they would be employable at a fairly basic level.

Trainers said that not all trainees achieved the full qualification aimed at (C&G skills test certificate, NVQ level 2 or equivalent), but in several courses the majority would *if* they stayed long enough. Most of the courses were modular, or would be more so with NVQs, and a trainee who managed only some of the requisite units would get a 'record of achievement' for them and could, given the opportunity, continue elsewhere. (An exception was the Channings Wood business course which had a progressive syllabus, but the trainer said that 87 per cent of his students completed the course.)

But a course of six or even twelve months, resulting in a C&G skills test or NVQ level 2, does not make a tradesperson. Many inmates were aware of this and of course the trainers were too. R042 said:

> I tell them: 'You won't be a bricklayer when you leave here, but you'll be a good labourer. You'll be able to work with a bricklayer, understand what he wants and what he's doing. When looking for work, aim for a small firm and ask for a labouring job at first. If you get on well with the bricklayer, because it's a small firm there'll be opportunities for you to do a bit, pick up a trowel now and then. If you show ability he may develop you, you'll get more experience, you'll learn.'

Other trainers made similar remarks. The courses were not apprenticeships but they imparted basic skills which, provided jobs were available (and that, of course, was another matter), could help a willing worker get a foot on the ladder.

Answers from prisoners interviewed

In order to assess what training was received by inmates interviewed for the study we now use the sample of eighty-eight who were later followed up after their release. During the prison interview we asked people about the kinds of work and training they had done, or were still doing, and the qualifications attempted, at any time during the current sentence. In the follow-up interview we checked (in most cases) to update that information to the date of release, so as not to omit any training that might have taken place in the last few months. Now we use this data to try to indicate in several ways how much training those eighty-eight people did.

First, focusing on daytime occupations during sentence, we noted that twenty-three of the eighty-eight had embarked on a training course (whether or not they completed it), twenty-eight had been involved in education, and eighty-five had been engaged in prison work. These categories overlapped: altogether forty-seven people (53 per cent) had done work only, thirty-eight (43 per cent) had done work plus training or education (or both), and three (3 per cent) had done only training or education (or both). Considering that some of the prison jobs might have imparted vocational skills, it seemed likely that a substantial proportion of the eighty-eight might have received some skills training through daytime occupation during their sentence.

Next we asked the eighty-eight whether they had learned, or started (or continued) to learn, any kind of vocational skill from *any* activity during sentence, whether it was from prison work, a training course, day or evening classes, physical education, work outside the prison or anything else. Forty-five people (51 per cent) said they had done so. They listed between them a great variety of skills, including nearly all the ones that have been mentioned in this chapter and in Chapter 2. Then we enquired whether these forty-five people had attempted a qualification, and if so how far they had got. The answers are shown in Table 2.

Table 2 shows that altogether twelve of the forty-five who acquired some kind of vocational skill obtained a certificate which recognised their achievement in completing a course, or learning a skill, which required several months or longer. The majority of these people completed a course leading to C&G skills tests and obtained the full certificate. Six people did some C&G skills tests or equivalent

Table 2 Qualifications achieved, or partly achieved, by forty-five inmates who started (or continued) to learn a vocational skill during sentence

Qualification		No. of inmates
Obtained HND or GCSE	2	
Obtained full C&G skills or basic certificate, or NVQ level 1 or 2	7 }	12
Obtained college certificate of completion/achievement for a course lasting several months	3	
Record of achievement for some C&G skills or units of NVQ level 1 or 2	6 }	8
Obtained certificate for a small course (e.g. health and hygiene, or basic first aid)	2	
None at all		20
No information		5
Total		45

for NVQ and obtained a 'record of achievement' for them. Two others did a smaller course, such as that in health and hygiene for food handlers, and obtained the certificate. (Several others also obtained this certificate along with a C&G one.) But twenty people, as far as we could tell, obtained no qualification nor any credits towards one. About five others we had no information.[7]

The reasons why nearly half the group obtained no kind of certificate, and six other people obtained only a partial one, were of various kinds. Some people in prison jobs, especially kitchens, felt at the time that they were acquiring a little skill but there was no structured training and no certificate. Some people took courses which apparently were uncertificated at the time. Some people started a course but then lost interest and dropped out. Others had to stop part-way through for reasons beyond their control, of the kinds we saw earlier. And several were caught by the difficulties in 1992–3 over NVQs, and did not receive the qualification they and their trainers had hoped for. So although half the eighty-eight people during their sentence felt they were learning (or had begun to learn) some kind of vocational skill, only a quarter had derived from it any kind of paper with which to try to impress an employer; and, as already mentioned, even the qualifications which people did get were well below the level of a skilled tradesperson.

Nonetheless, the achievements in 1992–3 of this sample of eighty-eight, who were fairly representative of prisoners sentenced to a year or more, compare favourably with the national NVQ figures for prisoners. The first twelve people in Table 2 either obtained an NVQ or probably would have done had their training taken place two or three years later; similarly the next six can be regarded as gaining some NVQ units, bringing the total of such people to eighteen, or 20 per cent of the sample. Had it not been for the teething troubles of NVQs a few more people who received no certificate or record of achievement for their training might have got one, thus raising the total proportion of the sample with NVQ units to perhaps 25 per cent, of whom half got a full NVQ. Nationally, the 1995–6 figures of 3,156 prisoners registered for NVQ training and 1,837 full NVQs attained (p. 129) are 13 per cent and 7 per cent respectively of the number of prisoners received in 1995 who were sentenced to a year or more. This comparison between the sample and national NVQ figures is rough in several respects[8] but it suggests that the research sample got more training than did the national average three years later. Here we recall that four of the six research prisons were 'training' ones which had been chosen partly because they were officially thought to provide good training (p. 25, note 91).

OUTSIDE TRAINING SCHEMES, AND COMPARISONS WITH PRISON

To compare prison training courses with some of the training going on outside we made short visits to four organisations which, funded through TECs, provided training for unemployed people under the government's Training For

Work (TFW) scheme. They were selected for the research (with the aid of the TECs) as schemes particularly sympathetic to unemployed people with 'special needs' (though they had other trainees too). One would expect them to be more geared than the average scheme to the training needs of ex-offenders, and thus they were particularly interesting as comparators for prison training.

The four schemes were all large ones with between 125 and 300 trainees. Two were run by voluntary organisations and two by private companies, and each was within the 'catchment area' of one of the six research prisons. Their trainees included some young people (doing Youth Training) but most were adults, and at three schemes most were men, the fourth having men and women in equal numbers. All four accepted ex-prisoners along with other people, and recruited applicants through jobcentres, other agencies including the Probation Service, and direct by press advertising or word of mouth. Under the government rules adult trainees received £10 a week on top of their DSS benefit, plus help towards the costs of travel and (if appropriate) of childcare.

A major point of interest was the content of the training these outside schemes provided. While between them their courses covered a wide range of subjects there was an emphasis, not so apparent among courses offered in prisons, on service and business occupations: the leisure industry, caring skills, retailing and business administration. Other subjects included arts and theatre administration, warehouse and stores, energy conservation and manufacturing practice. Two schemes offered some construction industry skills, but a third (in a depressed inner-city area) had stopped construction courses because job prospects were so poor. All four schemes offered training in information technology. All had provision to help recruits who lacked the basic education necessary for going straight into a main course, and all gave training in jobsearch skills.

Qualifications offered in nearly all the courses were at NVQ level 2. The prison training courses also were working towards this level, though when we first saw them NVQs were not so widely available. Managers at two of the schemes said that the majority of their trainees attained level 2, though for some the length of funded training, which was flexible for individuals but averaged twenty-six weeks, was not enough. Many prison courses also ran for up to six months, but (except at Kirkham) most inmates' weekly hours of attendance would be less than the minimum of thirty required of trainees at the schemes.

Another big difference from prison courses was that, in accordance with government policy, the schemes relied heavily on employers in the same occupations to provide some training, along with work experience. The length of a trainee's stay in a work placement varied between trainees and between schemes, but the average appeared to be about ten weeks. One training officer described enthusiastically his scheme's arrangements: after induction most trainees would go to a placement host for systematic training on four days a week, spending the fifth day back at the scheme base to receive more general training and support. Those learning information technology did so at the base and a few went out to college, but both groups eventually moved to employers for practical experience.

This planned mix of training and work, all aimed at helping the trainee to get a qualification, contrasted with the generally weak and inconsistent arrangements we found in prisons for linking courses with work.

Placement hosts were often hard to find, except at one scheme for which a band of sympathetic employers had set up a special network of support. One of the other schemes would pay a host up to £200 in 'inefficiency costs' to take a trainee who had been unemployed for six months. It appeared that only a small proportion of trainees – 15 per cent at one scheme, 6 per cent at another – were kept on by employers after their placements, but three schemes said that their success rate, as measured by the proportion of leavers going into employment or into further education or training, was about 40 to 50 per cent. Most of nine trainees briefly interviewed by the researcher at two schemes were pleased with the training they were getting.

Altogether, despite the sceptical view of government training schemes taken by some people (including ex-prisoners – see p. 160), and despite the unavoidable differences between outside life and the constraints of prison life, it seemed that these four training schemes pointed to some ways in which prison vocational training might be improved. Overall, the kinds of training the schemes offered were more in tune with outside job prospects, a situation which was helped by their contacts with TECs and local employers. Scheme staff could make more use of such links than prison trainers, who felt they were officially discouraged from doing so. At the schemes the mix of skills training, work experience, jobsearch techniques and (if needed) basic education, together with personal support, meant that for a trainee the whole period could be planned to address his or her individual needs and enhance employability. By contrast prisoners, despite the frequent willingness of trainers and other staff to take a personal interest in them, were liable to be moved about the system and placed in prison occupations with often little regard for continuity and their other training needs. This is the realm of sentence planning, which we discuss later. Meanwhile we now describe a prison training scheme which combined features from inside and outside and which, while it lasted, was in some ways a model of what might be done.

THE 'OPTIONS FOR LEARNING' SCHEME AT CHANNINGS WOOD

This special scheme ran in Channings Wood prison from mid-1992 to March 1995. It was funded by Devon and Cornwall TEC as a Training For Work (TFW) scheme and called, like the TEC's other TFW schemes, Options For Learning (OFL). It was administered at the prison by a manager and support staff appointed specially for the purpose, and the actual training was carried out by prison trainers, teachers and work instructors for OFL trainees in the same way as for other inmates whom they trained and supervised.

To be eligible for OFL a prisoner had to be within eighteen months of his expected release date. Then, like TFW trainees outside, he received an individual assessment and a personal training plan which took into account his abilities and past experience, his hopes for the future, and the kinds of training which could be offered: in his case the training provider was the prison. By mid-1993 there were OFL trainees in all the Channings Wood training courses, in basic education (which the TEC agreed could be regarded as vocationally relevant) and in the tailors, gardens and the officers' mess. A year later the list had expanded to include the laundry, woodwork and physical education, in all of which NVQs to level 2 had become available. OFL trainees had to aim for these qualifications, and in addition they received personal support and guidance from the scheme's administrators, and jobsearch training in the pre-release course. The basic education was often delivered on a part-time basis alongside other skills training. From September 1993 OFL inmates were also offered a 'personal development' course run by the administrators as part of their 'holistic' approach to meeting trainees' needs.

Inmates in the OFL scheme were paid, in addition to their prison 'wage', up to £10 a week extra, corresponding to the £10 a week which trainees in outside TFW schemes received in addition to their benefit money. (An OFL inmate working at least thirty hours a week, as was possible in, for example, the officers' mess, received the full £10. Most others got less because their prison working hours were shorter: the average was £8 a week.) The OFL money was put aside until the inmate's release. He then received half of it, and the other half thirteen weeks later by sending a claim in which he also reported whether he was in full-time employment, self-employment, further education or training; if he had achieved any of these 'positive outcomes' he received a bonus of £50 as well as the second half of his OFL money. (Prison staff welcomed this opportunity of receiving, through the OFL administrators, news of the progress of ex-inmates they had trained.)

Funding allowed the scheme to offer about seventy-five places, though whether an inmate could join OFL also depended on there being a vacancy in the course he wanted. Popularity among inmates grew steadily: by mid-1993 there were sixty-eight OFL trainees and a hundred on the waiting list. By mid-1994 a total of 255 men had passed through the scheme and reached their check date of thirteen weeks after release. While at Channings Wood twenty-eight of these had gained an NVQ at level 1 and nine at level 2; by twelve weeks after release fifty-two (20 per cent) had achieved a 'positive outcome'. This figure, though lower than the success rates quoted by outside schemes visited, is nevertheless not discouraging for a group composed wholly of ex-prisoners, as will be seen from the information on our follow-up sample in Chapter 6. Scheme staff said that during its last year the success rate was nudging 30 per cent, and was particularly high among ex-trainees who had taken the personal development course.

Five OFL trainees at Channings Wood were interviewed briefly for the research: two in the industrial cleaning course and three in horticultural mechanics. Four of them hoped on release to become self-employed, and all were enthusiastic about the scheme. One man, due for release in two weeks, had been in OFL for seven months, achieving the business studies diploma and a C&G certificate in horticultural mechanics, as well as saving £272 in OFL money for his release. He hoped to set up in business rebuilding and customising motor cycles.

The Channings Wood OFL scheme was an innovative and imaginative venture. Devon and Cornwall TEC funded it by money allocated for training unemployed people with 'special needs', reasoning that that category could include prisoners. Channings Wood inmates had a monetary incentive to participate (as well as the other benefits to them) because of the extra £10 a week, and the prison had incentives too, receiving £35 a week for every training place plus a bonus in respect of each trainee who achieved an NVQ or a 'positive outcome'. It was hoped that the prison's share would be ploughed back into facilities for training.

Much hard work was necessary in the first year to establish the scheme and win the trust of prison staff, but by mid-1994 it appeared to be flourishing strongly, with enthusiasm from staff and inmates and the success rate rising. It is particularly interesting in the context of our research for several reasons:

1   The TEC was involved directly in the prison. It advised on the suitability of prison training, and funded some.
2   The scheme's staff had a holistic approach. Trainees received an individual assessment and training plan, personal support and guidance throughout their training in addition to vocational skills, and jobsearch help near release.
3   The training was combined with practical experience in related prison work.
4   Trainees' pay enabled them to save some money against their release.
5   Feedback information on ex-trainees' progress was available to prison staff.

In these respects the Channings Wood scheme was a pointer to developments we would wish to become general, and which are discussed in Chapter 7.

At the end of March 1995 Devon and Cornwall TEC were obliged by a directive from the Employment Department to withdraw the funding. The reason was understood to be a government policy that one department should not subsidise another's activities (a matter loosely spoken of as 'double funding') – in this case, that prisoners' training should not be paid for by both the Employment Department and the Prison Service. Channings Wood managers wanted to keep the OFL scheme going but could not, and it was wound down a few weeks later. The NVQ training of Channings Wood inmates, which the OFL scheme had largely 'kick-started', continued and grew, but the distinctive features of the scheme – listed above as (1), (2), (4) and (5) – were lost.

PROBLEMS AND POTENTIAL FOR THE VOCATIONAL TRAINING OF INMATES

We have seen in this chapter that by 1995–6 an appreciable minority of prisoners were receiving training aimed at NVQs, and that four of the six research prisons were perhaps offering more than the national average despite fears over budget cuts. Vocational training was imparted in full-time courses typically lasting several months, in some other education classes (including PE) and to some inmates during their prison work.

Work instructors had mixed views on the importance of training (p. 117), but many would have liked to give more to inmates who were willing to learn. But in the workplace their efforts could be hampered by many factors: pressure to meet production targets or service deadlines, the short hours and interruptions of the prison working day, high turnover of workers, the need to watch and manage discontented inmates, security restrictions and limited budgets. Trainers leading courses also suffered from short hours and interruptions, security restrictions and budget constraints, but in other respects their task was more straightforward. They selected their recruits, who by and large were well motivated, and they could concentrate on training. They felt more able than work instructors to give their inmates specific advice for the future. They sometimes contacted employers or gave references, but like other prison staff they believed that such actions were officially frowned on and they would have liked feedback about the progress of ex-trainees.

Prisoners in training courses, on average, derived much more satisfaction from what they were doing than those engaged only in prison work. But the majority who trained, whether in courses or in work, acquired only low levels of skill, and a major cause of this was lack of continuity and co-ordination by prison management. Yet it seemed that prisons had much potential for delivering vocational training, and we now list some practical suggestions which were made by prison staff at all levels, prisoners, and a few other people. In some cases prisons were already putting these into practice, and others had plans to do so. The following are not in any particular order.

Woodwork   Give interested inmates more training in all the basic hand tools; this would be useful at least for DIY. Make a greater variety of products. Open the workshops for evening classes in carpentry. Organise small teams of workers (say four people) to assemble a complete batch of a product (say 200 tables) from start to finish, including every stage of assembly plus spraying and packaging, and have competitions between teams; this would encourage teamwork, increase skills training, and give interest and a sense of achievement.

Kitchen, catering   Integrate catering classes much more with practice in the kitchen, co-ordinating the work of kitchen staff and catering trainer. Get an outside catering firm to take charge of prison meals, using inmate helpers and training them as catering assistants. Expand a prison's catering service to prepare meals for other groups in the community as well, such as hospitals or day care centres. Develop sales of trainees' products to staff. Enable trainees to run a small room as a restaurant for staff and special visitors.

Gardens Grow more food. Enable a team of inmates to run a polytunnel as a business, producing tomatoes, for example; pay them more realistic wages, with bonuses for exceeding production targets.

Tailors, sewing Drastically reduce the tailors' shops to small workrooms employing just those inmates who are genuinely interested, and teach them to make whole garments; also cutting, designing and other aspects of the clothing trade.

Printing Use only modern equipment. Link up with training courses in office skills, business studies and computers: with these trainees, develop printing and publication services as a business to departments of the prison.

Light assembly Redevelop workshops to do light engineering work with some skill content; co-ordinate with training courses in welding, sheetmetal work and engineering.

Works/construction industry courses Change the emphasis of Works inmate labour from prison maintenance to training. Co-ordinate a throughput of inmates from CIT and other relevant courses (like welding) so that these trainees 'graduate' into the Works department for practice and consolidation of skills. Then, when they have done so, send them out of the prison on community work, thus making vacancies in Works for more trainees; prison maintenance will get done along the way. Obtain more community work, for example from local authorities on the maintenance of council houses. Develop a course in basic household maintenance (e.g. simple plumbing and electrical skills) for some inmates for DIY.

Stores Combine with training in computers and warehouse work.

Motor vehicles Develop or expand training courses in motor mechanics. Invite staff to be customers, and include business skills training. Offer services to community groups outside, e.g. maintaining council lorries. Develop a business in car restoration: this would be labour-intensive, would train inmates in several skills (motor mechanics, welding, spray painting, electrical wiring, upholstery, car valeting) and would produce end results that they could see and be proud of.

Office skills, computers Enable trainees from these courses to help with administrative and clerical work, and especially with the business enterprises of prison industries.

Business studies, retailing   Set up a shop, run by inmates, to sell prison produce and manufactures. Arrange trade between different departments of the prison, and involve inmates in administering it.

General   In all training, whether in workshops or courses, involve the education department in teaching inmates literacy and numeracy as required. This might be best done by teachers coming into the workshops and working alongside instructors and trainers.

These were specific suggestions. But there are also wider issues concerning the training of prisoners for future employment, namely: the relevance of prison work to the world of work outside, and the importance of addressing in an integrated way a prisoner's other needs which may affect his or her chances of success. These topics, already foreshadowed in this and earlier chapters, will be addressed in Chapter 7. But first, in Chapter 6, we examine how far the ex-prisoners in our study used their experiences of prison work and training after their release.

6   Sink, float or swim: release from prison

INTRODUCTION

In this chapter we follow the fortunes of the eighty-eight people in our sample of released prisoners to see how far their experiences of prison work and training improved their chances in the labour market. We look also at their financial circumstances, their further involvement in crime, and the ways in which, looking back on it a few months later, they viewed their time in prison. But first we examine the question: why is getting work important?

Avoiding future crime

During the research interviews with prisoners, 108 who were within three months of release were asked whether they intended to try to avoid crime in future. Sixty-eight gave a definite 'yes'. The others qualified their answers in some way, though twenty of them indicated that they wanted to avoid serious crime. But not nearly all those who wanted to felt sure that they could. Some examples:

R508, aged 22, has been serving his first prison sentence of fifteen months for theft. He is determined not to come back. 'This crime is the first and the last time.'

R530, aged 26, serving a year for reckless driving, has had six previous sentences for a variety of offences. He now has a girlfriend who has stood by him during this last one. 'I may end up in a couple of fights, but I'm not going out of my way to get them.' ('What about other things, drugs and so on?') 'No. I've done thirteen years now, that's long enough....It's up to me to stay out, if not for my own sake, for hers.'

R647, aged 44, has a long record of offending including thefts to fund his drug habit. ('What will happen when you are discharged this time?') 'I promise myself, like I've done in the past, I say to myself: right, this is it, this is the last time. But – saying that while you're locked up and keeping it up when you go out I find are two different things.'

This picture of good intentions, hopes and doubts was similar to that found by Burnett (1992) who interviewed male recidivist property offenders before and after they left prison. Before release over 80 per cent said that they wanted to avoid further crime, although considerably fewer felt confident of being able to. After her follow-up, one of Burnett's conclusions was that among those (57 per cent) who had re-offended the majority were not as committed to crime as formerly and were uncomfortable with their involvement in it: 'A sizeable proportion...are tantalisingly close to being conventional, law-abiding citizens.'[1] As will be seen later, many of our sample of eighty-eight tried hard to avoid serious offending.

What things could help?

One hundred and one of our prisoner interviewees, including eighty-one of those who said they wanted to keep away from serious crime, were asked what things could help them to do so. Out of a list of ten possible items they gave the highest ratings to 'enough money to live on' (rated important by 90 per cent), 'my own willpower' (89 per cent), and 'a job' (84 per cent). (The remaining items, which included family support, accommodation, avoiding alcohol or drugs, and four others, were rated important by up to 79 per cent.)

'Enough money to live on' will be examined later in this chapter, with evidence from the eighty-eight ex-prisoners about the money they had at the time of release, their subsequent sources of income, and their financial commitments and problems. The emphasis placed on 'willpower' is significant: later we will see that some felt they had used their time in prison to gain self-understanding or self-control, and in Chapter 7 we discuss issues of personal responsibility and competence.

The third most highly rated item was 'a job'. It is a major premise for this book, and one for which there is a great deal of evidence, that having worthwhile legitimate work reduces the likelihood of a person's further involvement in crime. Braithwaite in 1980[2] said:

> There have been many studies in Great Britain and America which show with a remarkable degree of consistency that prisoners who find stable employment upon release have about half (and sometimes less than half) the probability of being reconvicted compared with releasees who have a pattern of unemployment.

He cited fourteen such studies. Crow *et al.* in 1989[3] said: 'In one study after another it has been shown that probationers, ex-prisoners and others are significantly more likely to re-offend at some later date if they are unemployed', and cited ten British studies of which only two were also on Braithwaite's list. Motiuk in 1996[4] described further recent research with similar findings. Andrews and Bonta in 1994, after a large review of research looking for predictors of criminal behaviour in individuals, included 'an unstable employment record' in the set of 'major risk/need factors' which they regarded as well established.[5] We do not assert that there is a simple link between being unemployed and committing crime; on the contrary, the link is made complex by many other factors, some of which will become apparent in the course of this chapter.[6]

We now turn to consider the employment prospects of our sample of eighty-eight, beginning with preparations for their release from prison.

PREPARATIONS FOR RELEASE

Pre-release courses

In the year in which we first met these prisoners, officers at all the research prisons except Maidstone ran pre-release courses, usually lasting one or two weeks, for sentenced inmates nearing release, a dozen or so at a time. The format varied somewhat with the length of the course and between prisons, but typically the two officers in charge of a course would run some sessions themselves and bring in specialists, often from outside the prison, for others. These people would give advice and lead discussions with the course members on a range of 'survival' topics: DSS benefit entitlements, budgeting, health matters like alcohol and drugs, communication skills and, especially, jobsearch. Inmates would practise filling in application forms, learn interview techniques using role play and video, and hear advisers from the Employment Service, probation and voluntary agencies. Information would be given about training courses, jobclubs and other Employment Service facilities, and the question of disclosing a criminal record to a potential employer.

Except at Kirkham, the provision of these courses at the men's prisons was insufficient for all inmates who would have liked to attend one. At Liverpool, with a population of over 1,100 (including people on remand, some of whom would also have been interested) the course of one or two weeks running forty-four weeks a year did not meet the demand. At Channings Wood the course stopped every now and then because its staff were taken off for other duties, and eight Channings Wood inmates in our follow-up sample had been prevented from attending for that reason. R511 said that soon after he arrived at Channings Wood he was put into a pre-release course which ran for four days just as a show for visitors. 'What they done, they just come round and said you, you and you, and as soon as they left, we left.' He would have liked to go to the course properly before his release, but 'They're closing down, there's no one to run it.'

Not all inmates wanted to attend a pre-release course. Some thought they would not learn anything new, and some were in a prison job, such as the kitchen, where they earned more than they would have got for attending the course and where also, in a few cases, they felt the staff discouraged them from taking time off to go. Our sample of eighty-eight included twenty-seven who had attended a course during their most recent sentence. But twenty-two – a quarter of the sample – would have liked the opportunity and did not get it: because the course was not then available, or the inmate was not told enough about it, or his stay at that prison was too short for him to be considered eligible, or he was refused for other reasons. Seventeen others said they had not been interested, and in the remaining cases we did not know why people did not attend.

During the follow-up interviews the twenty-seven who had attended a course were asked what they remembered of it, and their answers gave a mixed picture. Altogether, fifteen felt it had been beneficial in some way. R584, for instance, from Holloway, spoke warmly of the prison staff and of the outside agency who had advised her on educational opportunities, which she was still pursuing by applying for a college place. Several people particularly appreciated the information they had received about DSS benefits, though R585 said, 'They tell you you're entitled to this and that, but when you come out – you try and get it!' As to jobsearch skills, nine people felt their pre-release course had been some use, but several of these also said they would have felt so more strongly if they had actually succeeded in getting a job. R515 remarked:

> It's useful if there's work about, but if there's none, if there are 200 applicants for every vacancy, you can be told how to fill in application forms till it comes out of your ears, you still won't get a job.

Statistically, the twenty-seven people who had attended a course were not more likely than the others to have found any work during the follow-up period.

Several people felt the pre-release course had helped them gain general confidence as they prepared to face the outside world. An interesting example was the following:

> R527 went to the pre-release course – 'a room with twelve strange people, you don't know any of them' – at a time when he had begun to reflect on his life and decide that he did not want to risk a fourth prison sentence. At the course sessions he looked round at his fellow-inmates and heard about their experiences of failure in life, and this bolstered his resolution. He found the forward-looking orientation of the course helpful too. 'When you leave here [the course room] of a night-time you switch off, you're back in prison again, you're back to wheeling and dealing in whatever you wheel and deal in. First thing in the morning, straight after a shave and a shower and everything else, you're back in here, your mind's switched on, being positive, and get on with the day.'
>
> ('Why do you think more people don't ask to come on the pre-release course?')

'Because they probably find: one, it's too boring, which it isn't, that's false information; two, they probably think, "Do you get the same wages?"... And they probably don't want – it's change again...to go into that room with total strangers. It's just like starting your sentence again, not knowing who is there, what to say.' R said that the confidence he got at the pre-release course was very helpful some weeks after release when he enrolled for a set of seminars in connection with his business plans. He was able to breeze into the room full of strangers so confidently, shaking hands all round and introducing himself, that the other students thought he was the tutor.

By spring 1996 when we made our updating visits to the prisons, provision for pre-release courses was still patchy. At Channings Wood they had stopped altogether, but were restarted in the summer after an influx of new officers enabled better staffing. At Highpoint officer-led courses had been running erratically. Liverpool's courses had been suspended for most of 1995 because officers were diverted to other work; by 1996 they were running again, though not often enough. Kirkham seemed to have had fewer problems.

In 1993 Highpoint was one of several prisons in which the Employment Department piloted a special course called 'employment focus'. Here inmates learned jobsearch techniques and received information about work and training opportunities. Before leaving they had an action plan, a contact with the Employment Service in their home area, and a place in an Employment Service programme if they wanted it.[7] But a year later Highpoint's course collapsed when the prison did not continue the Employment Department's initial funding.

The example of R527 shows how a pre-release course (by whatever name) could help a well-motivated inmate to look beyond the prison walls and develop the confidence necessary for successful jobsearch (see p. 163). It was regrettable that some people were deprived of the opportunity of a course because the prison had higher priorities for officers. But it will be argued later that a proper sentence and training plan would encourage inmates to use their whole sentence positively to prepare for release, including future employment. Then pre-release courses could add finishing touches, so to speak, instead of trying to achieve everything in the last few weeks, and some inmates might be less sceptical about their value.

The PRES hostel at Maidstone

Maidstone Prison did not run a pre-release course because so few of its inmates were near the end of their sentence, but in 1992 it had a hostel serving itself and ten other prisons in the Pre-Release Employment Scheme (PRES). The hostel had eleven places, and usually nine residents at any one time. These were men serving the last few months of a sentence of at least six years, and they were very carefully selected: prisoners other than lifers (who were automatically considered) had to apply a year before their expected release date, and the vetting process took six months. Hostel residents went out daily to ordinary jobs, they paid towards their board and compulsory savings, and once they had settled in and established a work pattern they could have frequent home leave at weekends.

Hostel staff worked closely with the local jobcentre, giving them advance notice of a new resident's coming and information about his education and qualifications, work and training he had done in prison. Jobcentre staff tried hard to find a suitable vacancy from those notified by employers. The new resident was also expected to hunt for work himself, going to the jobcentre the day after his arrival and searching the local press, knocking on employers' doors, and so on, all with support and encouragement from hostel staff. ('We give them a jump start,' said one staff member.) Despite the recession residents usually managed to find jobs and keep them till the end of their sentence, though after release most moved away from Maidstone.

One hostel resident, R540, was included in our follow-up sample. He found work for himself in Maidstone that was related to his previous career, and while at the hostel he continued studying for a professional qualification. By the end of his sentence he had saved a good deal of money, and several months later was in a responsible job (in another district) and obviously 'on the way up'. Talking about his time in the hostel he said:

> Six months' work is much better than six months' prison....Financially, security, family ties, your own self-being, attitude – when you're removed and alienated from people for so long you need time to adjust mentally, physically and in quite a few ways. Just to sit down and converse and feel confident again. All those things seem to be drained from you during a prison sentence.

The Maidstone hostel was an example of much that we recommend in Chapter 7, including liaison between prison staff and outsiders, and the opportunity for prisoners to work out from prison and pay their way as adults. But the hostel had only eleven places to serve inmates from eleven prisons. And by 1996 it had been closed down (and converted into a visitors' centre).

Holloway Prison jobclub and working out from prison

Ten minutes' walk from Holloway Prison in 1993 was a special jobclub, funded like other jobclubs by the Employment Service and run by the National Association for the Care and Resettlement of Offenders (NACRO), which Holloway inmates who had served at least half their sentence could apply to attend. At the time of our research seven were doing so (and the jobclub also took a few people referred by the Probation Service). Attenders were helped to look for employment: the club provided local newspapers, a telephone, typing facilities and so on, and the staff advised and encouraged. Information about possibilities for education and training was also available. Holloway inmates often went to the jobclub after finishing the pre-release course.

A woman who found a job would normally be allowed out of prison daily to do it until the end of her sentence. If it was for a voluntary organisation she would receive her prison pay, but those in paid employment were required, like the Maidstone hostel residents, to contribute to their board and lodging and to a savings account. A mother who had her baby with her in the prison's mother and baby wing would be allowed to take an outside job only in the last few weeks before release, and only if for that period she arranged full-time (twenty-four hours) childcare outside the prison. Staff explained that this was to avoid the risk of infection to other babies, but some mothers felt it was unfair.

Prison staff felt that going out of the prison to attend the jobclub (rather than it being inside the prison walls) helped to give women confidence in preparing for interviews with employers, and jobclub staff said that the proportion of people who stopped attending the club in order to go into work, full-time education or training was about 40 per cent. Like Maidstone hostel residents, not all Holloway women who found an outside job would be able to continue in it after release because their homes were in other parts of the country. But outside work, even for a short period, could help to build confidence for later jobhunting else-where. R587 appreciated having been able to work for a few weeks in an office, which exercised her word-processing skills and gave her a reference. R585 had used the jobclub facilities to apply for vacancies in her home town, helped by her home probation officer sending her local newspapers which the jobclub did not get. She was unsuccessful in these efforts, though after release she did take up a home study course about which the club had given her information.

In 1994–5 opportunities for Holloway inmates to go out of the prison were severely curtailed and attendance at the jobclub eventually ceased. But by mid-1996 a fresh start had been made, with jobclub sessions being held inside the prison, conducted by a jobclub representative who came in several times a week.[8]

Other ways of jobsearch before release

Most prisoners did not have the kinds of special opportunity just described to start work for an outside employer before the end of their sentence. But while still in prison they could make some enquiries about work prospects, depending on their inclinations and their contacts. At the time of release sixty-five of the eighty-eight people hoped to find work, and seven others wanted to pursue full-time education or training. (The rest did not want to look for work or training, or not yet, and some of their reasons are discussed later.) But of the sixty-five who wanted work only thirty-five took any steps to look for it before leaving prison, like asking relatives about job prospects, contacting former employers, or seeking help from anyone else. Some people used several methods. Among the whole sample of eighty-eight the commonest situation was that inmates' families or friends made some enquiries for work on their behalf: this happened in thirty-one cases (including a handful where the inmates themselves were not particularly interested). Altogether three people had a job firmly arranged before leaving prison, and several others had hopes which in the event were not realised. Home leave (which thirty-nine people said they had had) was usually spent in family contacts rather than jobhunting.

Prison education staff helped six people to apply for college courses, other prison staff helped in four cases and an outside agency in three. Probation officers (in prison or outside) helped in only five; although thirty-one of the eighty-eight prisoners were due for statutory supervision after release and others could ask for probation officers' help, it seemed that few thought the Probation Service would be able to assist them in finding jobs. Prison probation officers interviewed said their first priority with people about to be released was trying to ensure they had accommodation.

Altogether, in forty-three cases – practically half our sample – nothing was done before the date of release, by the inmate or anyone else on their behalf, to enquire for work, education or training. This suggests that, as was remarked in Chapter 4, many inmates saw little connection between life in prison and the outside world of work. The impression of isolation and discontinuity is reinforced by the fact that in most cases nothing was done by prison staff either to help inmates link up with job prospects outside.

A general note on pre-release provision[9]

Pre-release courses, the Maidstone hostel and the Holloway jobclub are examples from the six research prisons of ways in which prisoners could be helped before their release to move towards employment. The national provision in the early 1990s is described in the Prison Service annual report for 1993–4.[10] By 1996 all prisons were running their own pre-release courses, though from time to time they might be suspended if governors decided there were more urgent calls on staff time. As for the employment focus courses supported by the Employment Department, these had been growing in number, so that in 1994 fifty-four establishments were offering them and it was hoped that in 1995 at least sixty would do so. But then difficulties arose. Local Employment Service managers, like prison governors, were being given more control of their own budgets, as well as targets for placing clients in jobs, and a manager whose local prison discharged most of its inmates to other parts of the country had little incentive to go on funding a course there. In addition, when prison staff had to spend more time on security procedures and less on escorting inmates to courses, attendances fell, which further discouraged the Employment Service from supporting them. By the end of 1996 most employment focus courses were being wound down.

Maidstone's PRES hostel in 1992 was one of seven which between them provided 107 places, a number which remained constant for several years. But hostels were expensive in staff for their small numbers of residents, and by 1996 there were only five, with a total of seventy-three places. However, the pre-release employment scheme had expanded by means of resettlement prisons and units, where selected long-term inmates approaching their release date would spend some months engaged in pre-release training and prison work and then go out of the prison to work or training for their last few months. In 1996 there were six resettlement prisons and units, with approximately 560 places altogether.

Another contribution to pre-release assistance was made by NACRO's Prisons Link Unit (PLU), funded by the Prison Service, which trained prison officers to advise inmates on housing and employment. By 1996 all but two prisons had a pool of PLU-trained officers, and NACRO kept in touch and offered refresher training. Like other staff, however, these officers could be switched to other duties seen as more pressing.

Thus across the Service there was a variety of provision for helping inmates to prepare for release. But the vagaries of funding, together with the demands of security and other duties on staff time, meant that services could be erratic, so that in a population of between 50,000 and 60,000 prisoners a good many people, especially those with shorter sentences, must have been missed.

JOBHUNTING AFTER RELEASE

Methods and results

Now we resume the story of eighty-eight released prisoners. During the first few weeks after they left prison in 1992–3 seventy-one of these people (81 per cent of the sample) looked for work.[11] Most of them searched hard at first and by several methods: going to the local jobcentre, scanning press advertisements, approaching employers direct, using private agencies, asking families and friends. Though 83 per cent of the seekers looked at jobcentre noticeboards, only 22 per cent applied for jobs posted there, and none successfully; most of the others felt that the few vacancies they saw offered them nothing suitable. (Employers, for example, wanted fully skilled tradesmen, or asked for a car and telephone, or offered too little money or very unattractive work.) By far the most fruitful method was asking friends and relatives for work or job leads: 69 per cent did so and nearly half of them (twenty-three people) obtained some sort of work, but in many cases this was only casual and intermittent. Twelve people found work by other methods. Probation services apparently played little part in most people's jobhunting.

What sort of work did they look for? Few were prepared to take just *any* job, though many were willing to be flexible. R512, a former machine fitter and building worker, refused to apply for unskilled vacancies advertised by a battery manufacturer and a chicken processing plant because he feared the work would be unhealthy, though he would have considered other factory jobs if there had been any. R580, who between his several prison sentences had always worked outdoors, looked very hard for such jobs but refused the chance of factory work because he did not want to be inside. 'There's no point in doing something you don't like.' R550, a well-qualified engineer, took his time about jobhunting because he was uncertain whether to stay in the city or move around the country.

'I don't think I should go for a job where I won't get satisfaction.' Others were willing to try almost anything they felt they could do.

The majority of the jobseekers had, before their last prison sentence, acquired some kind of skill which they could offer an employer, though for most of them it was well below the level of a fully qualified tradesperson. A very few had professional or management skills. Most of the fully skilled wanted work in their trade, and some of the semi-skilled people would have preferred work using their abilities (for example, forklift driver, skilled building labourer, some experience as chef or in sales). But the majority of the semi-skilled as well as the unskilled were prepared to do a range of manual jobs (for example, general labourer, factory, warehouse, bar work). More than twenty looked for work on building sites, of which many had had previous experience. Altogether 85 per cent of those who had some pre-sentence skill tried to find work using it, though many were willing to do other jobs too.

Twenty people were seriously interested in setting up, or resuming, business for themselves. Their plans covered a wide range of activity: e.g. car repairs and dealing, catering, producing music, cleaning windows, childminding. The time until our follow-up interview was too short for most of such plans to have been realised, though seven people were then self-employed and others were preparing to be, some of them also looking for other jobs meanwhile.

People's individual experiences in searching for work were many and various, as the following examples help to show. Other cases later will illustrate particular points.

> R560, aged 28, had worked mainly as a forklift driver before his sentence. On release he went to London and looked for that or labouring work. His local jobcentre had no such vacancies, but after a month he registered for casual employment with a private agency which found him work almost every day, first as a dustman and later as a forklift driver. He arrived early each morning and was usually taken on. He would have preferred a full-time job but was glad to have that in the meantime.

> R521, aged 39, had worked for many years as a chef and had also run his own clothing firm. On his return to the Manchester area the local jobcentre got him two interviews for catering and sales vacancies but these were unsuccessful. Then he was engaged as chef by a friend who owned a restaurant, but lost that job a few weeks later when the business went bust. At the time of follow-up R was trying to raise the necessary capital to start a restaurant himself.

> R575, aged 42, when in employment had worked mainly on demolition and building sites, but had been out of work for more than a year before his last sentence. In prison he gained a C&G certificate in bricklaying skills. On release he went to London, thinking his job chances would be best there, and lived in a hostel. For the first three weeks he spent all of each weekday

tramping local streets in a search for building or any labouring work; he treated this period of jobhunting as a full-time occupation and wore out his prison-issue shoes in the course of it. He also looked in newspapers and at the jobcentre. By the time of the follow-up interview he had had only a few days' casual work, including helping to unload a lorry for which he was paid £15 a day.

R507, aged 23, with some previous skill in motor mechanics and experience as an industrial painter, came home to his parents in Liverpool. He looked regularly for work using the jobcentre, the local press and enquiries of friends, but to no avail. His father got him an interview for a painting vacancy but that went no further. He was offered two sales jobs but declined each because the pay was commission only, and he would have had to sign off the dole and then have no money until he achieved a sale. Moreover, one of those jobs was with a firm which had attracted attention in the consumer press for dubious (though not illegal) sales practices,[12] while the other was for selling a type of burglar alarm which R thought worthless. 'It was a useless product, no good – and I should know!'

Altogether, forty-two people (48 per cent of the sample of eighty-eight) did some kind of paid work (including self-employment) at some stage during the few months of our follow-up period.[13] Twelve found permanent jobs and seven got temporary ones, but half of those who obtained anything got only casual work, which in most cases was sporadic and in small amounts. A few people who did part-time or casual work were content with it, and a few were not seriously interested in employment anyway, though they occasionally did jobs for friends. But the great majority wanted a regular full-time job, and many of those who did not find one became more and more discouraged as the weeks wore on. The employment situations of the eighty-eight people at the time of our follow-up interview can be summarised as follows.[14]

1   Ten people were in full-time employment, while two were in substantial part-time or casual work and not seeking more. Eight others were running their own business or preparing to do so and not seeking other work. This subtotal of twenty out of eighty-eight people (23 per cent) may be regarded as working.

2   Fifty-six (64 per cent of the total) were unemployed and wanted work. Six of them were hoping to set up their own business but were searching for a job in the meantime. Eighteen had had some kind of paid work at some stage since leaving prison, ranging from a full-time job (in three cases) to various amounts of casual work which some were still doing. One was doing voluntary work but wanted a paid job. Two, unemployed so far, had a firm job due to start two days after our interview. Twenty-nine people (33 per cent of the total sample) had had no work at all and had no immediate prospect of any.

3   Ten other unemployed people (11 per cent of the total) were not looking for work. Four of them intended to do so eventually after sorting out other personal matters such as accommodation or the custody of children. The other six appeared discouraged, fatalistic or frankly not interested in legitimate employment, though some of them did minor casual work from time to time.

4   Finally, one man was too ill to work and one aged 66 was retired on state pension.

Interest in training

At our follow-up interviews we found sixteen people who were then seriously interested in taking training or further education to improve their job prospects. (All but one also wanted to find work, in some cases to tide them over till their other plans bore fruit, and all are included in the figures above on people's employment situations.) Two were already studying; four had applied for a college course and were awaiting the outcome, and five were considering applying to college. In seven cases people's plans were linked with training they had done in prison, and this will be discussed later.

Five people after failing to find a job were now interested in obtaining a place on a government-funded training scheme of the kind described on pp. 141–3, which would have given them up to six months' vocational training and work with an employer, and £10 a week in addition to DSS benefit. Three of them were eagerly awaiting the results of applications with which jobcentre staff had helped them; the other two had been disappointed when they were refused for lack of places, though they hoped to try again.

But apart from these five, the responses of people in the follow-up sample with whom we discussed the possibility of a training scheme were negative. Most were aware of such schemes, jobcentre staff having in many cases specifically drawn their attention to them. A few people felt they were being pushed into applying, or they had lost their earlier motivation, or had found that the only local scheme they knew of offered skills they already had. But the majority of unemployed ex-prisoners with whom we raised the topic were simply not interested. A frequent objection was that the pay was derisory and that there was no assurance of a job at the end of the training. Some men who felt like this pointed to their family responsibilities, but equally important were personal pride and the desire to avoid being exploited by employers. Other interviewees were frankly cynical, saying that in their view government schemes were just a way of reducing the unemployment statistics without providing real jobs.

FACTORS AFFECTING JOBHUNTING

Here we examine several matters which seemed to us to be important influences on ex-prisoners' jobseeking, and – with some of these matters – on the results.

Our data was a mixture. Some came directly from people's answers to questions on the topic, some from our own inferences from other things they said, and some from our observation of their situations at the follow-up interview. Several people spoke, directly or indirectly, about aspects of their lives which we felt were salient in other cases too.

Perceptions of high unemployment

As has been seen, the great majority of our sample wanted a job and many looked very hard for one, at any rate during the first few weeks. When we asked fifty-one at the follow-up interview the straight question as to why they thought they were unemployed now, by far the commonest reason offered was the recession: they believed there were very few jobs available. One man said he had telephoned about a painting and decorating vacancy and been told there were 400 other applicants. Other examples were the following:

> (Manchester) R532, aged 41 and with years of experience in steel fixing and roofing, has been round all his friends and lots of building sites asking for work. He has never had much trouble getting work before. But now his friends who are plumbers, electricians, etc., are unemployed themselves for the first time. 'There's no work going.'

> (Plymouth) R515 says he was released at the wrong time (late September). He wants outdoor work and there isn't much in winter. He has asked at the docks, in pubs, all his friends; he even went to the council and asked for street sweeping, which he would put up with meantime, but there's nothing. Now a fairground owner has given him some hope of a job in the spring.

There was some statistical evidence that people's willingness to look for work was linked with local unemployment rates. In the localities where the eighty-eight were living, unemployment rates[15] ranged between 6.3 per cent (York, October 1993) and 18.9 per cent (Newquay, Cornwall, January 1993). Although we found no evidence of a statistical relationship linking unemployment rates with the proportion of our sample who were actually in work, there was a suggestion that, counting employed and unemployed together, respondents' general keenness about work (as judged by us on a five-point scale – see p. 164) was linked with their local unemployment rate. Of the twenty-seven people who lived in places where the unemployment rate was 12 per cent or higher, fifteen (56 per cent) were judged to be keen about work or jobhunting, while among fifty-seven whose local rates were lower the corresponding number was forty-three (75 per cent).[16]

By the time of the follow-up interview some people's efforts to find a job had tailed off, though they would still have liked to have one. A small minority had not looked for work at all, believing from the outset that it was hopeless, as in the following case:

(Merseyside) R536, aged 28, has never been employed and has not looked for a job since release from prison. At school, says R, he and his peers got just a basic education, they were just brought up to be factory workers. He would do a factory job if there were any, but there aren't. Of all his former classmates he knows of only one who has had a job since leaving school; the others all went into government schemes. The only way to get a job is if your friends know of one. ('Are any of your friends in a job?') 'That's a hard question to answer. No, I can't think of any.'

Having a criminal record

In twenty-eight cases it seemed that this potential difficulty did not apply, either because the person had not been jobhunting or because no job application had yet reached that stage. For twenty-three others their prison record had apparently not been a problem: some were among those making business preparations, and others had been lucky enough to find sympathetic employers or ones who simply did not enquire about the matter. People who got casual work with friends or acquaintances were not usually embarrassed, and not all building site employers asked awkward questions (though see R513 in next example).

But for thirty-four people (39 per cent of the total sample, and nearly half the seventy-one jobseekers) their criminal record had been a real obstacle: in some cases because fear of having to disclose it had put them off applying for jobs, but more often because (they believed) their applications had failed on account of it. Typical in some ways (though not in the number of interviews) was the following case.

> R513, a personable and energetic young man determined to put his past behind him, has had five interviews for jobs as a building site labourer. Typically the employer is impressed by R's certificate of achievement from a building operatives training course, but when R says he has come out of prison the employer's interest fades. None has refused him to his face and some have praised his honesty, but he has had no job offer and he has seen some of those vacancies re-advertised. He has not applied to a local Army building site, thinking that security there would automatically bar him. He sees hotel jobs advertised but thinks he would not be considered for them either.

This young man eventually applied for a training scheme place, and at the follow-up interview was awaiting the outcome.

Acceptable wages

Thirty-six of the jobseekers were asked what minimum take-home pay they would accept, and their answers spanned a wide range. Five said they would take 'anything more than the dole', while at the other end of the scale six wanted a minimum weekly wage of £200 or more. In this group of thirty-six there was no statistical relationship between the minimum pay they wanted and their domestic circumstances. Several men living with their partners and children told us they could not afford to take a low wage (e.g. not less than £150 per week), but so also did some single men living in their own flats or lodgings, who feared the loss of housing benefit if they came off income support. And several made it clear that personal pride would deter them from taking a job at a wage they felt was paltry (e.g. £3 an hour). (As already mentioned, others rejected the idea of a training scheme for the same reason.)

Family worries

Several people had decided at the time of release to delay looking for a job until they had sorted out other problems. R577, for instance, concentrated on searching for a house for his partner and their three children, who during his imprisonment had lived in a one-bedroom flat. He had trade skills and was confident he would be able to get work when he felt ready. Other people, though wanting work, seemed unable to focus clearly on job-hunting. R539, for example, at the time of follow-up was making only desultory attempts, though at first he had looked hard without success. At our interview he described his difficulties in resuming normal family relationships after coming home from prison, and he was also preoccupied with a court case involving one of his children.

Bewilderment

R540, quoted on p. 154, expressed the lack of confidence which a person could experience on emerging from prison into the outside world, and which was clearly affecting some interviewees even three or four months later. R550 after his second prison sentence said, 'When you first come out of prison it knocks you sideways for a week, and it takes you six months to get your confidence back.' R566 spoke of 'an overdose of sensory perception...it's very strange'.

This state of mind could impede jobhunting. For example, R571, who at our first prison interview had seemed determined to take charge of his life after three years inside, found on release that he was frightened in crowds, and this put him off going to the jobcentre which was in the busiest part of town (though he did look hard for work in other ways, and eventually applied for a training scheme place). R534, who before his six-year sentence had been a highly skilled tradesman in a responsible position, said at follow-up, when he was still unemployed, that he had not yet got over the feeling that everyone he met immediately knew he was a criminal; at the beginning of the interview he had asked the researcher whether she minded sitting in the same room with him. R514, after describing his wanderings since release, said, 'My head's full of shit.'

Lack of commitment to legitimate work

Finally, a minority of people seemed to have little or no interest in legitimate employment, though they may have felt differently at an earlier stage in their lives. R533, a middle-aged man, had in his youth been a train stoker, but this was a redundant skill and he had not worked for years, making a living (when not in prison) by burglary and by doing odd jobs for acquaintances in return for favours. After release he returned to the same life, not having expected to do anything else. R536 (p. 162) may be included under this heading too.

We tried to classify eighty-four people by the strength of their motivation for work or jobhunting at the time of the follow-up, as judged by us from their situations and everything they said. Forty were assessed as being very keen to work; eighteen as nearly so; nine as wanting work but choosy; nine as only mildly interested; and eight as not willing to work or try. Among the last seventeen mentioned (20 per cent of the sample), who at that stage seemed very little committed to the idea of work, several were involved in further crime, which we discuss later.

In this section we have looked at several factors which, in different combinations for different people, seemed to influence many ex-inmates' jobhunting or its results. We have not included some obvious ones like lack of transport (which was mentioned by one in ten of the unemployed) or lack of skill and qualifications, which is treated in the next section. But we have tried to give some small indication of the complexity of people's lives, and to show that for many ex-prisoners looking for work – let alone finding it – was not a simple matter. This suggests that if people's time in prison is to be used to train them for employment, as we shall argue later that it should, other needs besides vocational skills will have to be addressed. These matters are discussed in Chapter 7.

DID PRISON WORK AND TRAINING HELP?

Forty-two people found some kind of work at some time during the few months of the follow-up period, but in only five cases was it related to the type of work, skilled or otherwise, which they had done in prison. To explore the central question of whether prison work and training could help in obtaining any kind of work after release, two methods were used. First, a set of statistical analyses was carried out to see whether any link existed between people's experience of prison work and training and their chances of being in employment at the time of the follow-up, taking into account their pre-prison employment record and skill. Second, a qualitative analysis was made of information on all but one of the forty-five people (p. 140) who had begun to learn a vocational skill in prison, to see whether they tried to use it after release and what factors influenced their attempts.

Statistical analyses

These are described in Appendix 3. Pre-prison employment record was measured by whether or not the person had been in work for most of the year immediately before sentence, and pre-prison occupational skill was measured by three levels. Prison experience was measured in three ways: the kind of daytime occupation the person had had during sentence (work, training or education, or both), whether any vocational skill had been learned, and whether any certificate had been gained (see p. 140). Six analyses were carried out (by three-way tables) to see how these factors (in alternative combinations) were related to the probability of being employed at the time of the follow-up interview.

The results were all negative. Employment at follow-up was strongly linked to pre-sentence work record, and alternatively to pre-sentence occupational skill; but neither of these links was materially altered by what the person had done in prison. For people who had been employed in the year before sentence, the chance of being in work at follow-up was about 50 per cent, no matter what their daytime occupation in prison had been. For people unemployed (or in some other state) the year before sentence, doing prison training or education instead of prison work, or adding training or education to prison work made no difference to their 13 per cent chance of being in work at follow-up. As for previous occupational skill, 40 per cent of the people whom we counted as fully skilled (tradesperson, management or professional) were in a job at follow-up, compared with 22 per cent of the semi-skilled and 11 per cent of the unskilled; but adding education or training to prison work did not improve the employment chances of the unskilled or semi-skilled. Similar results were obtained when the measure of prison experience was whether the person had started to learn a vocational skill during sentence. There was a slight suggestion that obtaining a certificate might be linked with motivation to look for work, in that none of the people who got one were among the small group who at follow-up were unemployed and not jobhunting, but the difference was too small to be statistically reliable.

These negative results appear to show that to the people in our follow-up sample prison training made no difference to their employment prospects on release: an outcome which, if true, would be disappointing for prison staff who try to train inmates in vocational skills. In pondering on the findings we must bear in mind two points. The first is the limitations of the statistical data: the small size of the sample, the crudeness of the measurements and the tiny numbers in some cells of the tables. The second point is that people's experiences cannot be adequately expressed in neat statistics: we must look further and more sensitively at their situations. So our second method of analysis was qualitative, examining individually all the cases of people who while in prison had begun to learn a vocational skill. This enquiry is set out in the next four subsections and, as will be seen, some small positive findings emerged.

Attempts to use prison skill

Forty-five people said that in prison they had begun (or, in a very few cases, continued) to learn some kind of vocational skill. In one of these cases we did not know whether the person had tried to use it in his unsuccessful search for work after release. The other forty-four can be summarised as follows.

1   Twenty people were definitely planning, or had already tried, to use their prison skill in work or training that was related to it. Only three had obtained some work using their prison skill; four planned to use their prison skill later but were doing or seeking unrelated work meanwhile; thirteen had looked for work using their skill, so far without success, though three of these had now applied for training which would build on it.
2   Four people had so far sought only unrelated work, regarding their prison skill as a possible 'second string' for the future.
3   Fourteen people had looked only for unrelated work or training.
4   Six had not looked for work or training at all (including one who was seriously ill).

So nearly half these people had tried, or were still hoping, to use the skill they had learned (or begun to learn) in prison, while about as many others had looked only for unrelated work, and a few had not looked at all. We now enquire into possible reasons for these differences.

Factors affecting the use of prison skill

Examination of all the forty-four cases suggested that a number of factors helped to determine whether ex-prisoners tried to use a prison-acquired skill, and whether those who tried succeeded. Some of these factors have already been seen in relation to jobsearch, and they are relevant now too. As before, factors interacted with one another and appeared in different patterns for different people. We set out below what seemed to us to be the main ones, and then give some illustrations, describing people's situations as they were at the time of follow-up.

- Self-image: whether the kind of skill learned in prison fitted with the person's self-image, interests and chosen lifestyle (before imprisonment and/or after it).
- Energy: the extent of the person's determination and ability to sort out his or her life on release, and overcome distractions while doing so.
- Incentive: whether the skill learned gave the person positive encouragement which was lacking before.
- Self-confidence: how far the person could cope with the mental shock of leaving prison.
- Relevance: whether the prison skill was similar to any kind of work outside.

- Job vacancies: whether they existed in similar work outside.
- Previous occupational skill that the person had gained before imprisonment.
- 'Bird in the hand': luck in getting a job regardless of prison skill.
- Level of prison skill: the extent to which this equipped the person to apply for available vacancies, and to combat his or her disadvantages in competing in the labour market. Disadvantages included criminal record, inadequate pre-sentence occupational skill (in many cases), and sometimes personal matters like self-confidence or appearance (such as tattoos).

Illustrations

Self-image, previous occupational skill, energy

R501, a businessman before sentence, took training courses while in prison in industrial cleaning and in computer skills. On release his strongest desire was to make money. He used computer skills, but not cleaning, in further business ventures.

Bird in the hand

R545 in prison began to learn bookbinding and enjoyed it, but on release he wanted to find work quickly to support his family. A friend recommended an employment agency which asked no questions about criminal records, and through it R obtained warehouse work which he hopes will be permanent. He still thinks of bookbinding as a possible interest for the future.

Self-confidence, previous occupational skill

R587 learned some office skills, which were new to her, during her sentence. But on release she felt self-conscious about being an ex-prisoner and too shy to venture out and look for office jobs. She had pinned her hopes on being re-engaged (in unskilled work) by her former employer, but was disappointed. At follow-up she was doing some casual work at home, using her skill as a dressmaker, and planning to train as a childminder, which would use skills she had learned through motherhood.

Incentive, energy

R512, who had had several custodial sentences resulting from fights, took a part-time course in prison in physical education and became very keen to train as a PE instructor. At the time of follow-up he was waiting to get into college for this, and looking (unsuccessfully) for other work (using his pre-sentence building experience) in the meantime.

Self-image, previous occupational skill

R511 felt that his prison work in the tailors' shop had taught him skill on sewing machines, but he saw it as 'no use to a man'. After release he was largely unemployed, but did some casual work repairing and dealing in cars, which he had done before.

Self-image

R508 before sentence had always done labouring jobs. He thinks of himself as a labourer and since release has looked only for such work, so far without success. He uses his prison cooking skill for himself at home.

Relevance

R531, who had learned weaving during his sentence, looked round after release and could find no weaving industry anywhere near his home town (in Yorkshire).

Incentive, job vacancies

R503 before sentence was unskilled and unemployed. In prison he obtained a C&G certificate in industrial cleaning, and on release looked for cleaning and other jobs. The jobcentre got him an interview for cleaning work three weeks ago but he has heard nothing since. He lives in a rural area where there are few jobs.

Lack of previous skill, level of prison skill, incentive, job vacancies

R578, previously unskilled and unemployed, worked in prison as a gardener (after dropping out of a CIT course he found too difficult) and was trained by his work instructor to NVQ level 1 (though he received no certificate because of the muddle over NVQs). After release he looked very hard for unskilled work and for gardening. He managed, with the help of his prison training and a reference from his instructor (a rare instance – see p. 116) to get two weeks' gardening work through an employment agency, which he enjoyed. That was the only work he could find during the five months of the follow-up period, and at our second interview, which took place in autumn, he was hoping rather forlornly for more.

Comments

The reader may notice that this list of nine cases begins with people who at follow-up were in substantial work, moves through others who had some work or were planning further training, and ends with five who were largely or wholly unemployed. When we looked at the kinds of prison skill which people had already used, or were planning to, and the kinds in which others had tried to find work but failed, comparisons were difficult because of small numbers. But the seven people who had used or planned to use a prison skill included four who had taken a course in business start-up, computers or word processing; while the thirteen who had failed to find related work included four with prison skills in building, two in engineering and four in catering (as well as the weaver R531 and the cleaner R503). It seemed that the efforts of the six who had learned a little building or engineering had been frustrated largely by lack of low-skilled vacancies in those trades, while the four who tried for catering work found that employers wanted better qualifications than they could offer (and they had personal problems too). Two of those four and one of the 'builders' were at the time of follow-up applying for a place on a training scheme.

Taking the statistical and qualitative analyses together, the general conclusion from this section must be that, overall, the effect of prison training on people's chances of employment was small. For a very few people it enhanced their prospects; it gave some people an incentive and hope for the future; for a few it provided a foundation for further training; and some used their new-found skills for DIY. But for many the level of vocational skill acquired in prison was too low to offset the handicaps with which they re-entered a very competitive labour market; and for others their prison skills did not seem relevant to working life outside. The results suggest that it is not only vocational skills that matter: personal qualities like self-image and confidence are important too. In Chapter 7 we will argue that prisons, *if* they were adequately resourced for proper sentence planning, would have a real opportunity to offer inmates help to address these personal needs together with relevant vocational training, and that such a holistic approach would greatly increase their prospects of finding work. But first we look in this chapter at some other topics explored in the follow-up interviews, beginning with money.

ENOUGH MONEY TO LIVE ON?

Money available after release, and financial problems

On leaving prison three-quarters of our sample (sixty-seven people) had very little money: only the discharge grant of about £40 (or, in the cases of twenty-seven who had convinced the prison staff that they had no home to go to, £80) plus not more than £20 cash in their pockets. Four people had more than this through their earnings during sentence: the one with most was R540, who while in the Maidstone PRES hostel (see p. 154) had saved nearly £2,000 in his outside job, and the next was R508 who, by contrast, had managed to save £70 from his prison pay. Ten people had money waiting for them outside, in savings or (in at least two cases) from the proceeds of crime. (In the other seven cases we did not know what money people had.)

At least sixty-four people (73 per cent) signed on for DSS benefit. (Eight did not, and we had no information on the matter for sixteen.) The majority of those who signed on received payment (which for nearly all was income support) two weeks later, and thereafter regularly unless their circumstances changed. A few people suffered distressing delays, but such cases seemed to be a small minority. Applications to the Social Fund for a grant or a loan were, however, a different matter, and many people had experiences which, while influenced no doubt by their own situations, also supported the common criticism that the Social Fund was a lottery.

It seemed from what people said at the follow-up interview that at least thirty-six (41 per cent) had been in serious financial difficulties at some stage since their release. Leaving aside failed applications to the Social Fund, we found that at least twenty people had difficulties with benefits (often housing benefit or special benefits) through bureaucratic delays and muddles. Nineteen people had come home from prison to face old debts or to incur fresh ones, for household bills, loans from relatives or other people and, in a handful of cases, outstanding compensation orders from previous convictions. At least sixteen people had multiple money problems.

People who at the time of release had had little more than the discharge grant available to them were more likely to be in financial difficulties during the follow-up period than those who had had more: in the former group thirty out of sixty-one (49 per cent) had difficulties compared with only four out of fourteen (29 per cent) in the latter group.[17] This difference will be discussed later.

Domestic situation and sources of income at the time of follow-up

At the follow-up interview forty-nine people (56 per cent of the sample) were living as single people, either on their own (in a flat, lodgings or hostel) or with their parents or other relatives. Eleven were living with a partner but without dependent children. Twenty-five were living with their partner and dependent children, and one other was a single parent, so that altogether 30 per cent of the sample had children with them to support and care for. Several of the others contributed to the support of children who did not live with them.[18]

Sixty-eight people (77 per cent of the sample) were claiming benefit[19] which for the great majority was income support. Forty-three of those people had no other income; the other twenty-five did, in most cases casual earnings which they did not declare to the authorities (see below). Only nine people were supporting themselves wholly by legitimate earnings. Eight not claiming benefit were supported wholly or partly by family (usually spouse or partner) or by friends, and these included some people who were preparing to set up in business. Ten people altogether appeared to be living partly by crime[20] in addition to other income.

Undeclared earnings

Nineteen people were earning money which they did not declare while claiming benefit. In nine cases the amounts were small, the least being the £40 which R575 (p. 158) had earned in total during three months. Ten people were getting more substantial or regular sums, like R511 whose casual car dealing brought him 'several hundred now and then'. R567, living with his partner and two children, was regularly moonlighting as a newspaper seller. ('You have to do extra jobs to support a family.') Most of the nineteen apparently felt justified in earning 'on the side' when they could, either because the amounts concerned were trivial or because, in their view, benefit payments were very low and they had not succeeded in getting a good job.[21, 22] R550's motive was slightly different. He eventually found well-paid work (see p. 157) but he had recently been divorced, and he continued to sign on as unemployed in the belief that doing so would reduce the maintenance he had to pay his ex-wife.

Level of financial comfort at the time of follow-up

At the interview we asked eighty-four people, and tried to assess from other things they said, how comfortable or otherwise their financial situation was. Seventeen people seemed to be at least reasonably comfortable but we classified forty-two, nearly half the sample, as 'only just managing, tight', and most of the remainder were worse off than that, twelve managing only with help from friends or relatives and a few having huge debts. Statistically the best-off were the small group living with a partner but without dependent children: we classified 40 per cent of them as 'comfortable' compared with only 17 per cent of those living in other ways. The worst-off group were, as might be expected, those living with dependent children: 62 per cent of them were 'only just managing, tight', though there was not much difference between this group and the 'singles', 52 per cent of whom also fell in that category.[23] The few people who depended partly on crime were scattered throughout the various living groups. Some examples follow.

Comfortable

R517 has a full-time job. His wife works and they have no children. He still has the travel warrant he received on leaving prison. 'It's not worth cashing.'

Only just managing, tight

R566 lives with his wife and their two small children. He has had two interviews for full-time jobs, but failed them because (he believes) of his prison record. Meanwhile his wife has returned to part-time work as a nurse to support the family, and R spends most of his time caring for the children. He receives £46 a week income support, he has had some casual cleaning work and he earns a little now and then by repairing friends' cars. He is awaiting the result of an application for housing benefit, and says the family manages with difficulty.

R548, his partner and 8-year-old daughter live on income support. R has had no work at all since leaving prison despite vigorous jobhunting. Housing benefit pays their rent but they have to meet all other bills. No debts, no other money coming in. R's application for a Social Fund grant was refused; his clothes are hand-me-downs from other family members.

Worse off

R515 lives with his parents and has been unable to find any work. He owes nearly £500 to his mother and over £1,000 to a finance company: before his sentence he had taken out a loan to pay a tax bill and then lost his job. The loan company is being patient and R makes regular payments. But his parents are subsidising him and his father is unemployed too. Friends help him out now and then.

R529, unemployed since release, is living on income support in a small council house with his wife and three children all under the age of 3 (and a large dog). They owe £400 in arrears of gas bills and (according to R) £1,600 in rent arrears which accumulated during two previous prison sentences. His probation officer is helping them negotiate with the gas company and the DSS, and R's parents and siblings have helped out, especially with Christmas presents for the children.

There was a relationship between the amount of money that had been available at the time of release and the level of financial comfort at follow-up. Of sixty-five people who had little more than the discharge grant only nine (14 per cent) seemed to be reasonably comfortable later, whereas of thirteen who had had more at the outset, seven (54 per cent) were.[24]

For sixty-five people[25] we compared their level of financial comfort against their sources of income, and despite small numbers the main message was clear. Most people depending only on benefit were struggling to keep their heads above water: only three out of forty-two (7 per cent) were classified as managing comfortably. Those who supplemented their benefit by casual or part-time earnings (which were usually undeclared) had a better chance of being comfortable: six out of fifteen (40 per cent) were. Those with regular full-time earnings were in the best position: six out of eight (75 per cent) were judged comfortable.[26]

The general picture emerging from this section on money is that for at least two-thirds of these ex-prisoners life in the first few months after release was a financial struggle. Most came home from prison with very little money in their pockets. Some had pre-existing debts and others incurred fresh ones, and for many the lack of full-time employment was a major obstacle to them in sorting out their lives.

Our findings are consistent with those of Hagell, Newburn and Rowlingson[27] who in 1994 made a detailed study of the financial circumstances of small groups of men just before and just after their release from prison. They found that the discharge grant, equal to approximately one week's income support and intended as a one-off payment to tide them over until income support (paid in arrears) was received two weeks after release, was nowhere near adequate for the purpose. A released prisoner is likely to have higher expenses in the first week or so than later on: for fares and telephone calls to agencies with which he or she must deal, as well as re-establishing social links; for re-connection of services or a deposit on accommodation; for clothes, as well as food and general household items. For the men in that study the discharge grant lasted only a few days and they then depended largely on help from relatives and friends. Among the recommendations made by Hagell *et al.* were that the agencies involved in addressing released prisoners' financial problems (including the Prison Service) should co-ordinate their work better; that prisoners near release should get more information and help in applying for benefit in advance of their release date; and that prisoners should be enabled to save more from their earnings from prison work.

Our follow-up interviews with ex-prisoners took place later than those in Hagell's study, and by the time we saw them most people's financial situations (whatever they were) had become more settled. But as well as finding that those who had had little more than the discharge grant to begin with were the ones most likely to have experienced problems, we found that a few months after release people's level of financial comfort was clearly linked with whether they were in full-time employment, living on benefit supplemented by casual work, or depending on benefit only. These results accord with common sense. It may also be remarked that people's life situations were complex and that one factor likely to contribute to financial comfort later would be financial stability and competence before going to prison.

But we now recall from p. 150 that when we asked 101 prisoners near release what would help them stay away from serious crime they gave top rating to 'enough money to live on'. In the National Prison Survey 1,470 inmates who were asked what would be useful to prepare them for release gave top rating to 'some money to help [me] live in the first few weeks out.'[28] And in Burnett's study the most frequent reason given for reoffending by those who did so was lack of money.[29] As our focus is on work, we point out at this juncture two ways in which the Prison Service could help ex-prisoners re-settle in the community and reduce their likelihood of further crime. One is to pay sufficient wages for prison work to enable inmates to save significant sums against their release; and the other is to give inmates work and training that will enhance their prospects in the labour market.

FURTHER OFFENDING

Numbers and kinds of offences

When first interviewed in prison, two-thirds of the follow-up sample told us that they were determined to try to avoid crime in future. Our impression from the follow-up interviews was that during the first few months most people certainly did try, including some who had been doubtful earlier. We asked people, and deduced from other things they said, whether they had broken the law in any way since release.

Forty-one people (47 per cent) admitted some infringement, but some of these would hardly be thought of by most citizens as 'crime': for example, minor motoring offences, being drunk and disorderly, smoking cannabis, taking discarded items from a refuse tip. Probably other people in the sample had done such things without telling us. The most common offence was social security fraud, in the shape of failing to declare earnings while claiming benefit. But here again there are distinctions, for the man who in three months did only a few days' work for £15 a day is not on a level with people who frequently earned several hundred pounds on the side (see p. 171). Three people admitted motoring offences of a more serious kind (like driving while disqualified), two admitted serious assaults, and nineteen admitted other crimes such as shoplifting, taking vehicles, burglary and handling stolen goods. Some people admitted more than one of these kinds of offence. In twenty-four cases we felt the interviewer did not elicit enough information for us to decide whether the interviewee had broken the law. Table 3 summarises the information we obtained, counting each person just once and with categories of offending in increasing order of serious-ness.

Table 3 shows that for thirty-six people (41 per cent of the sample) we recorded 'none' or 'minor'. Nine people (10 per cent) are shown as DSS defrauders but not in other categories. Nineteen (22 per cent) had committed other types of crime, and in ten of those cases it appeared that the person was

Table 3 Summary of illegal activities since release

Activity	No. of ex-prisoners
None whatever	23
Minor only (e.g. smoking cannabis, caught speeding, failing to declare very small or sporadic earnings)	13
Failing to declare regular or substantial earnings, but not other crime as below	9
Crime (e.g. burglary, assault, shop theft, taking vehicles) – sporadic or one-off	9
Living partly by crime	10
Insufficient information	24
Total	88

depending partly on crime for an income. In this last category the admitted offences were all property ones, but we suspected that some people were involved with drugs, about which respondents tended to be reticent.

The great majority of offences had not come to the notice of the police. Sixty-four people (73 per cent) had had no fresh contact with the criminal justice system since release. Nine had been arrested but the charge, if any, had been dismissed. Seven were awaiting a further court hearing, two had been convicted and were awaiting sentence, and five had been freshly sentenced, one to prison. So altogether during the follow-up period seven people (8 per cent) were reconvicted.

As would be expected, people who already had a criminal record before the last prison sentence were more likely to be involved in crime after release. Out of twenty-two who had not been to prison before, i.e. the least experienced, only four (18 per cent) committed crime other than benefit fraud during the follow-up period, while at the other end of the scale eleven out of the twenty-seven people (41 per cent) who had three or more previous custodial sentences (the most experienced) were involved in crime. But the more interesting point was that while 77 per cent of the least experienced kept out of trouble or were involved in only very minor matters, so did 48 per cent of the most experienced.[30] Clearly many people tried hard to avoid serious offending.

Links with unemployment and other problems

As Table 3 implies, the bulk of further offending by people who did it was for money or money's worth. We tried to assess how far offending was linked with people's employment situations. As with other analyses it was difficult to do this quantitatively because the numbers were so small, but we found that among twenty people who were working, or who were jobhunting but had had a reasonable amount of work at some stage, eight had committed no offence or only minor ones; nine had failed to declare substantial earnings; and three (15 per cent) had been involved in other crime. Thirty-six jobhunters who had had little or no work fell into just two groups: twenty-six with no or only minor offences and ten (28 per cent) involved in crime. Eight people who were not working and not looking for work also divided into two groups: two who kept out of trouble and six (75 per cent) who committed crimes. Although the numbers are very small, the increasing proportion of people involved in crime as one moves through the employment categories is worth noting.[31]

We had no doubt, from what people had told us about their lives, that in many cases unemployment and crime were linked, though the link was often not a simple one. The common element in many cases was the ex-prisoner's perception of his or her need for money, and this was often linked with other problems, including accommodation. Among our eighty-eight interviewees we judged that since release from prison eighteen had had severe problems with accommodation, thirty-six with money and fifty-five with finding employment (when they wanted it). Twenty-three had suffered two of these types of problem and nine had suffered all three; and of course the unemployed were prone to other difficulties too, including frustration, boredom and loneliness.

The ways in which people reacted to their problems, and the extent to which their reactions included breaking the law, varied widely between individuals. With regard to benefit fraud, we had the impression that most of the people who concealed their casual earnings from the authorities felt little compunction in doing so because they felt that benefit payments were insufficient to support a reasonable lifestyle, that they could not get a regular job at a decent wage, and that their cash-in-hand earnings contributed to independence and self-respect. As for more serious crime, many people were trying to avoid or minimise it, like R558 and R583 below. Some had lapsed occasionally when they saw it as the easiest, or the only, solution to an immediate problem. And a few others had, upon release or soon afterwards, slipped back easily into their old ways, without seriously expecting that their lives could be different or making much effort for change.

Some case examples

Very minor, and trying hard

R558, aged 27, was released after serving three and a half years for wounding and burglary. He used to be a heroin addict and did burglaries to get money; he had had six previous custodial sentences. This time he is at present determined to go straight. He is living with his mother, for whom he does odd jobs, budgeting his benefit money and looking for work, but he has no skills and little experience. He is desperate to get a job so as to be independent and keep out of trouble, but fears that if he cannot find it he may be tempted to go back to crime. So far his only breach has been smoking cannabis ('the odd joint with my brother').

Money problems and old habits

R583, who until his last sentence had kept out of prison for eighteen years, was released eight months ago. He is very short of money, resulting partly from the fact that after he moved into a rented house the housing office delayed for months in processing his repeated applications for housing benefit. An industrial painter by trade, he has been looking hard for work but there is nothing for him in his depressed seaside town. To supplement his income he does a small amount of handling stolen goods, making £10 or £20 every now and then. His contacts are local acquaintances from younger days. He is tempted to thieve himself but has so far not done so, though he knows many people who do. 'Everybody I talk to does shoplifting.' He does not want to go back to prison and worries about the risks he takes.

Back to crime

R506, aged 23, has lived mainly by crime since leaving school. In our prison interview he said he was not interested in work. 'I can earn more money illegally.' At the time of release he enquired about taking a training course, but lost the impetus when it could not be arranged immediately. He teamed up with a friend who was also an ex-prisoner, and together they have a small business selling cheap goods door-to-door. But this is also a cover for crime, which is equally profitable (R did not go into details). On the income from both occupations, plus DSS benefit, R supports his wife and children in modest comfort, and seems quite cheerful.

A tragedy

R549, aged 26, grew up in a run-down inner-city area described by one probation officer as 'a desert for work'. He had had almost no employment other than on government schemes. During his prison sentence (which was his fourth, and for burglary, like most of his other convictions) R managed to get himself off heroin, an achievement he was proud of. On release his overriding wish was to make a home for his two young children, whose mother (from whom R was separated) had agreed he could have them and who had been cared for by other relatives while he was in prison. He came home to his parents' small house and immediately set about searching for accommodation for himself and his family, but without success. The local council housing office said he would have to wait twelve months for a flat, and he felt the Probation Service did not help him either. As well as flat hunting he enrolled his children in school, bought them clothes and other things, and spent much time with them.

Meanwhile he was very short of money: he received income support for himself but nothing for the children. The DSS refused his application for a grant on the grounds that he did not have his own accommodation (but gave him a loan of £30 to be repaid at £12 a fortnight). As the weeks went on R felt increasingly under pressure for a flat and for money so that he could get his family together.

Two months after his release, feeling desperate, R went out at night and attempted to burgle a small shop. The security guard shot him and he died on the way to hospital. Soon afterwards a letter addressed to him came from the council housing office offering the hope of a flat.

PRISON IN RETROSPECT

Towards the end of the follow-up interview we invited eighty-six people to reflect on their last prison sentence and on their experiences since release, and to say whether any aspect of their imprisonment had been useful to them, in any way, since they came out. (We offered a list of seven possibilities to which they could add anything else they wished.) Altogether twenty-eight (33 per cent) felt they had benefited in some way by work, training or education they had done during their sentence. Thirty-eight (44 per cent) endorsed 'self-understanding, self-control' and twenty-eight endorsed 'social skills, getting on with people'. Twenty-six (30 per cent) said their sentence had been a deterrent. Twenty-eight said they had learned criminal expertise but only five said they had actually used it. Sixteen added other items, of which we mention some later. Twenty-five people (29 per cent) said they had learned nothing useful at all from their time in prison. We now look further at some of these responses, in the light of two of the chief factors which prisoners had earlier said (p. 150) could help them avoid crime: a job and willpower.

Skills for getting a job

The ex-prisoners' views on the work, training or education they had done in prison gave a broadly similar picture to that which emerged from our analyses on pp. 160–9. All but four of the group of twenty-eight who felt they had bene-fited in those ways had wanted to find work, and even though at follow-up sixteen were unemployed most of them still felt their prison training could be useful in the future. In contrast, another group of twelve people who had wanted to find work, and who during their sentence had engaged in some skill which at the time seemed vocational, felt at follow-up that prison had given them nothing useful by way of work, education or training. Examination of these two groups suggested that people's views, in hindsight, of whether they learned anything in prison that would help them get work outside were affected by the same factors that we have already seen as affecting their jobhunting and attempts to use their prison skill (if any): namely, the perceived relevance of prison work and training to work in the outside world and to the kinds of jobs they wanted; the availability of vacancies; the level of skill they had acquired; and the degree of energy, tenacity and single-mindedness they were able to muster in the face of very real difficulties.

It is significant that when we asked people at the end of the interview for suggestions to improve prison work and training, forty-three – half the sample – made a plea for more relevant work, more access to training (several mentioned especially building skills and motor mechanics), or higher levels of training. Twenty of those forty-three were people who had begun to learn some voca-tional skill during their sentence. Fourteen people suggested better pay for prison work, while others wanted more opportunities for doing outside work before release and for links with employers who were willing to consider ex-prisoners.

Willpower and related matters

More than two-fifths of our interviewees felt that they had used the time in prison to gain self-understanding or self-control, and one-third said they had

learned social skills, how to get on better with people. (One in five said they had
learned both.) Several of the extra items which respondents offered under
'anything else' could be put under those headings too: for example, self-understanding or self-control could include giving up smoking, getting off drugs,
taking a course in alcohol awareness; social skills could include learning respect
for other people and for authority, learning not to judge people by appearances.
Altogether, half our sample of ex-inmates felt they had been able to use their
sentence for some kind of personal improvement other than work, training or
education.[32]

We did not ask people whether they had taken part in courses designed to
help prisoners address their offending behaviour (see pp. 21–2), but several
volunteered the information that they had and had found them helpful. R534,
for instance, spoke appreciatively of the sex offenders' course he had undergone
and also of counselling he had received from a prison chaplain. R510, whose
sentence had been two and a half years for wounding, praised the course in
anger control at Dartmoor which he had attended for six weeks (and he would
have liked more): he said he had learned to understand himself and how other
people think, and had been able to restrain himself when provoked in a pub
fight some weeks after coming home.

We did, however, invite seventy-four interviewees to say what (in an ideal
system) they would have *liked* their prison sentence to do for them, given that
they had to serve it. By far the commonest answer, given by almost half, was a
wish for more or better training, while others responded in equally practical
terms referring to work, money or further education. Some wanted more advice
before leaving prison, and felt that they had not been offered enough help,
psychologically as well as practically, to prepare for the abrupt transition to
freedom. R579 expressed it by saying that leaving prison was like a young person
being brought up by his parents and then being shown the front door: 'OK,
we've done our bit, now out you go.' The bewilderment and lack of confidence
which could hamper jobseekers was noted on p. 163.

And some people's answers revealed that they wanted much more help
towards self-enlightenment than they had received, and they wanted the active
participation of prison staff in providing it. R579 said that during his previous
sentence in a Young Offender Institution the counselling sessions he received
regularly from his personal officer made him 'come away feeling as if I'd just
stepped out of a good shower', but in this last sentence at Highpoint his personal
officer had provided nothing like that, only a point of reference if he had any
welfare problems. R539 from Maidstone spoke in similar terms, saying that he
had wanted help but felt that the prison staff had not the time or resources to
give inmates caring personal attention, and that their attitude really was 'do your
time and get out'. R544 spoke for several former inmates of Liverpool when he
said he would have liked help to stop offending. 'They should show you how to
stop, drill it into you.' Altogether twelve people indicated that they would have
liked assistance in such ways.

These people were released from prison in 1992–3, and since then the

Service's provision of programmes addressing offending behaviour has expanded. In Chapter 2 we described what was available at the research prisons in 1996, and it is likely that if our follow-up sample had served their sentences then instead of four years earlier more of them would have had the opportunity of a course. On the other hand most such courses, apart from the programme for sex offenders, were very short: typically three or four days, a matter on which we comment on p. 210. The fact that half our sample had tried to use their prison sentence for learning self-understanding or social skills, and that some would have liked more assistance in these matters, suggests that the Prison Service has, potentially, a real opportunity to give prisoners training not only in work skills but also in the personal competence needed for success in life after release.

SUMMARY OF KEY FINDINGS FROM THE FOLLOW-UP SAMPLE

During the follow-up period seventy-one (81 per cent) of the eighty-eight people looked for work. Altogether forty-two (48 per cent) did some paid work at some stage, though in many cases it was only small amounts of casual work. At the time of interview twenty people (23 per cent) were in substantial employment. Fifty-six (64 per cent) were unemployed and wanted work. Ten (11 per cent) for various reasons did not want work. (Of the other two, one was ill and one was retired on pension.)

Sixteen people were interested in taking training or further education to improve their job prospects, but most of the unemployed were not interested in government training schemes.

Major influences on people's jobhunting, and its results, included: perceptions of high unemployment; having a criminal record; level of wages acceptable; family worries; bewilderment on coming out of prison; and lack of commitment to legitimate work.

Statistical analysis found no relationship between people's experience of training in prison and their job prospects on release; what mattered was their employment record before they went to prison. Qualitative analysis suggested that prison vocational training had made a small difference here and there. Factors influencing people's attempts to use their prison-learned skill, and the results of those attempts, included: whether the skill fitted the person's self-image and gave an incentive; the person's energy and self-confidence; whether the skill was relevant to outside jobs, and whether vacancies existed; luck; previous occupational skill; and the level of skill acquired in prison.

At the time of leaving prison three-quarters of the sample had almost no money other than the discharge grant of about £40 (or £80 for those with no accommodation). These people were more likely than others to experience serious financial difficulties during the follow-up period. At the time of interview three-quarters of the sample were claiming DSS benefit, and most of those people had no other income. Only nine people were supporting themselves wholly by legitimate earnings. Nineteen benefit claimants were also earning money which they did not declare, but the amounts varied widely. A few people were supported by family or friends, and ten appeared to be living partly by crime.

One in five appeared at the time of interview to be in reasonably comfortable financial circumstances, but we classified nearly half as 'only just managing, tight' while others were poorer still, a few having huge debts. The 30 per cent who lived with dependent children were worse off than others. Most people who depended solely on benefit were struggling; those who supplemented their benefit by casual or part-time earnings were a little better off; those with regular full-time earnings were most likely to be comfortable.

During the follow-up period twenty-three people (26 per cent of the sample) committed no further offences, and thirteen (15 per cent) committed only minor ones (like minor motoring offences, smoking cannabis or failing to declare small sums while claiming benefit). Nine (10 per cent) failed to declare more substantial earnings but did not offend more seriously. Nineteen (22 per cent) committed other types of crime like burglary, assault, shop theft or taking vehicles. (In the remaining twenty-four cases we had insufficient information.) Few of the offences had been detected.

There was a statistical link between people's further offending and their employment situation during the follow-up period. Among those who were working, or who were jobhunting but had had a reasonable amount of work at some stage, 15 per cent were involved in crime other than benefit fraud or minor matters. Among jobhunters who had had little or no work, 28 per cent were involved in crime. Among people not working or looking for work, 75 per cent committed crime. But the relationship between lack of work and further offending was not simple, because individuals reacted to their post-release problems in different ways. Many tried hard to avoid crime, and even among those people who had been in prison three or more times previously, nearly half kept out of serious trouble.

Looking back on their latest sentence, one-third of the sample felt they had benefited in some way by work, training or education they had done in prison. Half felt they had been able to use the time for some other kind of personal improvement: gaining self-understanding, self-control or social skills. When asked what (in an ideal system) they would have *liked* their prison sentence to do for them, given that they had to serve it, almost half wanted more, or better, training for work. Some wanted better psychological preparation for the transition to freedom. And one in six indicated that they would have liked much more help towards self-enlightenment than they felt prison staff had offered them, including advice on how to stop offending.

GENERAL NOTE

This chapter has been concerned with the experiences of eighty-eight ex-prisoners in the first few months after their release from prison, focusing on the topic of employment. Except in passing we have not touched on other important matters, like family relationships and housing, because the subject of this book is work. A comprehensive report in general terms of the issues involved in the resettlement of ex-prisoners has been published by the National Association for the Care and Resettlement of Offenders.[33] But we looked at the topic of money, which obviously is linked with employment and which prisoners had placed first among things that could help them avoid crime in future. We looked at the further offending admitted by our sample, and finally at 'willpower' which prisoners had also stressed as important. Our next and final chapter will bring all the research evidence together, along with some other material, and discuss its implications.

7 The challenge ahead

THE PURPOSES OF PRISON WORK

Over the last two centuries many ideas have been put forward as purposes for prison work. We saw in Chapter 1 that at different times work in prisons has been valued in terms of: teaching prisoners the virtues of labour; their moral regeneration; softening the pains of confinement; maintaining prisons; enabling them to run commercial enterprises with cheap labour, or at least to keep down their own costs; building public works; punishment and deterrence; control and discipline; imparting vocational skills; instilling work habits; 'treatment and training'; and simply keeping prisoners occupied. From time to time official inquiries have been held into prison work or into the whole prison system; the subject of work for prisoners has been carried along and swirled about by the changing currents of penal philosophy. Meanwhile prison staff have had to run prisons, and prisoners have had to do the work allotted to them. Over thirty years ago Cooper and King[1] concluded from empirical research that the aims of prison work in Britain were confused. The results of the exercise we reported in Chapter 4 (pp. 123–6) suggest that this confusion still exists.

In this final chapter we first set out the case for what we believe should be the *primary* purpose of prison work. Later we discuss the extent to which present arrangements fall short of meeting this purpose, and what changes are needed in order to achieve it.

What prison work should be for

One function of prisons is to protect the public, but prisoners are eventually released, and most of them sooner rather than later. Of the 64,000 prisoners who in 1996 were released after serving determinate sentences, 92 per cent had served less than twelve months from the date of their sentence.[2] Prisons are very expensive, and it is in the public interest that their protective benefit should carry over into the post-release period. Woolf, discussing the function of the Prison Service within the criminal justice system, said that part of the Service's role should 'be seeking to minimise the prospect of the prisoner re-offending after serving his sentence. This is fully consistent with the Prison Service's duty "to help them lead law abiding and useful lives in custody and after release." '[3]

Many prisoners have chequered work histories. The National Prison Survey found in 1991 that one in three had been unemployed just prior to their imprisonment;[4] of the people in our follow-up sample only 36 per cent had been in work for most of the year before their sentence; a NACRO survey of 3,000 prisoners in 1992 found that 89 per cent were likely to be unemployed after their release.[5]

There is much evidence from other research (see pp. 150–1) that offenders are less likely to re-offend if they are in employment. The House of Commons Employment Committee in 1991, considering prison work (see p. 15), took that as a major premise. In our study prisoners near release said that one of the three most important aids to them in avoiding further crime would be a job (p. 150); in the follow-up sample those who had had some work were less likely to be involved in crime (p. 175); most inmates had wanted a prison occupation which would use or improve their work skills or experience (p. 59); and half the follow-up sample pleaded that prisons should give inmates more relevant work and better training (p. 178). Prison staff thought that the best purpose of prison work would be training inmates in ways which could help them get a job after release (pp. 123–4).

From all this, we would argue that the *primary* purpose of work (and vocational training) in prisons should be to prepare and help prisoners – those who want to, and most do – to get worthwhile work when they leave. This need not preclude some of the other purposes: as we discuss later, inmates can still be expected to help maintain the establishment that houses and feeds them, and if some of the products of their labour can contribute to public funds, well and good, *provided that* the work is similar to work outside prison and the workers are fairly paid. But the most important aim, consistently emphasised, should be to sustain and improve prisoners' work skills so as to enhance their prospects of employment on release. If this aim is given priority it will also encourage inmates to be 'law-abiding and useful' inside prison: prisons will be easier to manage, as prisoners are occupied in ways which they themselves feel are constructive and forward-looking, meeting their individual needs.

This reasoning is consistent with the order of priority in which Prison Service HQ in 1992 listed its seven criteria for judging prison work (see pp. 16–17). The first criterion was whether the work is realistic compared with work outside; the second, whether it fits the aptitude of the prisoners; the third, whether it teaches and maintains skills which outside employers want.

In asserting that the primary purpose of prison work should be to fit prisoners for work outside we are repeating what has often been said in earlier times: in this century, by the 1932 Departmental Committee, for instance (p. 5) and in the 1950s with the official emphasis on 'treatment and training' (p. 6). But now in the 1990s there is much more evidence to form a solid base for the assertion, and to show in what circumstances, and with what changes to current practice, the purpose could be fulfilled. This chapter explores these issues, and we begin by looking at characteristics of the outside world of work.

PROSPECTS OF EMPLOYMENT IN THE OUTSIDE WORLD

Outside prisons the world of work is changing. Some changes have been going on for many decades, while others are more recent and are proceeding rapidly. Bearing in mind what has been seen of prison work, we examine some of the changes, drawing mainly on material published by the Institute of Employment Research at Warwick University and by the Skills and Enterprise Network.[6]

Kinds of work available

Certain industries in the UK are in severe decline. For example, between 1954 and 1994 the number of people employed in agriculture, as a proportion of the total employed (including self-employed), fell from 5.4 per cent to 2.2 per cent; in engineering it fell from 13.8 per cent to 7.5 per cent; in textiles and clothing, from 6.7 per cent to 1.9 per cent. By contrast, some other groups of industries have grown: for example, over the same four decades the share of total employment provided by hotels and catering rose from 3.2 per cent to 5.6 per cent; by banking and business services, from 3.4 per cent to 10.0 per cent; by health and education services, from 7.0 per cent to 18.2 per cent; by a group called 'other services', which includes among others personal services and the leisure industry, from 3.3 per cent to 4.9 per cent. In each of these examples the decline, or growth, was expected to continue to the year 2001. Other projections show that between 1996 and 2006 employment is expected to decline by 12 per cent in manufacturing as a whole, to rise by 13 per cent in distribution, hotels and catering, and to rise by 17 per cent in business and financial services. Employment in the construction industry is cyclical and liable to be severely affected by recessions (as in 1990–3); overall between 1954 and 1994 its share of the national total changed little, from 6.2 per cent to 6.1 per cent, and it is expected to show a small rise of 3 per cent over 1996–2006.

The distribution of occupations is changing along with that of industries. To start with 1981 and take examples, in that year 'corporate managers and administrators' were 6.3 per cent of the total number of people employed (excluding those in the armed forces) but by 1994 they were 10.6 per cent; over the same period the share of 'associate professionals' rose from 7.1 per cent to 9.5 per cent; that of protective and personal service occupations rose from 6.9 per cent to 9.1 per cent. In each of these cases growth was expected to continue to 2001. On the other hand, examples of declining occupations were skilled engineering trades, whose share fell from 5.7 per cent to 4.2 per cent between 1981 and 1994; plant and machine operators, falling from 12.8 per cent to 9.9 per cent; and 'other elementary occupations' such as labourers and cleaners, falling from 10.4 per cent to 7.3 per cent. It was expected that from 1994 to 2001 the number of plant and machine operators would be stable but that skilled engineering and elementary occupations would continue to fall. Projections for 1996–2006 showed a similar pattern: a rise of 10 per cent in managerial and administrative occupations, 15 per cent in associate professional and technical ones, and 17 per cent in personal and protective services; while craft and skilled manual trades were projected to fall by 4 per cent, plant and machine operators by 2 per cent, and 'other elementary occupations' by 1 per cent. For skilled construction trades the figures showed a rise of 8.2 per cent over 1981–91, a fall of 9.6 per cent over 1991–4, and a projected rise of 10.6 per cent over 1994–2001.

Thus the kinds of jobs available have changed. There are other changes too. Self-employment rose to 13 per cent of total employment in 1996 and was expected to go on growing. Part-time employment rose in the same year to 29 per cent, and 80 per cent of part-time workers were women; altogether, women were expected to be a majority of the labour force by the turn of the century. Many full-time jobs of the kinds traditionally held by men, especially manual workers, have been lost. There are fewer permanent jobs, while temporary and contract work is growing. White-collar employment has increased, while far fewer unskilled labourers are needed. Even in traditional skilled jobs the need for manual dexterity is being replaced by the need for skills in understanding and monitoring automated systems. Many jobs now require higher levels of skill, and the capacity to assume several roles and responsibilities.

Reasons for the changes

Some of the major reasons will be briefly noted here (not in any particular order). One is international competition and the globalisation of business. Firms in other member countries of the European Union can compete freely with British firms in the single market. Challenges come from developing capitalist economies in Eastern Europe and the 'tigers' of the Far East and the Pacific Rim. Transnational companies easily move their production to wherever labour can provide the right skills at the right price.

A second reason is the advance of new technologies. Computers not only replace routine clerical work and speed up communications, but they enable different functions in a business to be linked, thus impinging on the design of its jobs right across the board. They control manufacturing operations and systems. New materials, such as polymers and ceramics, affect designers and engineers. Bio-technology is a small but rapidly growing field. Along with new technologies is a growing concern for environmental matters: energy conservation, waste disposal and the control of pollution.

A third reason in Britain is demographic change. The growing number of older people in the population increases the demand for health care and personal services, and also encourages the growth of jobs in recreation and leisure as well as some in finance. As consumers, older people want high quality in goods and services.

The changes in employment and the reasons for them are largely independent of the business cycle. The recovery of Britain's economy from the recession of the early 1990s (which was the time of our main research in prisons) does not alter the obligation on the Prison Service to take account of the developments just described.

Personal qualities needed for employment

The sources from which the above material is largely summarised also indicate the kinds of personal qualities people need for good prospects of employment. They include the following:

* Higher levels of skill and, for many jobs, multiple skills rather than a single one; vocational qualifications;
* Information technology skills, for jobs at all levels;
* Business and enterprise skills, both for self-employment and for employees;
* Awareness of technological and environmental issues;
* Willingness to be flexible in hours, length and conditions of work;
* Self-management, initiative, being able to take responsibility;
* Adaptability, willingness to retrain ('lifetime learning');
* Individual responsibility for one's own career development;
* Skills in interpersonal relations, for effective communication with colleagues and customers.

PRISON WORK AND TRAINING AS PREPARATION FOR EMPLOYMENT OUTSIDE

We now review prison work and training in the light of this information on employment prospects. In doing so we shall use, among other material, the comparisons made in Chapters 3, 4 and 5 between prison occupations and those outside. Recalling also the examination in Chapter 6 of factors which seemed to influence whether ex-prisoners tried to use their prison skills in looking for jobs, we structure this section under three headings: the relevance of prison work to work outside; the provision of vocational training in prisons; and the utility of prison work and training for developing other personal qualities required for success in the outside world of work – responsibility, initiative, confidence, adaptability, interpersonal skills, etc.

Relevance of prison jobs to outside employment

The comparisons in Chapter 3 show that in actual content – products and processes – many kinds of prison work are very like their counterparts outside. In regard to gardening, farm work, machine sewing, laundries and Liverpool's leather workshop, for example, there were close similarities. Operations in the furniture factory we visited were not as de-skilled as those in the wood assembly at Channings Wood but were otherwise similar, while the outside weavers and printers used more modern machinery than some we saw in prison, though the prison weaving shops have since been modernised. The biggest difference we observed was that between prison kitchens using traditional methods and the hospital catering service which used automated cook-chill; this illustrates the tendency still existing in prisons to use labour-intensive processes rather than automation. As for Works jobs, maintenance of buildings is much the same in prisons as out, but inmates' use of tools is often limited. The quality of prison products, generally speaking, is comparable to those outside.

Our comparisons of prison work with work outside were limited to one or two outside firms for each type of work, and the firms may not have been wholly typical. But the best indicator of similarity between prison work and outside work is the fact that NVQs are now available for a wide range of prison occupations. The main exceptions to this match in content between prison and outside are unskilled manual light assembly work, which is now rare in outside industry, and the work of prison orderlies, for which there is no general outside equivalent.

So we see that most prison work is like outside work in content. But its relevance to the outside world in terms of job opportunities presents a much more mixed and doubtful picture. A comparison between Table 1 (p. 61) and the figures cited on pp. 185–6 shows a serious imbalance between the kinds of work many prisoners are engaged in and the kinds of work in which they are likely to find jobs after release. Nearly half of working prisoners are on domestic duties (as cleaners, servery assistants and so on), which for the most part are unskilled despite prisons' training courses in industrial cleaning. (Of course prisons have to be cleaned, but it need not take half the workforce to do it: see p. 197.) After the domestic workers one of the largest groups (albeit much smaller than the domestics) is those engaged in 'contract services' work, usually comprising unskilled manual assembly operations, of which one governor (R070) said, 'I suppose occupational therapy is the best way to describe it.' The total of these two groups of unskilled prison workers is out of all proportion to the demand for unskilled workers in the labour market. Of course there are other kinds of unskilled work too, in prison and out, but the comparison just made is sufficient to point up the imbalance.

The industry which, after domestic work, employs most prisoners is clothing and textiles. The number of prisoners sitting at sewing machines is in sharp contrast to the drastic reduction in such employment indicated by the IER figures (p. 185). R054, the head of inmate activities at one of the research prisons, said:

> It seems to me to be important that if we are trying to produce the work ethic then we do that in a realistic manner by producing realistic work. We are really banging our heads against a brick wall to say go and sit at the

tailors' shop machine and that will make you a good worker, because it won't.

The IER figures, however, may not tell the whole story. Huws' research on homeworkers in 1996[7] found they included many clothing workers who were probably unrecorded in official statistics. An investigation by Berens and Johnston into some clothing factories in London in 1996[8] found immigrants employed at very low wages in illegal conditions. Such jobs are unlikely to be sought by ex-prisoners even if they have learned sewing skills during their sentence. R091, the industrial manager at another of the research prisons, after recalling that historically the sewing industry was set up in prisons simply and cheaply to aid self-sufficiency, suggested that it had grown in Third World countries for the same reasons, and then said, 'I suppose in a way you could see the Prison Service as a mini Third World country, couldn't you?'

Some other kinds of prison work may be much more in step with opportunities outside. Prison kitchen workers are a relatively large group, and employment in hotels and catering is growing though many such jobs are poorly paid. Some skills are transferable: few ex-prisoners will find work on farms, but tractor-driving and fencing are done in other contexts too. And the fact that an industry is in decline does not necessarily mean there will be no jobs left in it: engineering workers will still be needed, though in fewer numbers than formerly and with some different skills.

The important message from our comparisons is that prisons should make every effort to arrange that the kinds of work they require prisoners to do are matched as far as possible to outside labour markets. This means taking advice from local employers and TECs as to what occupations offer good prospects in the localities to which their prisoners will be released. The figures we have cited are only an outline of some national trends, but regional and local figures are available: in particular, TECs regularly produce surveys showing occupational trends and skill shortages in their own areas. Prison governors should make use of such material, as some already do. (The workshops at the rebuilt Manchester Prison were set up after the prison management sought advice directly from local employers on what skills were in demand locally.[9] It is significant that a tailors' shop was *not* included.) The involvement of local employers and TECs is discussed further on pp. 201–4.

Vocational training

A second message from our examination of outside employment trends is the need for would-be workers to have good vocational skills. Vocational training in prisons was the subject of Chapter 5, and here we briefly review three aspects: the kinds of training offered, prisoners' access to training, and the levels of skill they acquire.

Kinds of training

Prisons between them offer an impressive range of kinds of vocational training – in structured courses, in other education classes, and 'on the job' in prison work. It is important that the skills taught should match those required in local labour markets: as with work, TECs should be asked for guidance. It is also important for the kinds of training offered to take into account prisoners' existing skills, interests and hopes for work on release, as we discuss later. Here we note two points from the advice on employment prospects summarised on p. 187: that people should acquire multiple skills rather than single ones, and that certain skills are needed across a wide range of jobs.

An example of the potential in prisons for multi-skills training is the construction industry courses. These interest many prisoners, often because they have previously done some work in building. Although jobs in construction were badly hit by the recession of the early 1990s the industry has made some recovery, and the variety of skills it uses gives opportunities not only to tradesmen but also to semi-skilled workers who are prepared to be flexible and adaptable. (A salient feature of our follow-up sample was the number of ex-prisoners who *were* willing to be flexible and do almost any work they could, albeit 'on the side' if all they could find was casual employment.) Training inmates who are interested in a variety of building skills would improve their chances of work (and such skills would also be appreciated for DIY). It was noticeable that among the six research prisons in 1992 Highpoint offered five kinds of construction course while Kirkham offered only one. Most prisons should provide several kinds of construction training course. Then inmates who arrived already possessing some skill in one aspect of building work could learn another, and those whose stay was long enough could take more than one course.

Skills needed across a range of jobs include, obviously, skills in information technology. Every prison should provide training in computer skills for as many inmates as can benefit, and staff should encourage inmates to take advantage of this provision. Much the same goes for business studies. Not everyone will want to run their own business, but an understanding of how businesses operate and the development of enterprise skills will increase ex-prisoners' general employability. It was noticeable that the outside training schemes visited, while covering between them a wide range of topics, gave more prominence to computers and business skills than we found in the six prisons. Computer and business skills training could be linked to various kinds of prison work, as we suggest later.

Access to training

A general impression from the research prisons was that, overall, inmates' access to training was quite limited compared with the amount of inmate labour devoted to production. This varied between the six establishments, the emphasis on production being greatest at Kirkham and perhaps least at Maidstone, but altogether the vocational training of inmates did not receive high priority. Many of the courses had long waiting lists. Inmates were often expected to do a spell of three months or so in the production workshops first, and by the time their turn came round for a course they might not have enough time left to do much of it – if indeed the trainer would still accept them at that stage, which was by no means always the case. Training opportunities for inmates in VPUs were very restricted compared with those in other wings. Even in the workplaces the training many inmates received was only the minimum necessary to fit them into the swing of production, not the wider range of skills tuition which instructors had the potential to offer. On the whole, despite the progress of NVQs and commendable efforts by prison managers to defend training against budget cuts, it seemed that vocational training was not a high priority in the prisons' activities.

This situation should be changed. Prospects of employment in the outside world are greatest for people who are trained in relevant skills, and prisons should therefore give much more emphasis than at present to provision for inmates' vocational training.

Levels of skill acquired in prison

The rough comparison on p. 141 between national NVQ figures and those for the research sample of eighty-eight people suggests that in 1995–6 prisoners in general gained less skill than those in the six research prisons had gained three years previously. Yet during our fieldwork it seemed clear that many inmates were not reaching the levels of skill which prison training had the potential to offer them. Several factors contributed to this situation.

Many inmates doing prison work were restricted in the amount of skill they were allowed to use or aspire to. For example: in kitchens, except at Holloway, inmates chopped vegetables and stirred pots, but the instructors did much of the real cooking; in woodwork shops inmates operated machines but the instructors set the machines up; in Works departments inmates generally acted as 'bag carriers' to the staff tradesmen and their use of tools was very limited. This general picture forms a contrast with that described by McHutchison in 1991 in her research on prison industries in New South Wales. There, inmates in Corrective Services Industries (CSI) workshops could progress through four levels termed 'unskilled', 'semi-skilled', 'skilled' and 'proficiency'. In CSI timber workshops (which produced items similar to those made in the woodwork shops at Channings Wood and Liverpool) 'unskilled' inmates used hand tools but 'skilled' inmates set up the machines such as bandsaws, routers and drills. In CSI metal fabrication shops (which produced, for example, tubular steel furniture) 'skilled' inmates set up machines for cutting, bending, drilling and welding. Inmates worked their way up the skill levels, learning from one another as well as from the staff, and there were also integrated training courses. McHutchison said, 'A culture exists in the workshops where those with skills are highly regarded.'[10] In our study, although there were different grades of work in the workplaces, the top skill levels available to most inmates seemed much lower than those described for CSI. Inmates should be allowed, and encouraged, to practise higher levels of skill in prison work.

A related point is the de-skilled nature of the operations we saw in prison workshops, for example in the wood assembly shop at Channings Wood, or in the tailors' shops generally. Prisoners found this very boring, as was mentioned in Chapter 3. Several outside employers said that current industrial practice was moving in the direction of increasing, not decreasing, the skill in production operations, and that if any vacancies occurred they would most likely be for versatile workers who knew how to make a whole article (e.g. for 'sample sewers' in clothing manufacture: see p. 82). Although instructors in the prison workshops did allow their inmates to move round and learn various operations, it seemed that with different organisation of the work inmates could be trained to be more versatile (and would get more satisfaction). Production routines in workshops should be reorganised to allow prisoners to learn how to make complete articles.

Discontinuities in training hindered prisoners' acquisition of skill. One cause was the frequent lack of co-ordination between training courses and prison jobs, which was discussed on pp. 135–7. Another was the transfer of prisoners around the system with scant regard for the stage of training they had reached (pp. 137–8). Both these matters are the concern of sentence planning and co-ordination of regimes, which we discuss later.

There is also the simple point that daily hours of training should be longer than the five or so hours a day which are current practice in most prisons. (The same goes for prison work too, of course.) Inmates in training courses told us it was frustrating to arrive in the morning, set up their materials (e.g. for brickwork) and then, after only two hours or even less, have to stop to go back to their cells for lunch, and then the same again in the afternoon. Others made the point that a two-hour meal break spent largely in lying on one's bed was not conducive to mental effort when the work session eventually resumed. Proper working hours of seven a day would enable inmates to learn more skills in the time available during their sentence. This, of course, would have implications for staffing hours and rosters.

How much training is possible?

On p. 141 it was noted that in 1995–6, estimating from national figures, the number of prisoners gaining some NVQ units was only about 13 per cent, and those achieving a full NVQ only about 8 per cent, of the number of prisoners sentenced to a year or more. Prisoners sentenced to a year or more comprise fewer than half (38 per cent in 1996)[11] of all who pass through the system. Clearly the provision of NVQ training even for this minority has a long way to go. For the majority who have a shorter time to serve after sentence (on average, less than five months), a full-time course leading to an NVQ may not be feasible in many cases. But these inmates, like others, should receive a vocational assessment at the beginning of sentence, and then (unless needing education) they should be placed in suitable work. A suitable prison job would be one which maintained any existing skill and helped to increase it by on-the-job training, including NVQ units (and accreditation of prior learning) wherever possible. Thus shorter-sentence prisoners, like others, should be included in the system of employment throughcare which we outline on pp. 204–7.

Responsibility and encouraging personal competence

R621, a prisoner working in the Maidstone print shop and serving two years, said:

> There's a great feeling of frustration, and almost emasculation, at having somebody, anybody, tell you to do things, and having no control over whether you do them or not. But the nature of prison is that, is control by others, and I don't see how really they can combine the two – self-control and keep you in prison.

R056, a prison education officer, said:

> [Inmates] become anaesthetised after a while, they just become dependent, like cripples really....Prisons are full of all sorts of contradictions – 'treatment and training' and then we have people having to *ask* for pens and papers, etc., and can I do this and do that. Most people leave all that about the age of 10, yet we impose it on people of 50. Then we wonder why when we kick them out they are bloody useless.

Imprisonment necessarily involves loss of freedom to run one's own life. Yet, to the fullest extent consistent with its duty of keeping prisoners in custody, the Prison Service should seek to limit the damage caused by incarceration and to encourage inmates in the exercise of personal responsibility.[12] In view of the qualities needed for future employment (p. 187) this is especially relevant to the area of prison work.

In Chapters 3 and 4 we saw how strong is the tendency of much prison work to discourage inmates' personal competence rather than to foster it. Much of the work is not of their choosing and they do not perceive it as relevant to their lives before or after release. Much is performed at very low levels of skill and the workers are given very little responsibility for making decisions about what they do. They feel little commitment to it; it gives them little interest or sense of achievement. They are paid at rates comparable to children's pocket money which they can spend on 'extras'; they are not required, or enabled, to pay their way or budget their money like adults. Some of their supervisors, especially in the large workshops, while generally kind and good-humoured manage them in ways reminiscent of the schoolroom.

Scope for responsibility was more in evidence with some kinds of work (and with some staff and some inmates) than with others. For example, a gardens worker who managed his or her own patch and could decide within limits what to plant in it, as did some gardeners at Highpoint, had opportunity for a sense of commitment to the work. So did the drains-clearer and the glazier at Liverpool and Maidstone (p. 86) who were key workers allowed to carry their own tools. Learning to handle animals on the farm could give some prisoners a completely new and positive experience and a real sense of achievement (see, for example, R533, p. 76). And often staff tried, as occasions arose, to give their workers responsibility and dignity (e.g. R023, p. 107).

Working closely with staff in a one-to-one relationship or a very small team, as for instance in some Works jobs, could help an inmate develop interpersonal skills in a way that was much less likely to occur in a tailors' workshop where four instructors supervised fifty men. The potential of the workplace for fostering prisoners' skills in developing good relationships with authority figures as well as with fellow inmates is something that prison managers should examine in regard to every kind of prison work. And here something may be said about the work of inmate orderlies, clerks and, to a lesser extent, No. 1s. These workers can be in an uncomfortable position: relied on by staff, but possibly despised as toadies by other inmates (see p. 102). To the extent that an orderly, clerk or No. 1 is performing a worthwhile, skilled and responsible work role, it can be an opportunity for him or her to develop in maturity (see R686, p. 110). If, on the other hand, he or she is treated by staff as a pet (p. 101) the relationship is unlikely to be helpful.

Two measures could help to counteract the negative attitudes of other inmates towards No. 1s and similar workers. The first would be to enable and encourage *all* inmates in the workplace to attain the highest possible level of vocational skill. This would promote a workplace culture in which skills were respected (as in the New South Wales CSI workshops) and adult dignity enhanced: a No. 1, as one of the most skilled, would be deservedly looked up to. The second would be to increase all inmate workers' pay substantially so that even the least skilled would gain self-respect from their own work.

The relevance of prisoners' pay to encouraging a sense of personal responsibility has been recognised by the Prisoners' Earnings Act 1996, which enables prisons to deduct from inmates' earnings (provided these are high enough) money towards their keep, supporting their families, victim support or crime prevention, and compulsory savings. Yet the number of prisoners whose wages are sufficient to allow this is still tiny, while the great majority continue in their state of dependence on other people to supply all their needs. At least some inmates recognise the importance of this issue (p. 112), and a further example arose during a post-release interview:

> R572: An inmate should have the opportunity (R suggests by paid community work) to earn money to help his family, to save for release, to pay board to the prison, and for spending money inside. This would give him the chance to do something for his family and thus for his self-esteem. 'You lose your self-esteem, you become useless in there...I don't want to sponge off nobody.' R still feels ashamed that when he was in prison he had to ask

friends outside to buy a birthday present for his wife, and that when he needed private cash she had to borrow from friends to send it in to him. He felt that even the clothes the prison gave him on discharge were a handout: 'You haven't *earned* it, they *give* it to you.'

Compared with most of our inmate interviewees who were doing prison work, those who were in training courses or education derived more sense of achievement, interest, and power over what they were doing and self-respect from their prison occupation. These are aspects of personal competence which are relevant to life outside. The essential difference between inmates in education and training courses and those in prison work was that, generally speaking, the former had *chosen* to do education or training because they felt it was relevant to their lives as people, not as prisoners, and they hoped to gain some personal benefit which would carry over into their release into the outside world. The conclusion from this must be that if prison work is to foster personal competence it must be work which is planned, for and with the inmate, to be relevant to his or her pre-sentence experience and to his or her hopes for work on release. This is to say, it must be part of employment throughcare and sentence planning, which we discuss later.

Altogether, how well does prison work, as exemplified in the six research prisons, meet the criteria which the Prison Service set in 1992 (pp. 16–17)? The answer must be: not well. Of the seven benchmarks comprising the first criterion (realism compared with work outside) the only one satisfactorily attained is 'production processes/technology'; and perhaps 'interaction with others' is partially met. On the second criterion (fitting prisoners' aptitudes) there is often a mismatch. On the third (teaching and maintaining marketable skills and qualifications) prisons' efforts with NVQs are creditable but there is a long way to go, and training has too low a priority. On the fifth criterion (prisoners' earnings) most prison work falls far short. The fourth, sixth and seventh criteria have not been part of our study.

A note on empowerment

The Prison Service would do well to ponder the implications of a survey conducted in 1994 by the Industrial Society, which asked 580 businesses about their experiences and intentions regarding empowerment.[13] Empowerment was seen as a process involving (among other things) the following changes. The workers nearest to a task are given the decision-making power and resources needed to carry it out; job boundaries are widened so that more tasks are covered and workers use more of their abilities and creativity; they feel they 'own' their jobs; they are likely to work in multi-skilled teams needing less supervision; supervisors are role models and facilitators rather than bosses; and the culture changes from one of command and control to one of co-operation and trust. Employees take more responsibility for their working lives. The survey revealed that while few firms were practising empowerment in 1994 it was a growing trend, and that firms already doing it found that the benefits included better service to customers, better use of workers' skills, lower costs or increased productivity, and greater competitiveness. If managers of prison industries would like to achieve these good things, perhaps they should consider how prison workers could be empowered.

PRISONS' POTENTIAL FOR INCREASING INMATES' EMPLOYABILITY

This discussion reviewing prison work and training has included ideas for positive development, and at the end of Chapter 5 we listed specific suggestions for improving vocational training which were made mainly by staff and prisoners during the research. We would maintain that despite their basic custodial function prisons have much potential for helping inmates towards success in employment, and we now look more closely at two topics: linking training with prison work, and making better use of the skills of the work instructors.

Linking training with prison work

There should be more co-ordination between training courses and related prison jobs. Prisoners who learn a skill in a trade training course should be enabled to practise and consolidate it in actual work, so that the course and the work come together, rather as in an apprenticeship, instead of being largely unconnected. On p. 136 examples were given where prisons were already doing this, and the list of ideas on pp. 146–8 includes suggestions for more. But in addition to specific trade skills we recall the advice (p. 187) that for best prospects of employment in the outside world people will need skills in information technology and in understanding business. So every kind of work in the prison should be looked at to see what opportunities it could offer for giving practical experience to inmates who have done, or are doing, training in computers and in business skills (and there should be many such inmates). Stores records, production targets, workshop organisation, records of training progress, Works maintenance records, arrangements for jobs done in the community, sales of prison produce and manufactures...there must be numerous opportunities that could be developed. Jobs like those of workshop office clerks should not be reserved for white-collar offenders who already have such skills, but instead should be seen as opportunities for training inmates in business practice.

A practical point concerns timetabling. It is advocated in much of this chapter that the thrust of prison work should be changed, to place the emphasis on training inmates for employment outside rather than on the production of prison goods, as was the traditional role of PSIF. But certain jobs in prison will still need to be done: meals cooked, clothes and linen washed, rooms kept clean. Inmates should be expected to help with such things as they might do if living in their own homes. So in areas of essential prison work like kitchen, laundry and cleaning there could be a division of labour. Inmates who are receiving vocational training in these occupations should be regarded as the prime workers, employed full-time to the extent that fits with their training, given the skilled tasks and enabled to practise their skills at the highest level possible. The unskilled tasks in such areas should be designated as domestic chores of which other inmates should do their share, part-time, before going off to their own work or training (or education) elsewhere in the prison.[14] Thus, for example, trainees on the industrial cleaning course could have responsibility for the complete cleaning of suites of rooms in the administration buildings or the education department (as was done at Channings Wood); but wing cleaning would be a chore to be done on a rota basis by inmates living in that wing for an hour a day (or a few hours a week) before they moved off to their own occupations. This arrangement would help foster a culture of respect for skill and training and would diminish the attractions of wing-cleaning work as an opportunity for 'skiving' or 'wheeling and dealing' in the illicit inmate counter-culture (see R653, p. 101).

So in each prison, managers should arrange for a survey of all the work that is done, and that *could* be done, by inmates, focusing on the following questions: What is the training content of this activity? How could it be increased? Is there an NVQ available? What training courses in the prison are, or could be, related to it? What is the potential of this activity for giving inmates on-the-job experience in computers and business skills? And at the same time essential unskilled tasks should be identified and designated as chores with which all inmates are expected to help. At an individual level, inmates arriving at a prison should be informed of the various kinds of work done there and of the ways in which they will be expected to help with it. This information should set out clearly what each kind of work is and what it is *for*, whether there is training with it and how the training is accessed; what the chores are and the arrangements for inmates to do their share.

Involving the work instructors

A strong impression from the research was that the work instructors' potential for training and helping prisoners was not being properly used. Many instructors we interviewed would have liked to do more training of inmates but other things got in the way: the pressure for production, the short hours and interruptions, the fluctuating numbers and, not least, inmates' lack of interest and motivation in many cases. And it seemed that the isolation of prisoners – in their cells in relation to the rest of the prison, and in the prison in relation to life beyond the walls – was to some extent reflected in the isolation of the work instructors, especially those who were civilians. Many we spoke with had little contact with other departments of the prison. They had little or no say in choosing their workforce, and when inmates were transferred out of their workshops they often heard little more about them. R071, a senior manager, said in 1992, 'I think it's a common feature of all prisons that instructors get pushed to one side and forgotten about.'

Yet the work instructors play a central part in many prisoners' daily lives. Inmates in their workplaces spend more time with them than with other prison staff (and if working hours were extended to thirty-five a week the difference would be greater still). Instructors not only teach inmates work skills and supervise their production but can listen to their concerns, liaise with other staff about their welfare, and generally try to ease the frustrations of prison life in ways which, even with the best will in the world, are often less open to uniformed wing officers (including personal officers) because of the latter's other duties and their changing shifts.

Recent Canadian research in prison industries has produced several results which are relevant here. It was found that work instructors who used techniques of active leadership (which could be acquired through training) improved prisoners' attitudes to their work: the inmates became more highly motivated and interested in their tasks, found the work more meaningful and felt more responsibility for its results.[15] Prisoners scoring highly on these attitudes (which were inter-related) were more likely to be judged by their instructors as good workers: dependable, co-operative, safety conscious and producing good quality.[16] Moreover, prisoners with these good work attitudes also rated themselves highly on generic work skills: co-operation, ability to solve problems, use initiative, work independently, and so on. The implication is that work instructors can help prisoners to acquire attitudes and transferable skills which will not only improve their production in prison industry but also increase their employability in other settings, and especially in the search for work after release.[17]

From what has been seen in earlier chapters, we would expect that instructors' success in motivating inmates would also be influenced by the kind of prison work they were engaged in. For responsibility and initiative to develop, opportunities to exercise them must exist. Prisoners' interest and willingness would also depend on whether they had been assigned to their prison jobs with some regard for their individual needs: motivation would be improved by placing them in work which they felt was relevant, giving them the training opportunities they wanted, and paying them at rates which enabled them to meet adult obligations. Work instructors should be involved in this process from the beginning: their important role should be recognised and developed. They should be enabled to work closely with teachers, training course tutors, inmates' personal officers and other prison staff as appropriate in planning and progressing inmates' work and training 'careers' throughout sentence. And they should be permitted, and encouraged, to put inmates near release in touch with outside job opportunities and to give references, and should be allowed to keep in touch with ex-inmates about their work and training if they wish. (See p. 207 for a note on Prison Rule 81.) In short, work instructors should be enabled to play a large part in *employment throughcare*, a concept we discuss on pp. 204–7.

Braithwaite[18] has suggested that it should be one of the duties of work instructors to help their prisoners find jobs on release; that workshops should record the number of placements they get; and that shops with good placement records should have preference for further investment and expansion while those which find no jobs are allowed to dwindle. This would help ensure that kinds of prison work matched opportunities outside, and would give instructors a strong incentive to train inmates. To this we would add the desirability of giving work instructors the leadership skills which can result in improving prisoners' work attitudes and general employability.

Through all these ways instructors' jobs would become more satisfying, and now we bring in another point from Canadian research.[19] Some of the generic employability skills – such as problem-solving, initiative, responsibility, self-management, interpersonal skills – are similar to those taught (often by cognitive methods) in other programmes for prisoners which directly address their offending behaviour (see p. 210). Work instructors can help inmates practise them in the workplace. The corollary is that instructors should be fully involved in prisoners' sentence planning, which is part of the wider perspective on prison work to which we turn later (p. 207).

The proposals discussed in the last two pages would do a great deal to overcome the isolation of the work instructors which Dawson[20] had described in 1972 (see p. 127) and which we found still existing twenty years later. Work instructors should be enabled to play a central role in the life of the prison and, working with other staff, to make a full contribution to the development of inmates' abilities.

Industrial prisons?

From time to time, especially since the Anson Inquiry of the 1960s (see pp. 7–8), the Prison Service has considered setting up industrial prisons. These may be defined as ones where the prisoners spend a full working day in industrial production and all other activities take place outside working hours. The former Chief Inspector of Prisons, Sir Stephen Tumim, has advocated a model like some in Europe where the inmates work inside the prison, supervised by prison staff, but are actually employed by an outside company which sends in materials and equipment and pays them real wages.[21] An alternative model is for the prison itself to run the industry, the inmates still working full time without interruptions (except for meals), rather like Coldingley Prison in its first years (p. 10).

Coldingley never paid real wages, and gradually its attempt to be an industrial prison faltered in other respects. R053, governor of one of the six research prisons, said in 1992 that the concept of an industrial prison had never really been put into practice in Britain despite all the talk of it in the 1970s:

> You could say, in a subconscious way, the Prison Service has never really been committed to the concept of industrial production, because if they had we would have people working eight-hour days with half-hour lunch-breaks on site. We'd actually make different arrangements, but we haven't.... There is not a collective will to do it, because we have never really satisfactorily dealt with the purpose of imprisonment.

If the Prison Service were to adopt the policy that the primary purpose of prison *work* is to fit prisoners for employment on release, the issue would be clearer, though establishing the practice would not necessarily be easy. It would not matter whether a prison was called an industrial one as long as its kinds of work realistically matched outside labour markets, inmates worked a full day, for wages sufficient to enable them to meet adult responsibilities, and the work included vocational training. Vocational training is as important as the other points; it is no longer enough to think that prisoners will acquire 'good work habits' if they spend the day in unskilled factory work, because times have moved on. Learmont suggested that political and trade union objections to industrial prisons (that they would take jobs away from outside workers) could be met by focusing on import substitution, the prisons producing goods which would otherwise be imported from countries where labour is cheap.[22] But surely this is short-sighted, because such jobs will not be available to ex-prisoners. As for a full working day, prison managers and staff would have to face up to this issue and arrange shifts and duty rosters so that working prisoners could stay at work. Blocks of time, in full days or weeks, could still be set aside for such things as offending behaviour courses, so that inmates attending them would be like workers in outside industry who are sent away for training.

Coldingley's governor in 1995 hoped that the prison could be redeveloped as an industrial one.[23] He envisaged a new factory, built in partnership with a private firm; a 39-hour working week for all inmates; training leading to NVQs, aided by the education department; revised staffing structures and attendance systems; and selection of prisoners so that Coldingley received fewer who were unfit for the workshops. The question of pay remained (though at that time some prisoners in the workshops could earn £30 a week in an incentive scheme). In 1997 it was reported that the management of Coldingley's industries was to be transferred to a private prison company with the intention of maximising inmates' work opportunities.[24]

Braithwaite has suggested that when a prison is considering setting up a new industry a sequence of seven questions should be posed.[25] Only if the answer to the first is 'yes' should the second be asked, and so on. The first five questions are: (1) could the industry be set up without causing insuperable security problems? (2) would it give its prisoner workers intrinsic job satisfaction? (3) would it teach them marketable skills? (4) could its products be marketed? (5) would it make a profit? If the answers to all these were favourable, costing exercises would be mounted to answer questions 6 and 7, about the return on capital invested and the ratio of the latter to the number of prisoners employed. To this sequence we would add, between 4 and 5: could the prisoners earn realistic pay?

INVOLVING OUTSIDERS

Outside agencies can be involved in prisons in ways which can enhance prisoners' prospects of employment, and such links, besides making a very practical contribution, help to reduce the isolation of inmates and staff from the rest of the community. In this section we look at two groups in particular: local employers, and Training and Enterprise Councils.

Local employers

These have already been mentioned in the discussion of industrial prisons. Local employers can be an invaluable resource in helping to make prison work relevant to outside, but there are pitfalls as well as potential gains. At present the commonest way for private firms to be connected with prison work is as customers for prison-made goods, either through the open market or through contracts as in the light assembly workshops. If in making the products prisoners learn skills for jobs on release and if they are reasonably paid, well and good. But if their prison work is unskilled and poorly paid then they are being exploited in the same way as underpaid homeworkers. The prison's chief aim should be to train inmates in marketable skills rather than to make money for the prison.

Another form of collaboration is for a private firm to take over completely the running of a prison industry (or workshop), supervising the workers, marketing the products and sharing the proceeds with the prison. This situation is much less common than it was in the last century when prisoners' labour was shamefully exploited (especially in North America).[26] But recently the Prison Service has become interested in reviving the model with proper safeguards, and there are other forms of co-operation, as will be seen.

In whatever way a private company is involved with a prison in providing work for inmates, tension is likely to arise between the aim of making money and the aim of rehabilitating prisoners. If in the joint venture the prison gives priority to the latter, it in effect becomes what Davies[27] has referred to as a 'social firm': an institution which, while still seeking to operate as a business, provides realistic work experience and training for people who would otherwise be handicapped in the labour market. This is surely a worthy objective for the Prison Service. Lightman[28] has suggested that if a private company sets up within a prison (with due protection for prisoners) the company's goal of profit will inevitably conflict with the goal of providing rehabilitative work experience and training, but that nevertheless the company's work and training are likely to be more realistic than the prison system in isolation would provide. Therefore the subsidy which the partnership entails – from the government to the employer – is socially justified. The chief benefit to the inmates, suggests Lightman, is that they are enabled to see themselves as part of the normal labour force rather than as prisoners. Again, this is surely a desirable outcome.

Since 1993 the Prison Service has endeavoured to interest private sector companies in forming partnerships of various kinds with prisons. It has been uphill work. Flynn,[29] discussing likely benefits and problems, points out that prisons differ in their regimes, security requirements, populations and facilities, so there can be no uniform approach; there are issues concerning access to the prison, communication with its staff at various levels, and availability of prisoners as the workforce; and while some prison managers are keen others are more cautious, as are employers despite PES's marketing efforts. (A degree of caution may well be justified: nobody would want to risk a repetition of the Prindus scandal of the 1980s.) By February 1996 PES listed twenty projects (involving seventeen prisons) as partnerships in operation and fifteen more as under discussion, though not all of them involved the private company in running prison workshops. At the five male research prisons practically the only form of collaboration we found at our updating visits was that companies were customers for prison products, usually under contract. They were barely involved in training, except at Maidstone where at the beginning of a contract (perhaps once a month) the firm's production supervisor would spend a day or two in the workshop setting up equipment and training instructors and inmates. Maidstone's management encouraged these visits to show firms what the prison could do, but no company did ongoing training or recruitment for the future. By contrast, in 1993 one of the best partnerships was the Reed scheme at Holloway (p. 43) where the company trained inmates to be office workers in exactly the same way as its employees outside, paid them £3 an hour, and gave them some hope of a job on release.

Another way in which local employers can assist prisons is by contributing to inmate development and pre-release courses, giving 'horse's mouth' advice on jobsearch techniques and interview skills. And they can help individual inmates by providing suitably trained ones with work experience placements during sentence and links to job opportunities on release. Several examples were achieved in the 'Beyond The Gate' project which ran in Kent prisons in 1993–5.

Beyond The Gate

In April 1993 the Prison Service and Kent TEC launched an effort to interest local companies in the eleven prison establishments in Kent, which between them held nearly every type of prisoner.[30] It was hoped to find employers willing to do any of the following: (1) provide short work experience placements for selected inmates, especially some who were training for NVQs; (2) provide jobs for inmates near the end of their sentence, who could then go out daily to work and would be kept on after release; (3) contribute jobsearch advice and training to pre-release courses; and (4) set up joint commercial enterprises with prisons which would provide work and training (and good pay) for inmates. The general aim was to raise employers' awareness of ex-offenders' need for jobs, show them what prisons were doing, and engage their interest in providing opportunities.

A serving officer from Canterbury Prison's resettlement unit was seconded to the TEC full time as Employer Liaison Officer (ELO) to build up the scheme. It was very hard work. During the first year approaches were made by mail and telephone to 1,000 firms, selected from the TEC's records according to their likely vacancies and need for skills which corresponded to the prisons' vocational training. When opportunities were offered, the ELO, working with prison staff, found suitable inmates and took them to the employers for interview. She also arranged for employers to visit prisons, and developed links with other outside agencies.

The end of the scheme's first year saw modest success on several fronts (though no commercial enterprise was established). Fifteen prisoners had been given work experience during their sentence, and eight near release had been placed in jobs. Five employers were participating in pre-release courses. Joint funding by a private firm, the TEC and the Prison Service enabled the charity Instant Muscle to send a full-time business adviser into the prisons to help inmates who were preparing for self-employment. Altogether nine of the Kent prisons had so far become involved in one way or another, and the ELO reported enthusiastic comments from employers who said their views on hiring ex-prisoners had changed. One firm was so impressed by the industrial cleaning course at Swaleside Prison that it sent some of its own staff to be trained there (for a fee). During the second year the ELO, in addition to her other work, developed a 'blueprint' for prisons to use in consolidating and expanding the scheme.

In March 1995 Beyond The Gate stopped. The TEC had funded it for two years on the understanding that then, when it was well established, the Prison Service would take over and continue it. But that did not happen. The ELO was moved to other duties and the scheme was wound down. By mid-1996 employers' involvement with Kent prisons was again mainly confined to their being customers for prison products, except at the resettlement units where some took a more active part.

Training and Enterprise Councils

Beyond The Gate, while it lasted, was an excellent example of co-operation between a TEC and the Prison Service. There have been many others. In 1993 the Employment Department published a comprehensive guide[31] to ways in which TECs could work with prisons, probation services and the Employment Service to help offenders into training and jobs. This document and the letter publicising it throughout the Prison Service early in 1994[32] listed ten TECs which were supporting a variety of projects in prisons in their areas. Among the activities were: providing local labour market information; funding the training of work instructors as NVQ assessors; facilitating the secondment of instructors to outside firms for refresher periods; supporting prison training courses; and funding the provision to individual inmates of vocational assessment and training plans. Another example, where (a very few) prisoners were included in an outside training scheme in 1995, is described by Roberts *et al.*[33]

At four of the six research prisons, at some period between 1992 and 1996, the local TEC had an important role. At Channings Wood, Devon and Cornwall TEC funded the Options For Learning scheme (pp. 143–5). Liverpool Prison was one of several in which Merseyside TEC funded NACRO to act as a training agency: NACRO representatives visited the prisons regularly to interview inmates, draw up personal training plans for them and put them in touch with training providers on their release. (In 1995–6 ninety Liverpool inmates received such a plan.) Maidstone Prison participated in Beyond The Gate. Kirkham Prison along with others facilitated research by Apex, funded by the two Lancashire TECs, which resulted in a 'skills audit' of Lancashire prisoners and an extensive set of recommendations on ways in which prisons could improve their training of inmates and TECs could help them do so.[34]

But, as has been seen, these hopeful enterprises were often short-lived. Options For Learning and Beyond The Gate stopped in 1995 when TEC funding ended. NACRO's training agency in Merseyside prisons ceased in April 1996 after TEC support was withdrawn; NACRO applied to the Probation Service for funds to continue it, but Probation Service 'partnership' money was available only for work with offenders in the community, not serving prisoners. The Lancashire 'skills audit' seemed to have very little lasting effect. At the five male research prisons, at the time of our updating visits in spring 1996, almost the only TEC-funded activity was some training for prison staff at Liverpool, and the impending appointment at Highpoint of a probation liaison worker specialising in education, training and employment. No labour market information was being sought or supplied.

The short-term, 'stop-go' nature of TEC funding, and the squeeze on prisons' budgets which made them unwilling to continue what others had started, meant that the hard effort which had been put into these projects was largely wasted. It takes much patient work to establish such schemes: to overcome employers' suspicions and ignorance of what goes on in prisons, and to overcome some prison staff's inward-looking attitudes and generate enthusiasm for building links with outside. Yet if after two or three years[35] the scheme stops, everything falls flat. Prison managers are inclined to see the TECs as 'talking shops' which do not understand the hard realities of running a prison; TEC managers think prisons ask for money but want to continue pursuing their own goals in isolation; prisoners who have been encouraged to train in the hope of access to jobs are let down; cynicism revives; and public money has been wasted.

EMPLOYMENT THROUGHCARE

Running through much of our discussion has been the theme of the need for continuity: between training and jobs within a prison, between training in different prisons, and between a person's training and work experiences in prison and those outside. We have seen that inmates are often assigned to prison work with little regard for their existing skills and aspirations (pp. 59–60); that their training is frequently liable to interruption (pp. 137–8); and that in many cases nothing is done before their release to link them with outside job opportunities which could use skills learned during sentence (pp. 156, 164).

The Employment Department's 1993 guide to TECs[36] envisaged that a prisoner's sentence plan would incorporate a training plan including: the possibility of training being provided by outside agencies as well as the prison; the gaining of NVQ units; the transfer of records of achievement; the accreditation of prior learning; and planning for the continuation of training after release. We would go further and advocate a system of *employment throughcare*. In this, prison staff and other people as appropriate would work with the inmate from the beginning of sentence to guide him or her through an individual programme of work and training linked to work on release, and co-ordinated in prison by the inmate's personal officer.

The essential first step would be a vocational assessment and guidance interview by someone skilled in such work. This would take into account the inmate's previous work experience, skills and aspirations, the labour market in the locality where he or she proposed to live on release, and (if necessary) guidance towards thinking realistically about the future, including an appreciation of ways in which the world of work has changed. Then a work and training plan would be drawn up to enable the inmate to make the best use of the facilities at each prison in which the sentence is served. During the early stages the people involved (besides the inmate) would probably be mainly prison staff such as work instructors, trainers and teachers, but outsiders could be involved too, in vocational assessment, in furnishing information about outside job opportunities, and as employers providing work in the prison. Later during sentence the balance might shift so that outsiders played a bigger part, with the inmate working out from prison, attending an 'employment focus' course, using a jobclub or other facilities run by outside agencies; but insiders could still participate, with work instructors and trainers contacting outside employers and giving references. After release outsiders, including the supervising probation officer where present, would play the main part, but support from prison staff should still be available until the released prisoner is fully settled into employment.

At each prison the plan would be monitored and co-ordinated by the inmate's personal officer. Personal officers would need to be well acquainted with the facilities for work and training in their own prison and at other prisons from which theirs received inmates or to which their prison's inmates were transferred. They would need some knowledge of outside opportunities for work and training in their prison's locality, and how to access specialist advice about them to help inmates near release. And they would be responsible for using all this information to put together, and maintain, a plan for each of 'their' inmates. The plan would be reviewed regularly, and would be flexible so as to allow room for the inmate to develop and, perhaps, stimulated by good experiences of prison work, education or training, to take up new career interests which had not been evident at the beginning. For inmates with very short sentences who will spend only a few weeks in prison, the plan (after the initial assessment) should focus on pre-release elements from the beginning, as well as including participation in suitable prison work with elements of vocational training, and educational help if required. Employment throughcare carried out in this way would give personal officers a very interesting and demanding role.

What of the Probation Service? The 'national framework document' for throughcare, published by the Home Office in 1993, says that throughcare embraces all the assistance given to offenders and their families by the Prison and Probation Services and outside agencies and ties in with all the training, education and work experience they are given. It is directed at equipping them to fit back into society, get a job and home and cope with life without reoffending.[37]

Later it makes clear[38] that in regard to convicted prisoners the tasks of seconded probation officers in prisons are largely concerned with contributing to sentence plans, risk assessments and offending behaviour programmes, and liaison with outside probation officers who will be supervising people released on licence. There is plenty of room here for other people such as work instructors to help with what we have called employment throughcare, and some of them would like to do so (p. 116).

As for post-release supervision, one of its objectives[39] is to reintegrate the offender into the community, and in recent years many probation areas have set up joint arrangements with the Employment Service, TECs and voluntary agencies to promote ex-offenders' employment prospects.[40] But a supervising officer's task of reintegrating an individual would surely be lightened if the ex-prisoner were already linked up with job opportunities through work done while in prison. Too often there is an assumption, which is reinforced by the separateness of funding, that the right time for a prisoner to start thinking about jobs is just before release, if not later, and that prison work is not relevant. The whole thrust of our argument is that it *ought* to be relevant, and should give the individual a continuous positive experience of work from the inside through to the outside.

Such a system of employment throughcare could gradually help prison managers to plan their provision of work and training to meet the needs of the prisoners they receive. Personal officers would have information on each inmate admitted to the prison, showing his or her needs as revealed by the initial assessment, the plan, and what had been done so far. This data could be aggregated over a period and analysed to give a profile of the prison's intake. Various groups would be revealed, defined by characteristics like previous work experience, stage of training reached, likely length of stay, and employment goals on release: with this information the prison's regime could be planned to address the needs of the different groups. Moreover, prisons would need to co-ordinate their regimes with one another, so that as prisoners moved between them at different stages their work and training plans could progress. All this would eventually result in more continuity of training and work experience for prisoners, and more constructive and efficient use of prisons' resources, than happens now. And among inmates who took advantage of the opportunities offered, as we believe many would, it would promote good behaviour and work co-operation in prison. They would feel that the work was relevant to the outside world and had positive value for them; they would have faith in the training; and all the time they would be encouraged to look out beyond the prison walls in preparation for their release.

Of course these ideas are not new. In 1991 Prison Service HQ, in planning the development of NVQs, proposed a framework[41] comprising steps very like much of what we have suggested, and also including a most important component which we discuss later: the need for prisoners to address offending behaviour and acquire skills of personal competence. Substantial elements of what we here call employment throughcare have already existed in some prisons, for some inmates, at some periods. Vocational assessment and guidance followed by a training plan featured in the Options For Learning scheme at Channings Wood (pp. 143–5), in NACRO's training agency work in Merseyside prisons (p. 203), and in an Apex project at Belmarsh Prison,[42] to name but a few examples. Vocational guidance can be offered by prison education staff, as in Channings Wood's New Horizons course (p. 37). Integration of prison work and training in inmates' 'action plans' was an essential part of the OFL scheme. And Beyond The Gate was an example of inmates being linked with outside jobs before release, as can happen elsewhere especially in resettlement units. The aggregation of data on prisoners' needs, to inform prisons' regime planning and co-ordination, was foreshadowed in the Prison Service's 1995 report on sentence planning,[43] though in 1998 it had barely begun.

A note on Prison Rule 81[44]

This rule is relevant to our recommendations that prison staff, including work instructors, trainers and others, should be able to help inmates with their arrangements for release, give them support in resettlement afterwards, and receive news of their progress. Rule 81 states: 'No officer shall, without the knowledge of the governor, communicate with any person whom he knows to be a former prisoner or a relative or friend of a prisoner or former prisoner.' The purpose of the rule is to protect prison staff and prisoners from harm that could occur if an ex-inmate (or inmate) abused a contact or tried to manipulate a relationship. But the rule is not a ban on contacts: it gives governors discretion to permit them. Governors should consider how any relevant sections of their staff (not just seconded probation officers) could help inmates with transition to release and with support following it, and should remind them that they may apply for permission whenever a suitable case occurs. Work instructors and others who may wish to contact employers, give references and so on, should not hesitate in seeking permission to do so.

A WIDER PERSPECTIVE

Our focus has been on prison work. But people are not sentenced to imprisonment in order to work, or because they have been unemployed:[45] they are sentenced because they have been convicted of crime. We will not attempt here a philosophical discussion of the aims of imprisonment. But in order to widen the perspective for examining prison work we will look at the second part of the Prison Service's mission statement: helping prisoners to lead law-abiding lives. How are prisons to do that?

What works

There have been a great variety of 'treatments' for offenders which aim to reduce recidivism, and many studies aiming to evaluate their outcomes. During the last two decades much work has been done to review such studies and synthesise their findings, seeking to draw out common principles which underlie successful treatments, and dispelling en route the pessimistic view of the 1970s that 'nothing works'. Two major reviews, encompassing others, of 'what works' have been carried out by McLaren (1992)[46] and by McGuire and Priestley (1995).[47] Among the principles of effective treatment programmes for offenders which they set out are the following.

- The programme should focus on those needs of the participants (offenders) which have clearly contributed to their offending.
- Preferably, it should use cognitive and behavioural techniques to teach the participants new, non-criminal ways of thinking and behaving.
- It should teach them practical skills to cope with personal and social problems.
- The programme should be 'multi-modal', recognising the range of the participants' problems and using a variety of methods to address them.
- It should match the methods of treatment to participants' abilities and learning styles.
- The content of treatment should match the needs of the participants, and the amount and intensity of treatment should be determined by the level of risk they present.
- Offenders should be involved in making the plan for their treatment, rather than it being imposed on them.
- The staff of the programme should relate to the participants with warmth and empathy, and in ways which encourage pro-social attitudes and behaviour. They should act as advocates for the participants, and link them to other appropriate services.
- Staff should draw on resources from the community, and establish positive links with outside.
- The programme must have integrity. This means, among other things, that it must be based on appropriate theory and be consistently run, by competent staff who stick to the design. It must have adequate resources, and management must not allow it to be weakened or diverted because of other demands.

These principles, plus others cited by McLaren and by McGuire and Priestley, are usually referred to in connection with treatments aimed directly at addressing offending behaviour of one type or another (and not just in prisons). But it is useful here to take them as a perspective from which to view the totality of 'purposeful activities' that prisons try to provide for their inmates: work, vocational training, education, PE, offending behaviour courses, pre-release courses and so on. What does this perspective imply? It implies that new prisoners will be assessed to find out what factors have been salient in their offending, and what things they need to reduce their likelihood of offending again. It implies that the activities and opportunities they are offered in prison will be matched to their individual needs. It implies that they will be encouraged in personal skills and responsibility, to run their lives in non-criminal and satisfying ways. It implies that prison staff who deal with them, in whatever activity, will help them to develop their skills and may involve the outside community in doing so. And it implies that these activities and opportunities will be available consistently, and will not be interrupted or withdrawn for reasons unconnected with the prisoner's behaviour. In short, it implies sentence planning, *and* the provision of those facilities which sentence plans indicate are required.

Sentence planning

Sentence planning in 1996, at least at the research prisons, seemed to have very little to do with the kinds of work to which prisoners were assigned, though sometimes it facilitated their access to training; it was more concerned with the provision of offending behaviour courses, many of which were very short. (See Chapter 2 and pp. 210–11.) By 1997 Prison Service HQ had developed a revised scheme of sentence planning, informed by 'what works' thinking and aiming at an integrated approach.

The revised scheme[48] had two main objectives: first, to prepare the prisoner for safer release; and second, to make the best use of the prisoner's time. It focused on the concept of risk: the risk the prisoner presented of reoffending when released, and of harmful behaviour during sentence to other people or to himself or herself. For a new prisoner the planning process was to begin with an assessment of risk and needs, and this would inform the first decision about security category and allocation to a particular establishment. Thereafter the aim was to manage the sentence in an integrated way, drawing on all the appropriate facilities and influencing all major decisions about the prisoner – assignment to work, education, training, special programmes, transfers to other prisons, temporary release and (for people sentenced to four years or more) release on parole. Staff running activities in which the prisoner took part were expected to contribute. And the Probation Service which would be supervising after release (because the scheme targeted only prisoners who on release would be under supervision – see below) was involved from the outset. The supervising probation officer would supply information, liaise with prison staff, and then, on release, take over the plan and continue work with the ex-prisoner aimed at reducing the risk of reoffending and helping resettlement. One can see how this ambitious framework could accommodate our proposal for employment throughcare.

The need for a holistic approach

Ideally sentence planning, accompanied by adequate provision, would enable all a prisoner's needs related to offending to be addressed in a holistic way. In Chapter 6 we saw that ex-inmates' efforts to get work, which they felt was important for avoiding further crime, were hampered not only by lack of vacancies and inadequate vocational skills but by other personal factors: lack of confidence and coping skills, bewilderment, family worries and so on. People wanted 'willpower'; many felt they had made some use of their time in prison for self-improvement, and some directly expressed a desire for help in overcoming criminal inclinations (p. 179). So a prisoner's sentence plan should address these matters. We would argue that inmates who felt during sentence that their needs for work skills *and* for social skills, confidence and ability to resist offending were being adequately addressed would be much more capable, on release, of participating in legitimate work and of staying out of crime: prisons' efforts on these two fronts would be mutually reinforcing. At this point it is appropriate to take a quick look at the provision in 1997 of offending behaviour courses.

Addressing offending behaviour

In 1996–7 Prison Service HQ set a new 'key performance indicator' for establishments: 'the number of completions by prisoners of programmes accredited as effective in reducing reoffending'. Detailed criteria and procedures for accreditation were developed, based very much on 'what works' principles, and by mid-1997 two kinds of accredited programmes were running in some prisons.[49] These were the sex offender treatment programme (core and booster) and two cognitive skills programmes: 'Reasoning and Rehabilitation' as developed by Ross *et al.* in Canada,[50] and 'Enhanced Thinking Skills' developed within the Prison Service. Accreditation of other programmes, especially on drugs, was under way. The programmes were intensive and designed, in the words of Prison Service HQ, to 'challenge the distorted beliefs which offenders use to justify their offending, make them face up to the harm they cause, and help them to develop the attitudes and skills which make it easier to avoid re-offending'.[51]

One cardinal feature of the accredited programmes was that they were very much longer than the short courses the research prisons were offering inmates in 1996 (see Chapter 2). The sex offender programme had always been substantial, and by 1997 its core course comprised about ninety 2-hour sessions and the booster about thirty. The Reasoning and Rehabilitation programme comprised thirty-six 2-hour sessions and Enhanced Thinking Skills comprised twenty. These two were thus a far cry from the small courses of up to about seven sessions (three to five days) which were typical of many in 1996 and which probation and prison staff had worked hard to establish. One wonders just how effective the small ones could be. 'It's done at a superficial level,' said a probation officer of those at her prison. At another prison the senior probation officer who had done much to develop them implied that all such a course could achieve would be to introduce the topic to interested prisoners and tell them what other resources might be available if they wanted to pursue it further. 'We open the door to the room, let him see the books on the shelves....Just a start-off to identify the problems.'

The accredited courses were available to only a minority of prisoners. Prison Service HQ considered that because of their length they would be appropriate only for people sentenced to more than eighteen months who could be sure of having time to complete the course. Not all such prisoners would be willing or judged suitable to attend: the existing courses were intended mainly for people who had committed violent, sexual or drug-related offences. It was aimed to provide 4,000 places a year, and in 1997 there were approximately 2,500.

Accreditation did not mean that other offending behaviour courses would necessarily be dropped, but one would expect that prison managers with an eye on the performance indicator might feel under pressure to give the accredited programmes priority. Thus again the majority of prisoners, especially people serving shorter sentences, would be likely to miss out.

Limitations and constraints

Sentence plans likewise were available to only a minority of prisoners. The 1997 revised scheme covers nearly all young offenders, but only about one-third of adults: those who after being sentenced have at least six months still to serve in prison.[52] Most adults, whose expected stay is shorter, are not required to have a plan (though they like others are subject to initial risk assessment, security categorisation and allocation). Moreover, even for people who do receive a plan there is no assurance that the needs identified during their assessment will actually be addressed. The pressures of increasing numbers of prisoners, tightened budgets and the overriding emphasis on security severely constrain prison staff's ability to provide the opportunities which sentence plans indicate are needed. Thus the majority of prisoners, even including some who have a sentence plan, are unlikely to be offered the integrated programme of activities which a 'what works' approach might imply they need to help them avoid re-offending. As things are, they are much more likely to go on being assigned to prison jobs in the uncoordinated way we have seen, interspersed perhaps with periods in vocational training, education or other things.

In 1993 the Inspectorate carried out a study of prison regimes[53] which found wide variations, even between prisons of the same type, in their provision of activities for inmates. Looking at the way prisons were scattered throughout the country, and addressing Woolf's concern that prisoners should be accommodated as near to their homes and communities as possible,[54] the Inspectors recommended that the prisons within any one geographical area should operate as a cluster, catering between them for all the different types of prisoners. Governors of prisons in a cluster, said the Inspectors, should work together to develop coherent regimes, and for prisoners with longer sentences who moved between establishments their sentence plan would link their experiences. The 1995 review of sentence planning[55] said that one of the objectives of sentence planning was 'to provide the information base for regime development and service provision, and the consequent strategic management of resources'. From these two proposals it follows that, within any cluster, information from prisoners' initial assessments should be aggregated over time to build up a profile of the population and the needs of its various groups. Managers of these prisons should co-ordinate their programmes so that prisoners moving between them would receive continuity of experience and progression in training, education, work and so on. (We have already alluded to this in regard to employment throughcare on p. 206.)

Although the Service's annual report for 1993–4 referred to intended clusters,[56] in 1996 there was practically no indication that any of the research prisons was co-ordinating its programmes with those of other prisons. In 1997 the sentence planning scheme still covered only a minority of prisoners, and the provision of activities to address even their needs was severely hampered by the pressures we have discussed and to which, to a large extent, each governor could respond in his or her own way. We have already referred (p. 24) to the Chief Inspector's criticism of this absence of planning and co-ordination.

THE IMPORTANCE OF PRISON WORK

From this wider discussion we now return to the topic of work, and argue that its significance has increased. Even if the Prison Service's intentions of 1997 are realised, by no means all prisoners will have a comprehensive sentence plan and not all will participate in an offending behaviour programme. But most adult prisoners will be at work for at least part of their sentence (and even people with very short sentences are likely to spend considerably more hours at work than they would in a small offending behaviour course). Thus it is important that prison work and vocational training should be developed in ways which make the most of their potential for helping prisoners not to reoffend. Such development would be entirely compatible with the Service's 1992 policy (pp. 16–17).

Findings of other studies

Most studies evaluating prison work and vocational training (or related schemes like work release and job placement for prisoners) have used the criterion of recidivism, and their findings have been very mixed. Braithwaite in 1980, after reviewing a large number, concluded as follows:[57]

> Vocational programs can have an effect on recidivism, but often they do not....The fundamental problem of program planning in this area is what Martin Rein has called the problem of discontinuity.[58] A number of component services are required to deal with any cycle of change. In the case of

vocational development the relevant component stages might be recruitment, screening, formal courses of training, on the job training, and job placement. Unless there is a continuous flow through all stages, then the program will have failed....There is at least some hard evidence to show that it is possible for vocational programs to reduce crime. The problem is that so far we have not been very good at using them, and that the people we are trying to change have been through such a long process of disillusionment and alienation that it is difficult for them to see the point, even in a program which offers the most concrete of economic and work satisfaction benefits.

Braithwaite wrote that in 1980, before the development of techniques which enabled more sophisticated research reviews and which led to the formulation of 'what works' principles.[59] But clearly Braithwaite was anticipating some of the points we have discussed in this chapter: the need for continuity and for addressing prisoners' other problems besides lack of vocational skills.

In 1992 McLaren, in her major exposition of 'what works' principles, reviewed studies of vocational programmes (as well as many others). In summing up that review she wrote:[60]

It is clear that work interventions have shown mixed results, and that experimentally rigorous studies which report positive outcomes have been infrequent....There is clearly potential for the further development of work interventions, particularly given their present high profile in correctional planning. Application of some of the suggestions above, and of the principles of effective interventions outlined on pp. 72–84 [here she was referring to 'what works'] could well improve outcomes in this area. It may well be that the failure of vocational interventions to reduce offending on a consistent basis may have less to do with the broad intervention type than with their failure to incorporate what is currently known about effectiveness into design and implementation.

Applying 'what works' to work

In Chapter 6 we assessed the outcome of our research sample's prison work and training primarily in terms of post-release employment rather than the avoidance of reoffending, though the connection between the two was examined. It was found that the follow-up sample's experience of work and training in prison appeared to make very little difference to their chances of obtaining jobs in the first few months after release, though a small number were still hoping to benefit from training. Now the discussion in the present chapter has suggested why the results were so negative: in a nutshell, the work prisoners are given should be relevant to the labour market and to their interests, and their other needs must be addressed as well. Prison work should be part of an integrated programme based on 'what works' principles.

Many of the ideas we have presented for improving prison work and training are in line with 'what works', as follows. Vocational assessment and guidance would involve diagnosing an inmate's strengths and weaknesses in relation to work, and identifying what would be needed in order to pursue a legitimate and satisfying career.[61] Inmates would participate in drawing up their work and training plans. Assigning inmates to suitable work and training (and we here assume these would be available) in accordance with their plans would match treatment to individual abilities and needs. Work instructors, relating to their workers with warmth, empathy and active leadership (as many already do), would encourage pro-social attitudes and behaviour. Instructors would collaborate with other prison staff so that inmates' problems were addressed in 'multi-modal' ways. Instructors could be trained to teach inmates personal coping skills and their application in the workplace. Instructors would be advocates for their workers not only in dealings with other prison staff but in linking them with outside employers and other agencies. Community resources, such as TECs and training schemes, would be drawn in (as can happen now) to help prison inmates and those making the transition to outside work. Finally, 'programme integrity' in regard to prison work and training *must* mean that their provision in prison matches outside labour markets, that they are adequately resourced, and that continuity and consistency of training and work experience are assured.

So realistic (and adequately paid) prison work, and employment throughcare with work instructors having a prominent role, could help released prisoners address several of the difficulties which impeded the research sample's attempts at resettlement. They would have more confidence, personal coping skills, relevant vocational skills and, above all, a sense that their time inside had not been wasted but had been used constructively to prepare for a law-abiding life 'on the out'. None of these things, of course, would alter external circumstances: the state of the job market, wage levels, employers' initial prejudices and so on. But they would help to give ex-prisoners equal opportunities with other workers.

Legge in 1978, drawing on published studies of prison work, argued that because of the nature of imprisonment and the prison system's confusion in defining its objectives, many of the values and practices normal in ordinary work became distorted and inverted in the prison situation.[62] Our comparisons in Chapters 3 and 4 between work in prison and outside suggested that much of this was still true in the early 1990s. But it need not be so: or at least, not nearly so much. If the proposals in this chapter were put into effect prison work could develop into an experience recognised by all concerned as positive, forward-looking and oriented to life outside despite taking place within prison walls. There is room for optimism.

Of course work is not a cure-all. The integrated system of sentence planning to which the Prison Service aspires would encompass many other things too. And it ought eventually to be extended to prisoners with shorter sentences: R100, a senior probation officer at one of the research prisons, pointed out that some of the people sentenced to less than twelve months may be among the most damaged individuals, often in and out of prison and not receiving supervision on release. Employment throughcare would not be a substitute for full sentence planning, but it would help a great many more prisoners, both short- and long-sentence ones, than receive adequate help now.

WOMEN PRISONERS' WORK

Our research did not treat women prisoners' work separately from men's, apart from the description in Chapter 2 of Holloway as one of the six participating prisons. Women were only 8 per cent of the sample of inmates (they form only 4 per cent of the prison population), and there were only five women in our follow-up sample. Resources did not allow us to focus on a larger number of women. In the descriptions of prison work and training women have contributed to the total picture (e.g. the Holloway sewing room, pp. 79, 80) and women are included in our case examples (e.g. R686, p. 110 and R587, p. 167).

Two major studies of women prisoners have recently been carried out by Morris *et al.*[63] and the Prisons Inspectorate.[64] They show that the circumstances, problems and needs of women in prison differ from those of men, some in the frequency with which they occur and some because they apply to women only. Women prisoners are more often in prison for the first time and therefore unfamiliar with the system. They are likely to be held far away from their homes, because there are only sixteen establishments for women (in 1998) and some of them are in remote country areas. At the same time, women in prison have more acute family worries: the majority are mothers of children under 16, and before coming into prison the mothers have been the primary carer and sometimes the only carer. Women need different healthcare from men, and many women who come into prison have severe medical problems. Many have been abused physically, sexually or psychologically; many seriously misuse drugs; many have attempted suicide or otherwise harmed themselves.

These features and others described in the two studies cited mean that, while both men and women prisoners should be treated as individuals and their problems addressed, women's needs require more attention from specialists and more sensitivity and skill from all staff who deal with them. (And the Inspectorate points out that caring for women is more demanding and stressful for prison staff than caring for men.) Certainly our impression at Holloway in early 1993 was that staff were trying hard to give prisoners individual consideration and to offer a wide range of activities and treatments.

What kinds of work and vocational training should be provided in women's prisons? The Inspectorate found that 70 per cent of the women they interviewed said they had not been employed before their imprisonment. When asked what would help them to avoid offending in future the majority felt they were unlikely to do that anyway, but the commonest answer from those who suggested anything was 'a job', closely followed by 'a home'. Prison work and training for women should be provided on the basis of equal opportunities: that is to say, women who hope for employment on release should, like men, be helped while in prison to acquire or maintain skills which suit their abilities and interests and give them good prospects in the labour market. At the same time, as was exemplified by several of our Holloway interviewees, not all want full-time employment, or not yet; some want to go out to work part-time and some want to stay as homemakers, at least while their children are young.

We asked male and female staff at Holloway for their opinions. Most thought women prisoners should be allowed to do the same jobs as men, except perhaps for very heavy ones, and should be encouraged to work for their living. A somewhat different view was expressed by R098, a male manager, who thought that women should be taught social and domestic skills as well as thinking about jobs.

> I don't want to say to them, 'You're only good for sewing, cleaning, cooking and housework.' But I do want to say to them, 'You really need to know about this, because there is going to be some idle bloke who's going to expect you to do that, and that's going to be your contribution towards the relationship maybe.'

He also thought women should be trained in making good relationships with men. 'These are things that women need to know, how to handle men.'

Holloway in 1993 provided a variety of jobs, by no means all of them domestic, though as at other prisons the majority of inmate workers were engaged in domestic and similar tasks (including sewing and cooking). Kinds of work and training at Holloway are listed on pp. 32–3 and 43, although in 1993 some of the courses were suspended and later there were worse problems. Morris *et al.*, studying three women's prisons (of which Holloway was not one) in 1993–4,[65] found that inmates' assignment to work was more concerned with occupying them, teaching them 'work habits' and servicing the prison than with teaching them marketable skills. Up to a point this echoes our findings in pp. 123–5. On the other hand, we may note the reported enthusiasm with which women inmates at Highpoint North in late 1996 took up the three construction industry training courses formerly offered to men (p. 42).

Changes in work in the outside world (pp. 185–6) may give female ex-prisoners better opportunities for jobs than male ones if they have the right skills. Office and business occupations, work in the leisure industry and personal services may offer good prospects to some. Women leaving prison and wanting jobs may need extra help with matters like budgeting and access to childcare. Everything we have said in this chapter about prisoners' employability – paying heed to labour markets, offering relevant work and NVQs, ensuring continuity, involving outsiders, teaching coping skills, addressing other personal problems – applies equally to women.

The principles are the same: find out what prisoners as individuals need, and offer it. But the practice may be more difficult in regard to women because they have some special problems, and because the female prisons are so scattered. Morris *et al.* found serious mismatches between women's needs and the services prison staff supplied.[66] The Inspectorate, while citing examples of excellent practice, found that there were many gaps, sentence planning was very patchy, and there was little co-ordination between the women's prisons though some were trying to arrange it. The Inspectorate pointed out the dilemma between, on the one hand, the need for continuity in training, education and treatment programmes as women prisoners were moved about, and on the other hand the need for them to be close to their homes. They recommended (among many other things) that 'multi-purpose variable security sites' should be developed; that small prison buildings in urban centres to accommodate women with short sentences should be considered; that a thorough analysis should be made of the needs of the female prison population, leading to national policies; and above all that a Director of Women's Prisons should be appointed to oversee and co-ordinate the management of the female establishments.[67]

CONCLUSION

Work, for most people, is a specially significant part of adult life. For the fortunate, work supplies not only income but personal satisfaction through the use of skills, a sense of achievement, companionship and social identity. And for ex-prisoners it can be a prophylactic against crime. Braithwaite has said, 'The most important potential value of prison industry is in helping prisoners to believe that legitimate work can be more rewarding than illegitimate work.'[68]

This last chapter has reviewed work-related ways in which prisons, *if* they were given the resources and the right conditions in which to operate, could help inmates to improve their lives. The help must be offered, not imposed. N. Morris has written of 'facilitated change, not coerced cure',[69] and Coyle has observed that attempting to force rehabilitation on people is both arrogant and ineffective.[70] Some prisoners, for a variety of reasons, will not want to change their lifestyles, and some may not be able to. But others do want to, and some prison staff would like to help them do so. We have shown that the Prison Service has the potential to make prisoners' experiences of work and training a substantial contribution towards their resettlement as law-abiding citizens. By setting the primary purpose of prison work as the preparation of inmates for work on release; by matching prison jobs to outside labour markets; by providing better access to more skilled training; by giving inmates more scope for responsibility; by engaging work instructors with other staff, prisoners and outsiders in a system of employment throughcare which would link inmates' experiences inside with outside: by doing all these things, the Prison Service could, in time, accomplish much.

However, prisons are not just about prisoners' work. They are about keeping people, some of them difficult and dangerous, in custody; about order, safety, and coping with violence and drugs; about medical services, education and facilities for visits; and about providing decent conditions for staff and prisoners while all these things, and many others, are carried on. Prisons are complex institutions, difficult to manage and extremely expensive. They are one of society's resources that should be used as sparingly as possible.

We have said little or nothing about many aspects of life for prisoners: the forced confinement, the separation from loved ones, frustration, boredom, drugs, bullying; health problems; recreational activities; or the inmate counter-culture except in so far as prisoners try to link it with their prison jobs. Prison is an unnatural environment, hugely disruptive of normal life no matter how much staff try to ameliorate its impact. King and McDermott say, 'Imprisonment can be seen as a massive process of social de-skilling,'[71] and one of the aims stated by the Prison Service for its revised system of sentence planning is 'within the context of lawful custody, to minimise the destructive effects of imprisonment'.[72] Therefore a prison sentence should be the punishment of very last resort. Nevertheless once a person has come into prison, some worthwhile experiences may be possible.

But although the Woolf Report brought hope, new policies and strenuous efforts for change, it seems that in the last few years the 'ever-deepening crisis' of which King and McDermott wrote in 1989[73] has returned, and that the Prison Service is once again fighting for survival. The number of prisoners continues to soar, overcrowding has increased despite more prison building, and budgets have been cut. In September 1996 when the prison population was 52,000, Richard Tilt, the Service's Director General, said:

> There is a need for very serious public debate. The Prison Service would like to do constructive things but this is jeopardised by a very fast rising population and budget reductions that do not seem to be sensibly achievable.[74]

The following month the Chief Inspector wrote:

> The most severe problems facing the Prison Service are shortage of money, and the danger signs that overcrowding, and the associated evil of inactivity, are doing real damage to all the progress that has been made over the past 4–5 years.[75]

Twelve months later the population had increased by another 6,000. In July 1997 the new Home Secretary (Jack Straw) reported to Parliament[76] on an audit he had requested of Prison Service resources and of the demands on it. The main findings included the following:

* In the three months following the general election on 1 May the prison population rose by the equivalent of the total capacity of four average-sized prisons, and far exceeded previous projections.
* The building programme approved by the previous government was already being outstripped by the rise in population.

- The number of prisoners held two to a cell designed for one had increased by 50 per cent since 1992.
- The level of purposeful activity for prisoners had dropped.
- There was a growing risk of prisons having to close because of inadequate maintenance.

The Home Secretary announced the allocation of £43 million extra over two years to provide more accommodation for prisoners. Yet in October 1997 the Chief Inspector, after publishing a damning report on conditions in Lincoln Prison, was recommending an urgent examination of the entire prison system, and saying, 'I must voice my concern that, to continue to cut resources while the prison population climbs inexorably higher, is in danger of becoming a process of *reductio ad absurdum* [reducing it to a farce]'.[77]

What is the explanation for these vast numbers of prisoners? In the writer's view, it lies in public attitudes to imprisonment and the pressure of public opinion on politicians and the courts. Surveys show that since the early 1990s public attitudes towards the sentencing of offenders have become harsher and support for the use of imprisonment has increased.[78] The Crime (Sentences) Act 1997, which changed the law on prison sentences and early release in ways likely to increase the population still further, was brought in by the last Conservative government (despite vigorous criticism from experts) and has been partially implemented by its Labour successor.[79] In July 1997 the Lord Chief Justice spoke of 'the present vengeful mood of the public' and said he had no doubt that the steep rise in the prison population was related to the pressure of public opinion on the courts. He called for a Royal Commission on crime and punishment.[80]

So the public wants a lot of people to be put in prison. But most of the time it does not show much interest in what happens to them inside. When there are escapes, when the Director General is sacked, or when disturbing practices like the shackling of hospital patients come to light the general public takes notice of the Prison Service, but otherwise it has little curiosity about the daily lives of most prisoners and little appreciation of the positive work the Service is trying to do. Of course the voluntary bodies, the pressure groups and the professional associations take a great deal of interest,[81] but among ordinary members of the public the usual attitude seems to be 'out of sight, out of mind'.

Far fewer people should be sent to prison: there are other ways in which the courts could deal with many of the offenders who now receive short sentences. If fewer people were in prison, prison staff would be able to give more attention to those who remained. Sentence planning could become a reality, and could extend to cover more inmates than it does at present. Staff would have the time and space to offer prisoners more individual care and consistent opportunities for personal development in the ways we describe; and gradually even inmates formerly cynical might become attracted by what was on offer. Managers would have the time and energy to develop and co-ordinate their programmes. To reorganise prison work and training in the ways proposed in this book would be expensive and would take time. But it would be a far better use of public money than building more and more prisons to become human warehouses where the only experiences are negative ones.

Public support is needed in other ways too. There should be more money, through TECs or other agencies, for worthwhile training and employment schemes linked to prisoners' work, and funded on a long-term basis so that the rug is not pulled from under them just as they are beginning to yield results. More employers are needed who are willing to engage with prisons and, with due safeguards, to offer jobs to ex-offenders trying to rebuild their lives.[82] Employers could see this as a contribution to crime prevention, and the Prison Service should resist attempts by companies and trade unions to invoke the old argument of lesser eligibility.[83] As Braithwaite has pointed out,[84] providing good jobs for ex-prisoners does more to reduce crime than providing the same good jobs for non-offenders.

The causes of crime are complex and interwoven, and they operate at both a personal and a structural level. Chapter 6 considered how participation in work, interacting with other personal factors, can influence ex-prisoners' likelihood of reoffending. The focus of this book has not been on structural factors affecting the crime rate, but it can barely be doubted that one of them is unemployment. (For recent reviews of the evidence, see Dickinson and Wells.)[85, 86] The Labour government is aiming at full employment for the twenty-first century.[87] The Prison Service, by reshaping work and training and by other measures, could assist ex-prisoners to share in that economy equally with other citizens, thus helping to ensure that the protection from crime which imprisonment gives the public can continue after the prisoner's release. But the Service cannot do it without the public's co-operation.

The Prison Service battling to do constructive things, and ex-prisoners struggling to rebuild their lives, need the support of an informed public. Are we – the voters, the taxpayers – willing to change our attitudes, and give them that support?

Appendix 1

Work instructors' aims

Thirty-one work instructors interviewed were asked: 'In your work with inmates, how much emphasis do you give to each of the following?' and offered a list of nine items, each to be rated on a five-point scale ranging from one point for 'not at all important' to five points for 'very important'. The mean ratings for each item, across all respondents, were then ranked, with the results shown in Table A1.1.

Table A1.1 shows that: (1) on average the instructors thought all nine aims were important (all nine received a mean rating above 3.00, the mid-point of the scale); (2) they had clear priorities, as shown by the order of the table, with 'producing high-quality goods and services' coming top and 'keeping management happy' coming bottom; (3) second-to-lowest priority was given to training inmates in vocational skills; (4) vocational training was the aim about whose importance they most disagreed (as is shown by its having the highest standard deviation). Twenty-four of the raters were PSIF work instructors and the other seven were not. By and large the ratings given by these two sub-groups were very similar.

Table A1.1 Work instructors' aims: ratings by thirty-one work instructors of the importance (on a scale of 1–5) of nine aims of their work with inmates

Aim	Mean rating	s.d.
Producing high-quality goods/services	4.71	0.46
Training inmates in good work habits	4.65	0.61
Producing goods/services on time	4.55	0.77
Promoting good working relations between inmates and/or between inmates and staff	4.54	0.58
Keeping inmates busy	4.48	0.68
Teaching inmates to respect good honest work	4.26	0.82
Keeping inmates happy	3.90	0.82
Training inmates in vocational skills	3.72	1.25
Keeping management happy	3.59	0.91

Appendix 2

Perceptions by prison staff and prisoners of the aims and purposes of prison work

At the end of the research interview with each prison staff member, and each inmate (in the main sample) who had had experience of prison work, the respondent was invited to complete some forms designed to explore his or her perceptions of the aims and purposes of prison work from several points of view.

Ninety-seven staff were given three forms with explanations, asking in effect:

1   Why do you think the Prison Service provides work for inmates, as the system is at present?
2   What, in your opinion, would be good reasons for providing work for inmates?
3   What do you think are inmates' reasons for working in prison?

One hundred and thirty-four inmates were given two forms with explanations, asking in effect:

1   Why do you think the prison authorities provide work for inmates in prison, and expect them to do it?
2   What are your own reasons for working in prison?

Each form offered a list of between thirteen and sixteen possible reasons for prison work. These had been derived from considering history (see p. 12), from general knowledge, and from suggestions made by staff and prisoners during a pilot study. Some of the reasons were common to all five lists, some to fewer, and some appeared just once. Some expressed similar themes in different words. The interviewee completing the form was asked to indicate the importance of each reason on a four-point scale (ranging from 'very' to 'not at all'). The tables in this appendix present the results in terms of the percentage of respondents who rated any reason as very or quite important, and the reasons are listed in the rank order defined by that set of responses (though the order was different on the original forms).

The 97 staff comprised 34 work instructors, 11 tutors in charge of vocational training courses and 52 other staff of all grades. (The number rating any one item varied slightly, the minimum numbers being 28 work instructors, 9 trainers and 44 other staff.) The 134 inmates comprised 106 serving sentences of between one and ten years who were within three months of release, and 28 others who were near the middle of a sentence of between four and ten years. (The number rating any one item varied slightly, the minimum numbers being 100 inmates near release and 23 mid-term.)

Table A2.1 shows what the staff think are the Prison Service's reasons for providing prisoners with work.

Looking at staff perceptions of official reasons, we see that this group of staff think the reasons for providing prison work that are most important to Prison Service HQ are giving inmates time out of cell (88 per cent) and keeping them busy (86 per cent). Almost equally important are training in skills (80 per cent) and work habits (79 per cent) which could help them get a job after release. Keeping the prison running is equally important (78 per cent), but a frankly commercial reason – offsetting the costs of the system – is somewhat less so (60 per cent). Enabling inmates to earn pocket money is rated at 61 per cent. Between 59 per cent and 71 per cent think work is provided for its value for inmates' characters – inculcating the work ethic, encouraging inmates to contribute to society and the prison community life, 'building character'. Fewer than half take the cynical view that the Prison Service just goes on providing work for inmates because it has always done so, though it is interesting that 44

Table A2.1 Staff perceptions of official reasons for providing inmates with work in prison

Reason	% rating reason as very important or fairly important to Prison Service HQ
To give inmates time out of cell, something to do	88
To keep them busy, stop them causing trouble	86
To give them skills which could help them get a job after release	80
To train them in work habits which could help them get a job after release	79
To help keep the prison running	78
To inculcate the work ethic, encourage inmates to respect legitimate work	71
Prisoners, like other people, ought to work as a contribution to society	70
Because work builds character	62
To give them the opportunity to earn money	61
As a commercial enterprise, to offset the costs of the prison system	60
To encourage them to contribute to the community life of the prison	59
They've always done it, so they just go on	44
To provide or maintain jobs for the staff	20
To punish inmates, because prison work is punishment	6

per cent say that. Only 20 per cent think prison work is provided to make or maintain jobs for staff, and only 6 per cent think it is provided as punishment.

Incidentally, while completing this form several staff suggested a further reason: that Prison Service HQ wanted to persuade public opinion that prisoners were kept usefully occupied. (This was not included in our analyses.)

Analyses not shown here compared the three sub-groups of staff – work instructors, trainers and others – on their ratings of the importance of these reasons to Prison Service HQ. The biggest difference was for 'contributing to the community life of the prison', rated as important by 67 per cent of the work instructors, 89 per cent of the trainers and only 48 per cent of the others. But otherwise there was no great divergence between the three sub-groups. So for the staff sample as a whole, we could say the Prison Service is perceived as providing work for inmates primarily for the purpose of managing the prison on a day-to-day basis – keeping inmates occupied and the prison ticking over; but also, nearly as important is the aim of improving inmates' chances of future employment.

Table A2.2 shows the staff's own views on what would be good reasons to provide prisoners with work.

Here we see that the aims of giving inmates work habits and skills for future employment are ranked highest (at 95 per cent and 94 per cent), closely followed by giving inmates time out of cell (92 per cent) and then by inculcating the work ethic (87 per cent). Enabling inmates to earn pocket money is also rated highly

Table A2.2 Staff views of what would be good reasons for providing inmates with work in prison

Reason	% rating reason as very good or fairly good
To train inmates in work habits which could help them get a job after release	95
To give them skills which could help them get a job after release	94
To give them time out of cell, something to do	92
To inculcate the work ethic, encourage inmates to respect legitimate work	87
To give them the opportunity to earn money	84
To encourage them to contribute to the community life of the prison	79
To keep them busy, stop them causing trouble	78
Because work builds character	76
Prisoners, like other people, ought to work as a contribution to society	72
To provide positive activity for its own sake	72
To help keep the prison running	62
As a commercial enterprise, to offset the costs of the prison system	53
To provide or maintain jobs for the staff	16
To punish inmates, because prison work is punishment	2

(84 per cent). The other 'character' reasons – contributing to society and the prison community, 'building character' – are rated as important by 72–9 per cent. All the reasons so far mentioned can be seen as having to do with treating inmates as people, rather than with the maintenance of the system (though 'time out of cell' can be seen both ways). If at this point we compare these ratings with what the same items received in Table A2.1, we see that staff rate all the 'people' items more highly as good reasons for inmates to work than they do as perceived reasons for official practice. By contrast, reasons to do with managing the system – keeping inmates busy, keeping the prison running, offsetting costs – are all rated lower as good reasons than as perceived reasons for practice. So although for any one reason the divergence between Tables A2.1 and A2.2 is not large (the biggest, in terms of percentage points, being for 'opportunity to earn money', where the implication is that staff would be more generous than HQ), overall there is a distinct difference in emphasis between the staff's perceptions of official reasons and their views on what would be good ones.

Again there was no great divergence in 'good reasons' between the three sub-groups of staff, the most notable being for 'keeping inmates busy', rated as important by 91 per cent of work instructors, 58 per cent of trainers and 75 per cent of other staff. 'Jobs for staff' – perhaps understandably – appealed more to work instructors (23 per cent) and trainers (25 per cent) than to others (9 per cent). Work as punishment was again dismissed as a reason by nearly all.

Table A2.3 shows inmates' own reasons for working.

This sample of prisoners give their own most important reason for working as 'to get through my sentence without trouble, as soon as possible' (92 per cent).

Table A2.3 Inmates' reasons for working in prison, as stated by themselves

Reason	% rating reason as very important or fairly important
To get through my sentence without trouble, as soon as possible	92
Something to do, to pass the time	84
Opportunity to get out of cell	81
To get a little bit of money	73
Interesting activity, helps to take my mind off prison	69
Opportunity to mix with other people, chat	60
To work off excess mental energy	59
I feel I ought to work, like other people in society	58
To comply with prison regulations	54
Learning or using work skills which might help me to get a job after release	52
Some prison jobs have good perks	47
To contribute to the community life of the prison	46
Getting work habits which might help me to get a job after release	45
To get a good parole report	42
I only work because the authorities make me	27
Working makes me feel less guilty about my crime	10

Next come two rather similar reasons: doing something to pass the time (84 per cent) and getting out of one's cell (81 per cent). Getting pocket money comes a little lower at 73 per cent. Next come reasons that are somewhat more positive: work as interesting activity, for social contact, for using mental energy, and the feeling that one ought to work (58–69 per cent). But working in prison as positive preparation for future employment, by learning skills and work habits, is endorsed by only about half the sample (skills 52 per cent, habits 45 per cent). The perks of prison jobs are an important reason to 47 per cent, and it may be that the 46 per cent who endorsed 'contributing to the community life of the prison' were thinking along the same lines. (We did not ask those inmates what they meant, but see R601, quoted on p. 120.) As to compulsion as a reason for working, three of the items refer to it: 'I only work because the authorities make me' (27 per cent), 'to comply with prison regulations' (54 per cent), and 'to get through my sentence without trouble' (92 per cent). The divergence in these three ratings suggests that overall, while inmates are aware of compulsion (and resent it: see R572, p. 121) they do not perceive it as an overwhelming reason for working. Forty-two per cent endorse the hope of parole as a reason (see below). Only 10 per cent say they work to relieve guilt.

A similar analysis compared the two sub-groups of inmates – 106 near release and 28 who were near the middle of a sentence of at least four years. On some reasons their ratings were fairly similar, but there were also some differences which suggested that the mid-sentence inmates saw their prison work in a more positive light than the near-release ones. More of them saw work as providing something interesting to think about (89 per cent compared with 63 per cent), and as using up mental energy (81 per cent compared with 54 per cent), more of them worked in order to comply with regulations (73 per cent compared with 54 per cent) and to contribute to the community life of the prison (65 per cent compared with 42 per cent). And more of them (71 per cent compared with 47 per cent) worked in the hope of getting skills useful for release.

This apparent difference in attitude between the two sub-groups cannot be explained by any differences in the kinds of work they were doing at the time of their interview: both were doing much the same range of kinds of work. But possible explanations are: (1) that many of the mid-sentence inmates, all of whom were serving at least four years, might have experienced a greater variety of prison work; (2) that because their release was further away they had more incentive than those near release to put up with their current situation and make the best of it; and (3) the majority of them were at either Maidstone or Holloway, prisons which allowed inmates a fairly free choice of occupation. As for parole, although all the mid-sentence inmates would (in theory) have been eligible for it at some stage, the proportion seeing work as increasing their chances was not much greater than among those near release (48 per cent compared with 41 per cent).

Table A2.4 shows staff perceptions of inmates' reasons for working in prison.

A comparison of Tables A2.4 and A2.3 suggests that (measured against inmates' statements to researchers) some of the staff's perceptions of inmates'

Table A2.4 Staff perceptions of inmates' reasons for working in prison

Reason	% of staff rating reason as very important or fairly important to inmates
To get a little bit of money	94
Something to do, to pass the time	92
Opportunity to get out of cell	92
To get through their sentence without trouble, as soon as they can	87
Opportunity to mix with other people, chat	87
Interesting activity, takes their minds off prison	79
Illegitimate perks of some prison jobs	77
To get a good parole report	75
They expect to work	56
Learning or using work skills which might help them to get a job after release	54
They only work because they are made to	51
Getting work habits which might help them to get a job after release	43
To contribute to the community life of the prison	17
To feel they are making a positive contribution to society	13
To relieve feelings of guilt	8

reasons for working are accurate and some are not. There is broad agreement on the importance of work for helping inmates get through their sentence (and pass the time and get out of cell). But staff think that inmates are more motivated by money than the inmates say they are (94 per cent compared with 73 per cent); in fact staff rank this reason highest. Staff also think that inmates are more motivated by the opportunity to socialise (87 per cent compared with 60 per cent), by perks (77 per cent compared with 47 per cent), by the hope of parole (75 per cent compared with 42 per cent), and that they need more compulsion to make them work (51 per cent compared with 27 per cent). Staff give inmates little credit for wanting to contribute to society (13 per cent) or to the community life of the prison (17 per cent), but it may be noted that the proportion of staff who think that inmates expect to work (56 per cent) is much the same as that of inmates who feel they ought to work (58 per cent). In short, while agreeing that inmates work in order to get through their sentence, staff are rather negative in some of their perceptions of inmates' other motives for working. However, staff are accurate in thinking that getting skills and work habits motivate only about half the inmates, as they are in believing that guilt plays a very small part.

Finally, Table A2.5 shows inmates' perceptions of the Prison Service's reasons for providing them with work.

The inmates are most inclined to perceive the authorities' reasons for prison work as being to keep inmates busy (80 per cent), to help keep the prison running (73 per cent) and to give them time out of cell (70 per cent). These three reasons have to do with managing the prison on a day-to-day basis. The next reason, the idea (attributed to the authorities) that prisoners ought to work (65 per cent), can

Table A2.5 Inmates' perceptions of official reasons for providing them with work in prison

Reason	% rating reason as very important or fairly important to the authorities
To keep inmates busy, stop them causing trouble	80
To help keep the prison running	73
To give inmates time out of cell, something to do	70
They think prisoners, like other people in society, ought to work	65
To make money for the prison	56
To use inmates as cheap labour	56
So that they know where the prisoners are	56
To train them in work habits which could help them to get a job after release	55
To encourage them to respect legitimate work	53
To give them skills which could help them to get a job after release	46
To make jobs for the staff	38
They think work builds character	38
To punish inmates, because prison work is punishment	29

be seen as part of the management theme too, especially as the other 'character' reasons – respect for legitimate work (53 per cent) and 'work builds character' (38 per cent) are placed lower. 'So that they know where the prisoners are' can be seen as management too, though it rates only 56 per cent. The ideas that the authorities use inmates' work to make money for the prison, or to exploit their labour, are endorsed by 56 per cent. Around half the inmates credit the authorities with providing work in order to give them skills (46 per cent) or habits (55 per cent) to help them with a job after release; this is much the same weight as inmates themselves put on these items as reasons for working. Items implying cynicism ('jobs for the staff') or antagonism ('prison work is punishment') come lowest on the inmates' list, though substantial minorities (38 per cent, 29 per cent) endorse them.

The two sub-groups of inmates (near-release and mid-term) had very similar patterns of responses. The biggest differences were that the mid-term inmates gave more emphasis than those near release to keeping the prison running (89 per cent compared with 69 per cent) and to making jobs for the staff (56 per cent compared with 34 per cent).

Comparing Tables A2.5 and A2.1, we see that inmates and staff show a fair amount of agreement in some of their perceptions of the official purposes of prison work: managing inmates (keeping them busy, and giving them time out of cell though staff rate that highest); and running the prison system, both in just keeping it going and in trying to use prison work as a commercial enterprise. But staff give the Prison Service more credit than inmates do for attempting to improve prisoners' characters and instil the work ethic, while on the aims of giving inmates useful skills and work habits inmates are much more sceptical than the staff. And while very few staff believe prison work is provided as punishment, over a quarter of the inmates feel it is.

An important final comment is as follows. Tables A2.1 and A2.2 together show that the great majority of reasons listed (all but 'they've always done it', 'jobs for staff' and 'punishment') are rated as important, whether as official reasons or as good ones, by over half the staff raters. These reasons express a wide range of possible purposes of prison work, and one interpretation could be simply that prison staff see prisoners' work as a multi-purpose activity. But the reasons are hardly all in the same direction, and indeed it could be argued that some are at odds with one another. For example, merely giving inmates 'something to do' is not the same as 'building their characters' or encouraging them to contribute to the community life of the prison; and training them in work skills for release may be incompatible with running workshops as a commercial enterprise to offset the costs of the system. These divergences suggest a second interpretation: that prison staff are confused about what the main purpose of prison work really is or ought to be. Similarly, Table A2.5 shows that all but the last four of the reasons listed there are rated by over half the inmate raters as important reasons to the authorities. These also are a wide range of different reasons, which could suggest either that the inmate raters perceive the authorities to be confused or that they themselves are confused as to the authorities' reasons for requiring prisoners to work.

Appendix 3

Statistical analyses of the follow-up sample

The aim of these analyses was to see whether the experience of prison work and training affected people's chances of getting work after release, taking into account their pre-prison work history. Three types of variable were used:

The dependent variable

The dependent variable, representing the chance of getting work after release, was taken as the person's employment status at the date of the follow-up interview, with the cases divided into three groups derived from the data summarised on pp. 159–60:

- Working or about to (n=22): the twenty people regarded as working, plus the two who had a firm job ready to start two days later.
- Unemployed, wants work (n=54): all but two of those who were then without a job but still wanted one.
- Unemployed, does not want work (n=10): those who were not then looking for work, for whatever reason.

The pensioner and the man too ill to work were omitted from analysis, so the maximum number of cases available was eighty-six.

The independent variable

The independent variable, experience of prison work and training (during the last sentence), was measured in three ways, derived from the data on pp. 140–1 on the amount of training people had received. These three ways were:

- Daytime prison occupation: whether this had been work only (n=47), education or training only (n=2), or work plus education or training (n=37).
- Acquisition of vocational skill: whether the person had started to learn any vocational skill (n=44) or not (n=42).
- Acquisition of vocational qualification: those who began a skill and received any kind of certificate, full or partial (n=19), those who began a skill but

received nothing (n=20), and those who did not begin a skill (n=42). (Data was missing in five cases.)

The control variable

The control variable, work history before the last sentence, was measured in two ways:

- Whether during the twelve months before coming to prison the person had been mainly employed (n=30), mainly unemployed (n=43), or in some other state (n=11). For some analyses the 'unemployed' and 'other' groups were combined. Two cases were omitted because of missing data.
- The person's level of pre-sentence occupational skill (as judged by the researchers) in three categories: fully skilled (tradesperson, management or professional) (n=30), semi-skilled (n=37), unskilled (n=19).

Analyses

Six analyses linking these three variables were carried out by three-way tables which are not shown here. But to set the scene for reporting their results, Tables A3.1 and A3.2 show the strong relationship between pre-prison work history and post-prison employment.

Table A3.1 shows that people who had been mainly in employment during the year before sentence (36 per cent of the total) were much more likely than others to be in work at follow-up: 50 per cent of these were, as opposed to only 13 per cent of all the rest. Those who had been unemployed before sentence included nearly all the people who at follow-up were not looking for work. But it is worth noting that the great majority of the formerly unemployed and the 'other' group who were still unemployed at follow-up wanted to work.

Table A3.2 shows a clear trend: as might have been expected, the more skill

Table A3.1 Eighty-four ex-prisoners: employment status at follow-up by pre-sentence employment record

	Employment status at follow-up							
	Working, or about to		Unemployed, wants work		Unemployed, does not want work		Total	
	n	%	n	%	n	%	n	%
During 12 months before sentence, R was mainly								
Employed	15	50	14	47	1	3	30	100
Unemployed, other	7	13	39	72	8	15	54	100
Total	22	26	53	63	9	11	84	100

Note: chi-square = 14.15, df = 2, P<0.001.

Table A3.2 Eighty-six ex-prisoners: employment status at follow-up by pre-sentence occupational skill

	Employment status at follow-up							
	Working, or about to		Unemployed, wants work		Unemployed, does not want work		Total	
	n	%	n	%	n	%	n	%
Pre-sentence occupational skill								
Skilled trade or higher	12	40	15	50	3	10	30	100
Semi-skilled	8	22	27	73	2	5	37	100
Unskilled	2	11	12	63	5	26	19	100
Total	22	25	54	63	10	12	86	100

Note: If the two 'unemployed' categories are combined to make a 3 x 2 table, chi-square for linear-by-linear association = 5.63, df = 1, P = 0.018.

people had before sentence the more likely they were to be in a job at follow-up. Forty per cent of the fully skilled were working, compared with 22 per cent of the semi-skilled and 11 per cent of the unskilled. But it may be noted that even among the fully skilled 50 per cent were out of a job and wanted one, and the proportions of jobseekers were higher among those with less skill. The few who were not looking for work were scattered through the three skill groups.

The six analyses and their results were as follows.

1 Employment status by daytime prison occupation, allowing for whether employed in year before sentence   No relationship. For people who had been employed the year before sentence the chance of being in work at follow-up was about 50 per cent no matter what their daytime occupation in prison had been. For people unemployed (or in some other state) the year before sentence, doing prison education or training instead of prison work, or adding education or training to prison work, made no difference to their 13 per cent chance of being in work at follow-up. The proportions in work, wanting work, and not wanting work remained much the same as those shown in Table A3.1 (allowing for tiny frequencies in some cells).

2 Employment status by daytime prison occupation, allowing for degree of pre-sentence occupational skill   No relationship. Daytime occupation in prison made no difference to the chances of being in work at follow-up, which remained practically the same as those shown in Table A3.2. In particular, adding education or training to prison work did not improve the employment chances of the unskilled or the semi-skilled.

This lack of relationship between employment status at follow-up and daytime prison occupation suggests either that prison training had no effect on subsequent job prospects, or that 'daytime prison occupation' was a bad measure of prison training. So we now turn to the other two measures of training.

3 Employment status by acquisition of vocational skill, allowing for whether employed in year before sentence   No relationship. People who had begun to learn a vocational skill in prison were not more likely to be in work at follow-up than people who had not begun a skill: what affected their chances was whether they had been employed in the year before sentence, as shown in Table A3.1.

4 Employment status by acquisition of vocational skill, allowing for degree of pre-sentence occupational skill   No relationship. People with no previous occupational skill, or who were only semi-skilled before sentence, did not have their chances of work at follow-up increased by having begun to learn a vocational skill in prison; nor did those with good skills before sentence. Again Table A3.2 tells the whole story.

5 Employment status by acquisition of vocational qualification, allowing for whether employed in year before sentence   No statistically significant relationship. This analysis, even more than analyses 1–4, was limited by tiny cell frequencies. The most notice-able difference was that none of the people who got a certificate were among the small group who at follow-up were unemployed and not looking for work; if this were a reliable finding it would suggest that getting a certificate might be linked with motivation. But all the differences in the table were too small, in too small samples, to be statistically reliable.

6 Employment status by acquisition of vocational qualification, allowing for degree of pre-sentence occupational skill   No statistically significant relationship. Results as for analysis 5.

Altogether, these six analyses imply that, statistically, vocational training in prison had no effect on people's chances of getting work after release: what mattered was whether they had been employed before going to prison, and the level of occupational skill they had had then.

Notes and references

1 INTRODUCTION

1 H. Woolf and S. Tumim, *Prison Disturbances April 1990: Report of an Inquiry*, Cm 1456, London, HMSO, 1991 (hereafter referred to as the Woolf Report).
2 The chief sources for this history are as follows: C. Harding, B. Hines, R. Ireland and P. Rawlings, *Imprisonment in England and Wales: A Concise History*, London, Croom Helm, 1985, especially chapters 5 and 6; M. Ignatieff, *A Just Measure of Pain: The Penitentiary in the Industrial Revolution 1750–1850*, London, Macmillan, 1978, especially chapters 3, 4 and 7; HM Commissioners of Prisons/Prison Department/Prison Service, *Annual Reports*, London, HMSO (hereafter referred to as the Annual Reports).
   Other sources, and references for specific points, are cited separately.
3 Ignatieff, *A Just Measure of Pain*, pp. 3–7.
4 E. Ruggles-Brise, *The English Prison System*, London, Macmillan, 1921, pp. 134–5.
5 Departmental Committee on Prisons (the Gladstone Committee), *Report* and *Minutes of Evidence*, C7702, London, HMSO, 1895. Pay is mentioned in minute no. 226.
6 Gladstone Committee, *Report* and *Minutes of Evidence*.
7 *Annual Report 1906–07*, p. 30.
8 *Annual Report 1907–08*, p. 44.
9 Departmental Committee on the Employment of Prisoners, *Report Part 1: Employment of Prisoners*, Cmd 4462, London, HMSO, 1933.
10 Home Office, *Prisons and Borstals*, London, HMSO, 1945, p. 10.
11 *Prison Rules 1949*, SI 1949/1073.
12 *Annual Report 1955*, p. 20.
13 L.W. Fox, *The English Prison and Borstal Systems*, London, Routledge and Kegan Paul, 1952, p. 179. The quotation is from M. Grunhut, *Penal Reform*, Oxford, Oxford University Press, 1948, p. 20.
14 All references here are to material in the first report: Home Office and Scottish Home Department, *Work for Prisoners: Report of the Advisory Council on the Employment of Prisoners*, London, HMSO, 1961.
15 Advisory Council on the Penal System, *The Regime for Long-Term Prisoners in Conditions of Maximum Security* (the Radzinowicz Report), London, HMSO, 1968, p. 40.
16 *Prison Rules 1964*, SI 1964/388. Rule 1 was: 'The purpose of the training and treatment of convicted prisoners shall be to encourage and assist them to lead a good and useful life.'
17 Home Office, *People in Prison: England and Wales*, Cmnd 4214, London, HMSO, 1969, para. 46.

18 D. Lipton, R. Martinson and J. Wilks, *Effectiveness of Correctional Treatment – a survey of treatment evaluation studies*, Springfield, Praeger, 1975, as cited by S.R. Brody, *The Effectiveness of Sentencing: a review of the literature*, Home Office Research Study no. 35, London, HMSO, 1976.

19 Brody, *The Effectiveness of Sentencing*.

20 Home Office, Scottish Office and Northern Ireland Office, *Report of the Committee of Inquiry into the UK Prison Services* (the May Report), London, HMSO, 1979, pp. 61, 67, 70, 72.

21 R.D. King and R. Morgan, *The Future of the Prison System*, Farnborough, Gower, 1980, p. 15.

22 J. Mott, *Adult Prisons in England and Wales 1970–1982: a review of the findings of social research*, Home Office Research Study no. 84, London, HMSO, 1985.

23 Home Office, *Circular Instruction 55/84*, London, Home Office, 1984.

24 I. Dunbar, *A Sense of Direction*, London, Home Office, 1985.

25 HM Chief Inspector of Prisons, *Annual Report for 1985*, HC 123, London, HMSO, 1986, p. 3.

26 R.D. King and K. McDermott, 'British prisons 1970–1987: the ever-deepening crisis', *British Journal of Criminology*, 1989, vol. 29, pp. 107–28.

27 National Audit Office, *Appropriation Accounts 1983–84. Vol. 6: Class IX Vote 8: Prisons, England and Wales (Home Office): Report of the Comptroller and Auditor General*, HC 614–VI, London, HMSO, 1984, p. v.

28 House of Commons Committee of Public Accounts, *26th Report, Session 1985–86: Prison Industry Losses* and *Minutes of Evidence*, HC 160, London, HMSO, 1986, paras 7, 9. The chairman's comment is reported on p. 2 of the *Minutes*.

29 National Audit Office, *Home Office Prison Department: Objectives, Organisation and Management of the Prison Service Industries and Farms: report by the Comptroller and Auditor General*, HC 93, London, HMSO, 1987.

30 This account is based on four sources: R. Caird, *A Good and Useful Life*, London, Hart-Davis, MacGibbon, 1974, and three reports by the Prisons Inspectorate: HM Chief Inspector of Prisons, *HM Prison Coldingley*, London, Home Office, 1986, 1994, 1996.

31 Quoted by Caird, *A Good and Useful Life*, p. 142.

32 The extent to which, even in the first few years, Coldingley workshops actually did match outside industrial conditions has been critically discussed by Caird (*A Good and Useful Life*) who spent ten months as a prisoner in Coldingley in 1970–1. He felt that what determined the working atmosphere was overwhelmingly the prison discipline, whose effects far outweighed features like clocking on and calling the workshop staff 'foremen' (which the prisoners never did).

33 HM Chief Inspector of Prisons, *HM Prison Coldingley*, 1994, pp. 2–3.

34 HM Chief Inspector of Prisons, *HM Prison Coldingley*, 1996, p. 17.

35 HM Prison Service, *Corporate Plan 1996–99*, London, HM Prison Service, 1996, p. 16.

36 HM Chief Inspector of Prisons, *Annual Report for 1988*, HC 491, London, HMSO, 1989, p. 15.

37 Woolf Report, pp. 1, 239, 241–2.

38 Woolf Report, pp. 372–3, 381, 386, 400–6, 431.

39 Woolf Report, p. 388.

40 Woolf Report, pp. 384, 388–90.

41 Woolf Report, pp. 388, 390–1, 393–4.

42 Home Office, *Custody, Care and Justice: The Way Ahead for the Prison Service in England and Wales*, Cm 1647, London, HMSO, 1991.

43 Home Office, *Custody, Care and Justice*, p. 5.

44 Home Office, *Custody, Care and Justice*, pp. 5, 12–13, 69–88.

45　Home Office, *Custody, Care and Justice*, pp. 78, 80.

46　Home Office, *Custody, Care and Justice*, p. 78.

47　Home Office, *Custody, Care and Justice*, pp. 78–9, 81–2.

48　The others were the Employment Department, Judge Stephen Tumim (HM Chief Inspector of Prisons), the Prison Governors' Association, the Prison Officers' Association, the Association of Chief Officers of Probation, the National Association for the Care and Resettlement of Offenders (NACRO), the Apex Trust and the Prison Reform Trust.

49　House of Commons Employment Committee, *Employment in Prisons and for Ex-Offenders*, HC 30, London, HMSO, 1991, pp. xvi–xviii.

50　Home Office and Employment Department, *Employment in Prisons and for Ex-Offenders: the government reply to the first report from the Employment Committee Session 1991–92, HC 30*, Cm 1837, London, HMSO, 1992.

51　HM Prison Service, *Briefing* no. 51, 14 July 1992, pp. 2–3.

52　Prison Service Industries and Farms, *Central Services: Working for prisons – for work in prisons*, London, HM Prison Service, 1993, p. 12.

53　*Annual Report 1992–93*, pp. 20–1, 24–5, 32–4.

54　HM Prison Service, *Briefing* no. 57, 12 February 1993, p. 2.

55　*Annual Report 1992–93*.

56　HM Prison Service, *Briefing* no. 66, 30 November 1993, p. 1.

57　J. Woodcock, *Report of the Inquiry into the Escape of Six Prisoners from the Special Security Unit at Whitemoor Prison, Cambridgeshire, on Friday 9th September 1994*, Cm 2741, London, HMSO, 1994.

58　HM Prison Service, *Director General's Newsletter*, 15 March 1995.

59　*Annual Report 1994–95*, p. 19.

60　J. Learmont, *Review of Prison Service Security in England and Wales and the Escape from Parkhurst Prison on Tuesday 3rd January 1995*, Cm 3020, London, HMSO, 1995.

61　*Annual Report 1994–95*, p. 28.

62　Home Office, *Prison Statistics England and Wales 1996*, Cm 3732, London, The Stationery Office, 1967 (hereafter referred to as *Prison Statistics 1996*), p. 1.

63　Home Office, *Statistical Bulletin: Projection of Long-Term Trends in the Prison Population to 2002*, London, Home Office, 1995.

64　Home Office, *Statistical Bulletin: Projection of Long-Term Trends in the Prison Population to 2004*, London, Home Office, 1996.

65　*Prison Statistics 1996*, Tables 1.2, 1.11.

66　*Prison Statistics 1996*, Fig. 1.5.

67　Penal Affairs Consortium, 'Rising numbers', in *Prisons – Some Current Developments*, London, PAC, January 1996, p. 2.

68　HM Prison Service, *Briefing* no. 71, 23 March 1994, p. 3.

69　P. Robson, 'Learning from scratch', *Prison Report*, 1996, no. 36, pp. 18–19.

70　HM Prison Service, *Director General's Newsletter*, 2 September 1993.

71　HM Prison Service, *Director General's Newsletter*, 2 September 1993.

72　Woolf Report, p. 451.

73　*Annual Report 1992–93*, p. 28.

74　HM Prison Service, *Report of the Review of Sentence Planning 1994/5*, London, HM Prison Service, 1995.

75　Home Office, *Custody, Care and Justice*, p. 69.

76　For a description of the sex offender treatment programme see S. Boddis and R. Mann, 'Groupwork in prisons', in Prison Reform Trust, *'A Good and Useful Life': Constructive Prison Regimes*, London, PRT, 1995, pp. 55–68. Later the core programme was lengthened to about ninety sessions and the booster to about thirty.

77　R.R. Ross, E.A. Fabiano and B. Ross, *Reasoning and Rehabilitation: a handbook for teaching cognitive skills*, Ottawa, The Cognitive Centre, 1989.

78 *Annual Report 1992–93*, p. 28.
79 See, for example, HM Prison Service, *Corporate Plan 1995–98*, London, HM Prison Service, 1995, p. 16.
80 *Annual Report 1994–95*, p. 26.
81 HM Prison Service, *Corporate Plan 1995–98*.
82 This was 'a comprehensive strategy intended to tackle the problems associated with the presence of drugs in prisons'. Planned components included increased searching, mandatory drug testing of inmates, better provision of treatment and support for misusers, and throughcare links with outside agencies. Implementation began in February 1995. *Annual Report 1994–95*, pp. 22–5.
83 Penal Affairs Consortium, 'Budgetary cuts', in Penal Affairs Consortium, *Prisons – Some Current Developments*, pp. 2–3.
84 HM Prison Service, *Briefing* no. 89, 18 December 1995, p. 1.
85 HM Prison Service, *Corporate Plan 1996–99*, p. 16.
86 HM Prison Service, *Briefing* no. 94, 28 June 1996, pp. 1–3.
87 Woolf Report, p. 296.
88 *Annual Report 1994–95*, p. 32.
89 HM Chief Inspector of Prisons, *Annual Report 1995–96*, HC 44, London, The Stationery Office, 1996, p. 2.
90 F. Simon and C. Corbett, *An Evaluation of Prison Work and Training*, London, Home Office, 1996. This is a short summary report of the Brunel study based on the field-work carried out in 1992–3. Pp. 2–8 describe most of the methods, apart from the 1996 updating visits and the gathering of additional material for depicting the national context.
91 Also the four training prisons (Channings Wood, Highpoint, Kirkham and Maidstone) were officially regarded as providing mainly good rather than average training. This was not a drawback either, because if the research findings were to support that view the prisons could be held up to others as examples of good practice.

   Dispersal prisons, which held about 8 per cent of all sentenced adult males including those Category A people requiring the highest security, were excluded for security reasons. But when interviewing prisoners in our sample we noted the experience of work or training in a dispersal which a few of them had had.
92 Throughout the book we use 'governor' to refer to a prison's governing governor (or deputy). Other governor grades are referred to by titles when appropriate (e.g. head of inmate activities), or else as managers of the prison.
93 Comparisons were made with data from three sources as follows: Home Office, *Prison Statistics England and Wales 1991*, Cm 2157, London, HMSO, 1992; T. Dodd and P. Hunter, *The National Prison Survey 1991: a report to the Home Office of a study of prisoners in England and Wales carried out by the Social Survey Division of OPCS*, London, HMSO, 1992; *Annual Report 1992–93*.

   Later comparisons using *Prison Statistics 1996* and regime monitoring figures for 1996 showed that the picture had changed very little, except that by that year the proportion of the prison population sentenced for drugs offences was somewhat larger than formerly.
94 The sample contained too few women (fourteen) to allow statistical comparisons between male and female inmates, but data from the women contributed to the overall pictures. Chapters 3 and 4 mention some ways in which practices at Holloway differed from those at the male prisons, for instance the incentives given to sewing workers and the scope for inmates' creativity in the kitchen. The specific topic of women prisoners' work is discussed on pp. 215–17.
95 Dodd and Hunter, *National Prison Survey 1991*, Table 2.6, with the percentages recalculated to omit people under 21.

96 Two of the eighty-eight were special cases. One was of a man who had been released later than expected and whom we found ourselves interviewing only four weeks after release instead of three months as planned; attempts at a second follow-up interview were unsuccessful. The other case was of a man who died two months after release and whose family offered us an interview at the three months point. In both these cases we felt that the amount of data gathered justified their inclusion with the other eighty-six cases in the follow-up sample. Apart from these two, three-quarters of the interviews took place between three and four-and-a-half months after release, and the others took longer, the longest interval (two cases) being eight months.

97 A request for an updating visit was made to Holloway in the same way as to the other five prisons. But in 1995–6 Holloway was beset by troubles which came to public notice in December 1995 when the new Chief Inspector of Prisons pulled his team out of Holloway in disgust at the deteriorating conditions. Months of adverse press publicity followed (especially about the shackling of maternity patients). In this situation Holloway staff in 1996 were too busy, trying to put things right for the Inspectors' return, to spare time for our research interviews. Our information on Holloway after 1993 was gleaned from the 1995 Board of Visitors' report, from press reports, and from writings by the Chief Inspector. See note 7 to chapter 2.

98 We did not look at prisoners' personal files, except in twelve cases during a pilot study, or seek or check information about individuals from any other source. We wanted to obtain both their views and their trust, in order to increase the chance of a successful follow-up. We did note from the prison records database a small number of items such as type of offence, sentence and dates relating to length of stay in that prison. All these items were checked with the respondent early in the prison interview, and thereafter we relied entirely on what he or she told us in confidence.

99 T. Hirschi, M.J. Hindelang and J. Weis, 'The status of self-report measures', in M. Klein and K. Teilman (eds), *Handbook of Criminal Justice*, Newbury Park, Sage, 1981, pp. 473–88.

100 J. Graham and B. Bowling, *Young People and Crime*, Home Office Research Study no. 145, London, Home Office, 1995, pp. 6–9.

101 In case examples and quotations throughout the book we have preserved the anonymity of prisoners and prison staff by giving most informants a number preceded by R (for respondent). These numbers were used only for the research and have nothing to do with any others. Numbers for prison staff begin with 0 or 1, and those for inmates with 5 or 6.

Some of the statistical comparisons, especially in the follow-up data, are based on small numbers, so while they reveal interesting differences in our sample they are not necessarily a basis for generalisation. In our reports of statistical findings the base number each time is the number of cases in which data was available on the particular point.

2 SIX PRISONS

1 HM Prison Service, *Annual Report 1994–95*, Cm 447, London, HMSO, 1996, p. 32.
2 HM Chief Inspector of Prisons, *HM Prison Channings Wood*, London, Home Office, 1995, p. 19.
3 HM Chief Inspector of Prisons, *HM Prison Channings Wood*, London, Home Office, 1991, p. 60.
4 HM Chief Inspector of Prisons, *HM Prison Channings Wood*, London, Home Office, 1993, p. 5.

5 HM Chief Inspector of Prisons, *HM Prison Channings Wood*, 1995, p. 16.

6 This description is taken partly from 'Inside job helps women prisoners to pay their way', *Daily Telegraph*, 27 April 1993, p. 9. It confirmed plans described to us by prison staff in February.

7 The main source of information for our description of Holloway Prison in 1994–6 is the *Annual Report for 1995* of the prison's Board of Visitors (London, Board of Visitors, HM Prison Holloway, 1996). Other points have been taken from R. McMillan (pseudonym), 'What went wrong at Holloway?', *Prison Report*, 1996, no. 34, pp. 8–10, and from press reports and writings by the Chief Inspector of Prisons as noted separately below.

8 J. Learmont, *Review of Prison Service Security in England and Wales and the Escape from Parkhurst Prison on Tuesday 3rd January 1995*, Cm 3020, London, HMSO, 1995.

9 Holloway Prison Board of Visitors, *Annual Report 1995*, p. 8.

10 HM Chief Inspector of Prisons, *Annual Report 1995–96*, HC 44, London, The Stationery Office, 1996, p. 14.

11 D. Ramsbotham (Chief Inspector of Prisons), 'Why we need to reform our prisons', *Reader's Digest*, January 1997, p. 53.

12 See, for example, the following: 'The shame I felt in chains – I just wanted to die', *Guardian*, 11 January 1996, p. 1; 'Prison mothers to stay in chains', *Independent*, 10 January 1996, p. 4; 'Mother in chains to sue', *Independent*, 12 January 1996, p. 3.

13 'Howard unchains pregnant prisoners', *Independent*, 19 January 1996, p. 2.

14 'Progress at Holloway Prison', *Independent*, 10 April 1996, p. 14.

15 'JPs accused of crowding jails', *Independent*, 14 June 1996, p. 8.

16 HM Chief Inspector of Prisons, *HM Prison Holloway*, London, Home Office, 1997, pp. 3, 134.

17 HM Chief Inspector of Prisons, *HM Prison Kirkham*, London, Home Office 1993, pp. 51, 83.

18 In 1993 Kirkham had been one of about a dozen prisons listed by Prison Service HQ as potential candidates for market testing. Later the threat receded, though the possibility of its return was still in the minds of Kirkham managers. But by 1997 it was clear that the short courses would not suffice for the performance indicator: see p. 210.

19 From 1992 to 1994 Liverpool had to accommodate extra prisoners while Manchester Prison was being rebuilt after the 1990 riot. By 1996 this was no longer required, and Liverpool's accommodation had increased through the completion of some refurbishment.

20 HM Chief Inspector of Prisons, *HM Prison Liverpool*, London, Home Office, 1993, p. 56.

21 HM Chief Inspector of Prisons, *HM Prison Liverpool*, 1993, pp. 57–8.

22 HM Chief Inspector of Prisons, *HM Prison Maidstone*, London, Home Office, 1996, p. 33.

23 HM Prison Maidstone, *A Prisoners Guide to HMP Maidstone*, Maidstone, HM Prison, 1996, p. 2.

24 HM Chief Inspector of Prisons, *HM Prison Maidstone*, 1996, pp. 11, 13, 50–2, 54, 55.

25 HM Chief Inspector of Prisons, *HM Prison Maidstone*, 1996, p. 66.

26 HM Chief Inspector of Prisons, *HM Prison Maidstone*, 1996, p. 68.

3 PICTURES OF PRISON WORK, AND COMPARISONS WITH OUTSIDE

1 Though it may be remarked that the Annual Report for 1994–5 had fewer such pictures than in previous years (five, on pp. 8, 12 and 13) and more showing security procedures (six, on pp. 10, 18–20). HM Prison Service, *Annual Report 1994–95*, Cm 447, London, HMSO, 1996.

2 In early 1992 when the research began the average weekly pay for inmates in work was £3.50. Pay varied with the type of work, and inmates in education or training courses were paid at a flat rate which was rather lower. Inmates working long hours, as in kitchens or on the Kirkham farm, received higher pay: some people on top rates might earn up to about £10. In December 1992, part-way through the research, a new pay scheme increased the average pay for inmates in work to £6 a week and gave prisons more flexibility to set their own rates (within overall budgets and subject to national limits). Further increases raised the average pay to £7 a week from April 1994. In our sample of prisoners interviewed the highest pay received was £9 a week before December 1992 and £12 afterwards.

3 H. Woolf and S. Tumim, *Prison Disturbances April 1990: Report of an Inquiry*, Cm 1456, London, HMSO, 1991, pp. 393–4.

4 Only three of our interviewees, all at Maidstone, said they had a sentence plan. Two of them had started it at Whitemoor which was then a new prison.

5 Most of the data shown in Table 1 for Prison Enterprise Services work has been taken from information supplied by PES, especially some relating to budgets for 1995–6 and 1996–7. The numbers of inmates employed in farms and gardens, and all the data for 'other' work, have been taken from regime monitoring statistics collated by Prison Service HQ for 1995–6. Such statistics were the basis for the 'profile of inmate occupations' which until 1991–2 used to appear in the Prison Service Annual Reports. Because of various problems of definition, interpretation, collection and processing, regime monitoring figures contain anomalies and inconsistencies, and should be taken only as a guide to the proportions of prisoners engaged on average in various types of prison occupation. Numbers of inmates employed as orderlies, clerks, etc., cannot be extracted from them. Prison Service HQ introduced new data collection arrangements in 1997.

6 Regime monitoring figures for 1995–6 show the number of inmates in education or training courses as 10,269 out of 45,030 'average population monitored', or 23 per cent; those in induction were 2,182 or 5 per cent.

7 The regime monitoring figures for 1995–6 show domestic workers as being 58 per cent of inmates occupied in male remand centres, 32 per cent in male locals, and 14 per cent in Category B and C prisons.

8 A PES leaflet describes engineering shops as producing, for example, sheetmetal lockers, welded gates and grilles, tubular furniture, and stainless steel catering equipment.

9 Prison Service Industries and Farms Board of Management, *Chairman's Report 1992–93*, London, HM Prison Service, 1993, p. 4.

10 Prison Service Industries and Farms, *Central Services: Working for prisons – for work in prisons*, London, HM Prison Service, 1993.

11 The figures for NVQs in 1995–6 in this chapter (and Chapter 5) are taken from statistics compiled by Prison Service HQ. These showed that in regard to catering, for example: (1) forty-seven prisons had received approval to offer NVQ certification, and we have taken this figure as the number actually offering training; (2) 182 full NVQ certificates were awarded, and we have taken this figure as the number of prisoners gaining a full certificate, as very few would be counted twice. Similar remarks apply to NVQ training in other occupational areas.

12 The (very approximate) NVQ equivalents are, respectively, between levels 1 and 2 and between levels 2 and 3.
13 The increase in ratio largely resulted from the closure of the light assembly workshop which had formerly employed inmates medically graded as fit only for light work. Some of these men were now being assigned to the gardens.
14 In an effort to overcome this image Channings Wood's new shop was named 'the repair and charity shop'.
15 U. Huws, *No Sweat! Why Britain's one million homeworkers need a new deal*, London, Trades Union Congress, 1996.

4 GENERAL FEATURES OF PRISON WORK

1 See pp. 16–17.
2 H. Woolf and S. Tumim, *Prison Disturbances April 1990: Report of an Inquiry*, Cm 1456, London, HMSO, 1991, pp. 391–5.
3 T. Dodd and P. Hunter, *The National Prison Survey 1991: a report to the Home Office of a study of prisoners in England and Wales carried out by the Social Survey Division of OPCS*, London, HMSO, 1992, p. 44.
4 Some prisoners earning 'real wages' were already subject to such deductions, as were those going out daily to ordinary jobs under the pre-release employment scheme. See HM Prison Service, *Annual Report 1992–93*, Cm 2385, London, HMSO, 1993, pp. 20, 30. But there were only tiny numbers of such cases.
5 HM Chief Inspector of Prisons, *HM Prison Manchester*, London, Home Office, 1996, p. 71.
6 Dodd and Hunter, *The National Prison Survey*, p. 36.
7 S. Dawson, *Industrial Work in a Prison Context: Problems and Potential*, London, 1972. Unpublished report to the Home Office, cited with the permission of the author and the Home Office.
8 S. Dawson, 'Power and influence in prison workshops', in P. Abell (ed.), *Organisations as Bargaining and Influence Systems*, London, Heinemann, 1975, pp. 151–86.

5 VOCATIONAL TRAINING IN PRISONS

1 We include among vocational training courses the construction industry (CIT) courses which are shown separately in the statistics. CIT courses were run by Works department staff until 1995. In that year responsibility for them at HQ was taken over by the Education and Training Advisory Service, but in prisons they might be managed by the Works department or another manager at the discretion of the governor, with the education department providing support.
2 HM Prison Service, *Briefing* no. 29, 31 January 1991, p. 1.
3 'NVQ achievement soars', *Prison Service News*, 1995, vol. 13, no. 5, p. 5.
4 At some prisons the hours for training were somewhat shorter. Under the daily routine, after breakfast and lunch working inmates were sent or escorted to their workplaces first, and when they were out of the way those attending training courses or education followed. On return the order was reversed.
5 P = 0.006. The mean score for trainees was not significantly different from that for twelve other inmates in daytime education, though theirs was slightly higher at 4.67.
6 For a description of this course see R. Jerred, 'Out of the wood', *Prison Service News*, 1991, vol. 9, no. 83, p. 4.

7 The figures in Table 2 may not be as exact as they look. For this information, as for much else on our sample of inmates, we relied on what they told us and did not check other sources for evidence one way or the other of certificates gained. It is doubtful anyway whether the prison files of all would have been complete in that respect.

8 Several points need explanation. (1) The NVQ statistics for 1995–6 were based on returns from only 111 prisons and the actual totals may have been higher. On the other hand, they included young offenders who are more likely to receive training than adults, so the figures for adults only would be lower than the totals. The research sample of eighty-eight were adults only. (2) The number of prisoners (including young offenders) received under sentences of a year or more in 1995 was 24,655 (*Prison Statistics 1995*, Table 1.13). This is a convenient figure against which to set the numbers of prisoners receiving NVQ training in 1995–6, although of course some of them would have started their sentence before 1995. (3) It is sensible for the time being just to consider prisoners sentenced to a year or more (who are about 36 per cent of the total, excluding fine defaulters). Prisoners sentenced to one year actually serve, under sentence, an average of five months. (*Prison Statistics 1995*, Tables 3.14, 4.12 and 5.11 taken together.) Five months would be long enough to enable a prisoner to take a four-month training course aiming at NVQ level 1 if all other circumstances were favourable, i.e. if he or she could start the training within one month from the date of sentence and remain in it without interruption. Of course, this would be unlikely to happen in practice for the various reasons explored in this chapter; also some prisoners would be trained at work rather than on courses. Nevertheless, it seems reasonable to hope that during five months under sentence an inmate might achieve some NVQ units.

Home Office, *Prison Statistics England and Wales 1995*, Cm 3355, London, HMSO, 1996.

6 SINK, FLOAT OR SWIM: RELEASE FROM PRISON

1 R. Burnett, *The Dynamics of Recidivism: summary report*, Oxford, Centre for Criminological Research, University of Oxford, 1992.

2 J. Braithwaite, *Prisons Education and Work*, Phillip, Australian Institute of Criminology, 1980, pp. 12, 23–4.

3 I. Crow, P. Richardson, C. Riddington and F. Simon, *Unemployment, Crime, and Offenders*, London, Routledge, 1989, p. 79.

4 L. Motiuk, 'Targeting employment patterns to reduce offender risk and need', *Forum on Corrections Research*, 1996, vol. 8, no. 1, p. 24.

5 D.A. Andrews and J. Bonta, *The Psychology of Criminal Conduct*, Cincinnati, Anderson, 1994, as cited by D. Andrews, 'The psychology of criminal conduct and effective treatment', in J. McGuire (ed.), *What Works: Reducing Reoffending*, Chichester, Wiley, 1995, pp. 35–62.

6 The studies cited by the authors mentioned rest on disaggregate individual-level data. For discussion of studies which use aggregate data to explore the complex relationships between unemployment and crime, see the following: D. Dickinson, *Crime and Unemployment*, Cambridge, Department of Applied Economics, University of Cambridge, 1994; J. Wells, 'Crime and unemployment', in K. Coates (ed.), *The Right to Work: the loss of our first freedom*, Nottingham, Spokesman, 1995, pp. 54–100; I. Crow, 'Employment, training and offending', in M. Drakeford and M. Vanstone (eds), *Beyond Offending Behaviour*, Aldershot, Arena, 1996, pp. 51–62.

7 HM Prison Service, *Annual Report 1992–93*, Cm 2385, London, HMSO, 1993, p. 33.

8 HM Chief Inspector of Prisons, *HM Prison Holloway*, London, Home Office, 1997, p. 114.

9 Most of the information for this note was supplied by Prison Service HQ. None was available for 1996 on the number of prisons running jobclubs or allowing inmates to go out for work or training. But it was likely that by that year the numbers of inmates working out, apart from those at resettlement units, would have been smaller than formerly because of the greater restrictions on temporary release. It was certainly so at the research prisons.

10 HM Prison Service, *Annual Report 1993–94*, HC 185, London, HMSO, 1995, pp. 28–9.

11 Of the others, three already had a job arranged before their release, thirteen did not seek work at all because they had other plans or were not interested, and one man died.

12 '*Which?* investigates pushy sales methods', *Which?*, November 1991, p. 604.

13 The follow-up interviews had been intended to take place three months after release, and 77 per cent were achieved at between three and five months. Most of the others took longer, the longest interval being eight months (two cases). At the time of interview three people were back in custody, and for them the follow-up data refers to the period up to their re-arrest. Data on one man who died two months after release (and whose family were interviewed) refers of course to that period.

A principal focus of the follow-up was the person's employment situation. Apart from the four people just mentioned and one other followed up after only one month, there were only four people in the sample whose job status at the date of follow-up was substantially different from what it had been exactly three months after release; for the great majority the employment picture was much the same whether the follow-up was three months or longer. (Of the last-mentioned four, three had had jobs but lost them, and one took a long holiday between jobs.) So in this chapter, for convenience and in order to make the best use of the data, we have used the whole follow-up period as the reference period for some topics like jobhunting efforts, and the date of the follow-up interview (or just before it) as the reference point for others like employment status and sources of income.

14 The information set out here is quite independent of whether the person was signing on as unemployed and claiming DSS benefit.

15 In each case we took the unemployment rate for the person's 'travel to work' area in the month of the follow-up interview, as published in the *Employment Gazette*.

Employment Department, *Employment Gazette*, London, Employment Department, monthly.

16 Chi-square = 3.39, df = 1, P<0.05 on a one-tailed test. As might be expected, the difference is in the same direction as that found five years previously by Simon and Crow among unemployed young people released from Youth Custody Centres: those who lived in areas of relatively lower (though still very high) unemployment were judged (by their supervising probation officers) to be making greater efforts to find work.

F. Simon and I. Crow, *Training Young Offenders: a comparative study of Youth Training Schemes and Youth Custody Centres*, London, National Association for the Care and Resettlement of Offenders, 1990, p. 39.

17 The difference is not statistically significant, but it is suggestive.

18 In two cases we had no information on the domestic situation.

19 Child benefit and housing benefit are not counted here.

20 Failure to declare earnings while claiming benefit is not counted here.

21 As well as cases where people failed to declare earnings, minor or substantial, we found several households where the respondent lived with his wife or partner and

their children did *not* claim benefit and earned some money by casual work, and Mrs R continued to claim benefit for herself and the children just as she had done while R was in prison. If there is any breach in such cases it is Mrs R's and we have not counted it against R. We met more than one Mrs R, careful manager of the family budget, who had decided, in view of previous difficulties caused by delays and muddles at the DSS, that this time the family's interests would be best served, and a steady income maintained, by not telling the DSS of R's homecoming until he found a regular job.

22 We found no case among our respondents of organised benefit fraud, or cheating by anyone other than individuals. But the following case of attempted fraud by an employer who advertised in the jobcentre is of interest.

> R583 (see p. 176) obtained just one interview through his local jobcentre, for a position as living-in handyman at a hotel taking in 'DSS' lodgers. This employer offered R the job on the condition that R would continue to sign on as unemployed and claim full benefit, and the employer would pay him merely pocket money. R refused.

23 These differences are not statistically significant.

24 This relationship is statistically significant: chi-square = 8.32, df = 1, P<0.01.

25 Omitting six who were supported by a partner, the one pensioner, ten people living partly by crime, and six for whom there was insufficient information.

26 For this 3 x 2 table, chi-square for linear-by-linear association = 20.25, df = 2, P<0.001, though this is inflated because of two small cell frequencies.

27 A. Hagell, T. Newburn and K. Rowlingson, *Financial Difficulties on Release from Prison*, London, Policy Studies Institute, 1995.

28 T. Dodd and P. Hunter, *The National Prison Survey 1991: a report to the Home Office of a study of prisoners in England and Wales carried out by the Social Survey Division of OPCS*, London, HMSO, 1992, pp. 72, 103.

29 Burnett, *The Dynamics of Recidivism*, p. 13.

30 The figures are as follows. Among twenty-two people with no previous custodial sentences, seventeen (77 per cent) committed no breaches or only minor ones, while five (23 per cent) had substantial undeclared earnings or were involved in other crime. Among fourteen people with one or two previous sentences the corresponding figures were six (43 per cent) and eight (57 per cent). Among twenty-seven with three or more previous sentences the corresponding figures were thirteen (48 per cent) and fourteen (52 per cent).

31 For the 3 x 2 table comparing the quoted percentages, chi-square for linear-by-linear association = 7.89, df = 1, P = 0.005.

32 As might be expected, younger people and people with little previous experience of prison were more likely to say they had gained self-understanding or social skills. Nevertheless, 41 per cent of those who had had three or more previous custodial sentences, and 45 per cent of those aged 30 or over, felt they had learned some self-understanding, social skills or both.

33 National Association for the Care and Resettlement of Offenders, *Opening the Doors: the resettlement of prisoners in the community*, London, NACRO, 1993.

7 THE CHALLENGE AHEAD

1 M.H. Cooper and R.D. King, 'Social and economic problems of prisoners' work', in P. Halmos (ed.), *Sociological Studies in the British Penal Services*, The Sociological Review, Monograph no. 9, Keele, University of Keele, 1965.

2 Home Office, *Prison Statistics England and Wales 1996*, Cm 3732, London, The Stationery Office, 1997 (hereafter referred to as *Prison Statistics 1996*), Tables 3.14, 4.12 and 5.11 taken together. The figures exclude time served on remand (which counts towards sentence), fine defaulters, and people sentenced to life imprisonment.

3 H. Woolf and S. Tumim, *Prison Disturbances April 1990: Report of an Inquiry*, Cm 1456, London, HMSO, 1991 (hereafter referred to as the Woolf Report), p. 242.

4 T. Dodd and P. Hunter, *The National Prison Survey 1991: a report to the Home Office of a study of prisoners in England and Wales carried out by the Social Survey Division of OPCS*, London, HMSO, 1992, p. 15.

5 National Association for the Care and Resettlement of Offenders, *Opening the Doors: the resettlement of prisoners in the community*, London, NACRO, 1993, pp. 5, 22.

6 The statistics cited in this section have been selected from two main sources. (1) Institute for Employment Research, *Review of the Economy and Employment 1995: Occupational Assessment*, Coventry, University of Warwick, 1995. Tables 2.3 and 3.3 have been drawn on for statistics for 1954–94 and projections to 2001. (2) Business Strategies Ltd, *Occupations of the Future*, London, BSL, 1996, as cited in Skills and Enterprise Network, *Labour Market and Skill Trends 1997/98*, Nottingham, Department for Education and Employment, 1997, Figures 2.5 and 4.2. These have been drawn on for projections from 1996 to 2006.

Statistics on self-employment, part-time employment and the participation of women have been taken from Skills and Enterprise Network, *Labour Market and Skill Trends 1997/98*, pp. 12, 15. Other material comes from pp. 1–17 of that publication and from Institute for Employment Research, *Review of the Economy and Employment 1996/97: Labour Market Assessment*, Coventry, University of Warwick, 1996, pp. 6–7, 11–17.

Material on reasons for the changes, and on the personal qualities needed for employment, comes mainly from two publications: Skills and Enterprise Network, *Labour Market and Skill Trends 1992/93*, Nottingham, Employment Department, 1991, pp. 16–22; A. Rajan, *1990s: Where Will the New Jobs Be?*, Tunbridge Wells, Institute of Careers Guidance and the Centre for Research in Employment and Technology in Europe, 1992, pp. 1–8, 20–7.

7 U. Huws, *No Sweat! Why Britain's one million homeworkers need a new deal*, London, Trades Union Congress, 1996.

8 C. Berens and L. Johnston, 'The high-street sweatshops', *The Big Issue*, no. 181, 13–19 May 1996, pp. 6–8.

9 HM Prison Manchester, *Taking Part: information booklet for prisoners* and *Information Pack for Official Visitors*, Manchester, HM Prison, 1994.

10 J. McHutchison, *NSW Corrective Service Industries and Offender Post-Release Employment*, Research Bulletin 14, Sydney, NSW Department of Corrective Services, 1991, p. 33.

11 *Prison Statistics 1996*, Table 1.13.

12 Woolf Report, pp. 372–3.

13 Industrial Society, 'Empowerment', *Managing Best Practice*, no. 8, London, Industrial Society, 1995.

14 This proposal is similar to one made by the Inspectorate in 1993. HM Chief Inspector of Prisons, *Doing Time or Using Time*, Cm 2128, London, HMSO, 1993, p. 75.

15 C. Gillis, *The influence of the CORCAN shop supervisor leadership characteristics on offender work attitudes*, unpublished Master's thesis, Carleton University, 1994, as cited by E. Fabiano, J. LaPlante and A. Loza, 'Employability: from research to practice', *Forum on Corrections Research*, 1996, vol. 8, no. 1, pp. 25–8.

16 M. Getkate, *The CORCAN Offender Work Attitude Survey*, Ottawa, Correctional Service of Canada, 1994, as cited by Fabiano *et al.*, 'Employability: from research to practice', p. 28.

17 C. Gillis, D. Robinson and F. Porporino, 'Inmate employment: the increasingly influential role of generic work skills', *Forum on Corrections Research*, 1996, vol. 8, no. 1, pp. 18–20.

18 J. Braithwaite, *Prisons Education and Work*, Phillip, Australian Institute of Criminology, 1980, pp. 151–2.

19 Fabiano *et al.*, 'Employability: from research to practice'.

20 S. Dawson, 'Power and influence in prison workshops', in P. Abell (ed.), *Organisations as Bargaining and Influence Systems*, London, Heinemann, 1975, pp. 151–86.

21 HM Chief Inspector of Prisons, *Annual Report 1994–95*, HC 760, London, HMSO, 1995, p. 19.

22 J. Learmont, *Review of Prison Service Security in England and Wales and the Escape from Parkhurst Prison on Tuesday 3rd January 1995*, Cm 3020, London, HMSO, 1995, p. 141.

23 HM Chief Inspector of Prisons, *HM Prison Coldingley*, London, Home Office, 1996, pp. 5–7, 17.

24 'Coldingley contract', *Prison Report*, 1997, no. 40, p. 15.

25 Braithwaite, *Prisons Education and Work*, pp. 184–5.

26 E.S. Lightman, 'The private employer and the prison industry', *British Journal of Criminology*, 1982, vol. 22, pp. 36–48.

27 M. Davies, 'Prisons as social firms: the way forward for prison industry?', in Prison Reform Trust, *'A Good and Useful Life': Constructive Prison Regimes*, London, PRT, 1995, pp. 35–48.

28 Lightman, 'The private employer and the prison industry', pp. 40–1, 46–7.

29 N. Flynn, 'Making workshops work', *Prison Report*, 1995, no. 30, pp. 26–7.

30 Information on the 'Beyond The Gate' scheme has been taken mainly from the following sources, supplemented by discussion with the scheme's employment liaison officer: HM Prison Service and Kent Training and Enterprise Council, *Beyond The Gate* and *The Blueprint*, Chatham, Kent TEC, 1994; Kent TEC, *Update*, October 1993.

31 Employment Department, *Partnership Initiatives: Helping Offenders into Training and Work*, Developing Good Practice/Equal Opportunities series, Sheffield, Employment Department, 1993.

32 HM Prison Service, *Advice to Governors*, 20 January 1994.

33 K. Roberts, A. Barton, J. Buchanan and B. Goldson, *Evaluation of a Home Office Initiative to Help Offenders into Employment*, London, Home Office, 1996, pp. 40–2.

34 N. Flynn, *Missing Links: recommendations for productive partnerships between TECs and the Prison Service*, London, LAWTEC Ltd/ELTEC/Apex Trust, 1993.

35 Or even less. Roberts *et al.*, *Evaluation of a Home Office Initiative*, describe seven initiatives in 1995 designed to help offenders (mainly in the community, but also including a handful of inmates from Bristol Prison) into training or employment, and involving TECs, probation services and other agencies in partnerships. Some of these schemes built on existing ones, but the specific initiatives which Roberts *et al.* evaluated were funded by the Home Office for *only six months*.

36 Employment Department, *Helping Offenders into Training and Work*.

37 Home Office, *National Framework for the Throughcare of Offenders in Custody to the Completion of Supervision in the Community*, London, Home Office, 1993, pp. 5–6.

38 Home Office, *National Framework for Throughcare*, pp. 28–31.

39 Home Office, *National Framework for Throughcare*, p. 20.

40 See, for example, Employment Department, *Helping Offenders into Training and Work*, pp. 20–4, and Roberts *et al.*, *Evaluation of a Home Office Initiative*.

41 HM Prison Service, *The Way Ahead: National Vocational Qualifications* (leaflet), London, Home Office, 1991.

42 The project at Belmarsh Prison was an ambitious attempt in 1992–3 by the Apex Trust, funded by South Thames TEC, to work in a new prison on two fronts. One was an effort to get local employers involved, rather as in Beyond The Gate. The other was to offer inmates vocational assessment and guidance followed by action plans which would use the prison's facilities (and, for people near release, facilities in the community). It was intended that an inmate's plan would inform decisions by the prison management about his assignment to occupations in Belmarsh and about his transfer to other prisons. But Flynn and Baines of Apex have described how the project ran into serious difficulties. Prisoners were transferred out with little regard for their action plans; timetables for using the workshops, training and education facilities were too inflexible to allow prisoners their choice of occupation; departments in the prison were competitive and defensive; and Apex felt that the project, despite having been endorsed by senior managers, was never wholly accepted by prison staff. The authors suggest that external organisations wanting to work in prisons can face major problems.

   N. Flynn and C. Baines, *Working It Out: Employment Guidance and Employer Involvement in Prisons*, London, Apex Trust and South Thames TEC, 1994.

43 HM Prison Service, *Report of the Review of Sentence Planning 1994/5*, London, HM Prison Service, 1995, page preceding p. 1.

44 *Prison Rules 1964*, SI 1964/388.

45 Or only very rarely, and never primarily. See I. Crow and F. Simon, *Unemployment and Magistrates' Courts*, London, National Association for the Care and Resettlement of Offenders, 1987.

46 K. McLaren, *Reducing Reoffending: What Works Now*, Wellington, New Zealand Department of Justice, 1992.

47 J. McGuire and P. Priestley, 'Reviewing "What Works?": past, present and future', in J. McGuire (ed.), *What Works: Reducing Reoffending*, Chichester, Wiley, 1995, pp. 3–34.

48 The description of the revised scheme is largely based on information supplied by Prison Service HQ.

49 The description of accredited programmes is based on information supplied by Prison Service HQ.

50 R.R. Ross, E.A. Fabiano and B. Ross, *Reasoning and Rehabilitation: a handbook for teaching cognitive skills*, Ottawa, The Cognitive Centre, 1989.

51 HM Prison Service, *Briefing on Offending Behaviour Programmes*, London, HM Prison Service, 1997.

52 Under the Criminal Justice Act 1991 young offenders are subject to at least three months' supervision after release. Adults sentenced to twelve months and over are on licence and under supervision from the date they are released until the three-quarters point of their sentence. The 1997 sentence planning scheme requires plans to be made for all young offenders who at the date of sentence have at least four weeks still to serve, and for all adults sentenced to twelve months and over who have at least six months still to serve. In *Prison Statistics 1996*, Table 3.14 shows that almost all young offenders would be included. Tables 4.12 and 5.11 show that most adults sentenced to more than twelve months would be included, but most of those sentenced to exactly twelve months would not. Table 1.13 shows that in 1996 adults sentenced to more than twelve months were 33 per cent of all sentenced adults received. (All these figures exclude fine defaulters.)

53 HM Chief Inspector of Prisons, *Doing Time or Using Time*.

54 Woolf Report, pp. 24–5.

55 HM Prison Service, *Report of the Review of Sentence Planning*, page preceding p. 1.

56 HM Prison Service, *Annual Report 1993–94*, HC 185, London, HMSO, p. 27.

57 Braithwaite, *Prisons Education and Work*, p. 54.
58 M. Rein, *Social Policy: Issues of Choice and Change*, New York, Random House, 1970, as cited by Braithwaite, *Prisons Education and Work*, p. 54.
59 See McGuire and Priestley, 'Reviewing "What Works?" ', pp. 7–9.
60 McLaren, *Reducing Reoffending: What Works Now*, p. 63.
61 In invoking 'what works' here we are not suggesting that in all cases offending has sprung from employment needs.
62 K. Legge, 'Work in prison: the process of inversion', *British Journal of Criminology*, 1978, vol. 18, pp. 16–22.
63 A. Morris, C. Wilkinson, A. Tisi, J. Woodrow and A. Rockley, *Managing the Needs of Female Prisoners*, London, Home Office, 1995.
64 HM Chief Inspector of Prisons, *Women in Prison*, London, Home Office, 1997.
65 Morris *et al.*, *Managing the Needs of Female Prisoners*, p. 10.
66 Morris *et al.*, *Managing the Needs of Female Prisoners*, pp. 53–4.
67 HM Chief Inspector of Prisons, *Women in Prison*, especially ch. 12.
68 Braithwaite, *Prisons Education and Work*, p. 185.
69 N. Morris, *The Future of Imprisonment*, Chicago, University of Chicago Press, 1974, pp. 13–18.
70 A. Coyle, *The Prisons We Deserve*, London, HarperCollins, 1994, p. 75.
71 R.D. King and K. McDermott, *The State of Our Prisons*, Oxford, Oxford University Press, 1995, p. 283.
72 HM Prison Service, *Manual for the Revised Model of Sentence Management and Planning*, London, HM Prison Service, 1997, para. 2.2.
73 R.D. King and K. McDermott, 'British prisons 1970–1987: the ever-deepening crisis', *British Journal of Criminology*, 1989, vol. 29, pp. 107–28.
74 R. Tilt, 'Rights, risks and rehabilitation 1996', *Criminal Justice*, 1996, vol. 14, no. 4, pp. 6–7.
75 HM Chief Inspector of Prisons, *Annual Report 1995–96*, HC 44, London, HMSO, 1996, p. 3.
76 House of Commons, *Parliamentary Debates*, 25 July 1997, cols 761–2.
77 'Jail conditions dreadful, says chief inspector', *Independent*, 16 October 1997, p. 4.
78 A survey by Social and Community Planning Research found that between 1990 and 1994 the proportion of people agreeing with the statement 'Too many criminals are let off lightly by the courts' rose from 79 per cent to 86 per cent, while the proportion agreeing that 'the prisons contain too many people who ought to be given a lighter punishment' fell from 48 per cent to 28 per cent. Another survey by the Home Office found that between 1992 and 1996 the proportion of people in England and Wales favouring imprisonment for a recidivist burglar rose from 37 per cent to 49 per cent.
    L. Brook and E. Cape, 'Libertarianism in retreat?' in R. Jowell, J. Curtice, A. Park, L. Brook and D. Ahrendt (eds), *British Social Attitudes: the 12th report*, Social and Community Planning Research, Dartmouth, Aldershot, 1995, pp. 191–209.
    P. Mayhew and P. White, *The 1996 International Crime Victimisation Survey*, Research Findings no. 57, Research and Statistics Directorate, London, Home Office, 1997. Additional information supplied by Ms P. Mayhew.
79 For an exposition of the Bill, an analysis of its likely consequences, and the views of critics, see Penal Affairs Consortium, *The Crime (Sentences) Bill*, London, PAC, 1997. The Act received Royal Assent in March 1997, though in 1998 not all its provisions, including those on early release, had been implemented.
80 'Top judge in plea for fewer jail sentences', *Independent*, 11 July 1997, p. 11.
81 The Penal Affairs Consortium, 169 Clapham Road, London, comprises thirty-three such organisations.

82 And in this respect the government's proposal in the White Paper *On the Record* in June 1996 for criminal conviction certificates can only be regarded as destructive. A full discussion of the issues involved in the White Paper has been given by the Penal Affairs Consortium. In 1998 the proposal had not been implemented.

   Home Office, *On the Record*, Cm 3087, London, The Stationery Office, 1996.

   Penal Affairs Consortium, '*On the Record*': comments on the White Paper of June 1996, London, PAC, 1996.

83 The argument that convicts are entitled only to a smaller share of society's goods than is given to the lowest rank of free men.

84 Braithwaite, *Prisons Education and Work*, p. 28.

85 D. Dickinson, *Crime and Unemployment*, Cambridge, Department of Applied Economics, University of Cambridge, 1994.

86 J. Wells, 'Crime and unemployment', in K. Coates (ed.), *The Right to Work: the loss of our first freedom*, Nottingham, Spokesman, 1995, pp. 54–100.

87 'Brown promises a job for everyone', *Independent*, 29 September 1997, p. 1.

Bibliography

Andrews, D.A., and J. Bonta, *The Psychology of Criminal Conduct*, Cincinnati, Anderson, 1994, as cited by D. Andrews, 'The psychology of criminal conduct and effective treatment', in J. McGuire (ed.), *What Works: Reducing Reoffending*, Chichester, Wiley, 1995, pp. 35–62.

Berens, C., and L. Johnston, 'The high-street sweatshops', *The Big Issue* no. 181, 13–19 May 1996, pp. 6–8.

Boddis, S., and R. Mann, 'Groupwork in prisons', in Prison Reform Trust, '*A Good and Useful Life': Constructive Prison Regimes*, London, PRT, 1995, pp. 55–68.

Braithwaite, J., *Prisons Education and Work*, Phillip, Australian Institute of Criminology, 1980.

Brody, S.R., *The Effectiveness of Sentencing: a review of the literature*, Home Office Research Study no. 35, London, HMSO, 1976.

Burnett, R., *The Dynamics of Recidivism: summary report*, Oxford, Centre for Criminological Research, University of Oxford, 1992.

Caird, R., *A Good and Useful Life*, London, Hart-Davis, MacGibbon, 1974.

Cooper, M.H., and R.D. King, 'Social and economic problems of prisoners' work', in P. Halmos (ed.), *Sociological Studies in the British Penal Services*, The Sociological Review, Monograph no. 9, Keele, University of Keele, 1965.

Coyle, A., *The Prisons We Deserve*, London, HarperCollins, 1994.

Crow, I., 'Employment, training and offending', in M. Drakeford and M. Vanstone (eds), *Beyond Offending Behaviour*, Aldershot, Arena, 1996, pp. 51–62.

Crow, I., P. Richardson, C. Riddington and F. Simon, *Unemployment, Crime, and Offenders*, London, Routledge, 1989.

Davies, M., 'Prisons as social firms: the way forward for prison industry?' in Prison Reform Trust, '*A Good and Useful Life': Constructive Prison Regimes*, London, PRT, 1995, pp. 35–48.

Dawson, S., 'Power and influence in prison workshops', in P. Abell (ed.), *Organisations as Bargaining and Influence Systems*, London, Heinemann, 1975, pp. 151–86.

Departmental Committee on Prisons (the Gladstone Committee), *Report* and *Minutes of Evidence*, C7702, London, HMSO, 1895.

Departmental Committee on the Employment of Prisoners, *Report Part 1: Employment of Prisoners*, Cmd 4462, London, HMSO, 1933.

Dickinson, D., *Crime and Unemployment*, Cambridge, Department of Applied Economics, University of Cambridge, 1994.

Dodd, T., and P. Hunter, *The National Prison Survey 1991: a report to the Home Office of a study of prisoners in England and Wales carried out by the Social Survey Division of OPCS*, London, HMSO, 1992.

Dunbar, I., *A Sense of Direction*, London, Home Office, 1985.

Employment Department, *Partnership Initiatives: Helping Offenders into Training and Work*, Developing Good Practice/Equal Opportunities series, Sheffield, Employment Department, 1993.

Fabiano, E., J. LaPlante and A. Loza, 'Employability: from research to practice', *Forum on Corrections Research*, 1996, vol. 8, no. 1, pp. 23–8.

Flynn, N., *Missing Links: recommendations for productive partnerships between TECs and the Prison Service*, London, LAWTEC Ltd/ELTEC/Apex Trust, 1993.

——'Making Workshops Work', *Prison Report*, 1995, no. 30, pp. 26–7.

Flynn, N., and C. Baines, *Working It Out: Employment Guidance and Employer Involvement in Prisons*, London, Apex Trust and South Thames TEC, 1994.

Gillis, C., D. Robinson and F. Porporino, 'Inmate employment: the increasingly influential role of generic work skills', *Forum on Corrections Research*, 1996, vol. 8, no. 1, pp. 18–20.

Hagell, A., T. Newburn and K. Rowlingson, *Financial Difficulties on Release from Prison*, London, Policy Studies Institute, 1995.

Harding, C., B. Hines, R. Ireland and P. Rawlings, *Imprisonment in England and Wales: A Concise History*, London, Croom Helm, 1985.

HM Chief Inspector of Prisons, *Annual Report for 1985*, HC 123, London, HMSO. 1986.

——*HM Prison Coldingley*, London, Home Office, 1986.

——*Annual Report for 1988*, HC 491, London, HMSO, 1989.

——*HM Prison Channings Wood*, London, Home Office, 1991.

——*Doing Time or Using Time*, Cm 2128, London, HMSO, 1993.

——*HM Prison Channings Wood*, London, Home Office, 1993.

——*HM Prison Kirkham*, London, Home Office, 1993.

——*HM Prison Liverpool*, London, Home Office, 1993.

——*HM Prison Coldingley*, London, Home Office, 1994.

——*Annual Report 1994–95*, HC 760, London, HMSO, 1995.

——*HM Prison Channings Wood*, London, Home Office, 1995.

——*Annual Report 1995–96*, HC 44, London: The Stationery Office, 1996.

——*HM Prison Coldingley*, London, Home Office, 1996.

——*HM Prison Maidstone*, London, Home Office, 1996.

——*HM Prison Manchester*, London, Home Office, 1996.

——*HM Prison Holloway*, London, Home Office, 1997.

——*Women in Prison*, London, Home Office, 1997.

HM Commissioners of Prisons/Prison Department/Prison Service, *Annual Reports*, London, HMSO.

HM Prison Holloway Board of Visitors, *Annual Report 1995*, London, HM Prison Holloway Board of Visitors, 1996.

HM Prison Service, *Briefing*, London, HM Prison Service, periodically.

——*Corporate Plan 1995–98*, London, HM Prison Service, 1995.

——*Report of the Review of Sentence Planning 1994/5*, London, HM Prison Service, 1995.

——*Corporate Plan 1996–99*, London, HM Prison Service, 1996.

——*Manual for the Revised Model of Sentence Management and Planning*, London, HM Prison Service, 1997.

HM Prison Service and Kent Training and Enterprise Council, *Beyond The Gate* and *The Blueprint*, Chatham, Kent TEC, 1994.

HM Prison Service Industries and Farms, *Central Services: working for prisons – for work in prisons*, London, HM Prison Service, 1993.

HM Prison Service Industries and Farms Board of Management, *Chairman's Report 1992–93*, London, HM Prison Service, 1993.

Home Office, *Custody, Care and Justice: The Way Ahead for the Prison Service in England and Wales*, Cm 1647, London, HMSO, 1991.

——*National Framework for the Throughcare of Offenders in Custody to the Completion of Supervision in the Community*, London, Home Office, 1993.

——*Statistical Bulletin: Projection of Long-Term Trends in the Prison Population to 2002*, London, Home Office, 1995.

——*Statistical Bulletin: Projection of Long-Term Trends in the Prison Population to 2004*, London, Home Office, 1996.

——*Prison Statistics England and Wales 1996*, Cm 3732, London, The Stationery Office, 1997.

Home Office and Employment Department, *Employment in Prisons and for Ex-Offenders: the government reply to the first report from the Employment Committee Session 1991–92, HC 30*, Cm 1837, London, HMSO, 1992.

Home Office and Scottish Home Department, *Work for Prisoners: Report of the Advisory Council on the Employment of Prisoners*, London, HMSO, 1961.

Home Office, Scottish Office and Northern Ireland Office, *Report of the Committee of Inquiry into the UK Prison Services* (the May Report), London, HMSO, 1979.

House of Commons Committee of Public Accounts, *26th Report, Session 1985–86: Prison Industry Losses*, HC 160, London, HMSO, 1986.

House of Commons Employment Committee, *Employment in Prisons and for Ex-Offenders*, HC 30, London, HMSO, 1991.

Huws, U., *No Sweat! Why Britain's one million homeworkers need a new deal*, London, Trades Union Congress, 1996.

Ignatieff, M., *A Just Measure of Pain: The Penitentiary in the Industrial Revolution 1750–1850*, London, Macmillan, 1978.

Industrial Society, 'Empowerment', *Managing Best Practice* no. 8, London, Industrial Society, 1995.

Institute of Employment Research, *Review of the Economy and Employment 1995: Occupational Assessment*, Coventry, University of Warwick, 1995.

Institute of Employment Research, *Review of the Economy and Employment 1996/97: Labour Market Assessment*, Coventry, University of Warwick, 1996.

Jerred, R., 'Out of the wood', *Prison Service News*, 1991, vol. 9, no. 83, p. 4.

Kent Training and Enterprise Council, *Update*, October 1993, Chatham, Kent TEC.

King, R.D., and K. McDermott, 'British prisons 1970–1987: the ever-deepening crisis', *British Journal of Criminology*, 1989, vol. 29, pp. 107–28.

——*The State of Our Prisons*, Oxford, Oxford University Press, 1995.

King, R.D., and R. Morgan, *The Future of the Prison System*, Farnborough, Gower, 1980.

Learmont, J., *Review of Prison Service Security in England and Wales and the Escape from Parkhurst Prison on Tuesday 3rd January 1995*, Cm 3020, London, HMSO, 1995.

Legge, K., 'Work in prison: the process of inversion', *British Journal of Criminology*, 1978, vol. 18, pp. 16–22.

Lightman, E.S., 'The private employer and the prison industry', *British Journal of Criminology*, 1982, vol. 22, pp. 36–48.

Lipton, D., R. Martinson and J. Wilks, *Effectiveness of Correctional Treatment – a survey of treatment evaluation studies*, Springfield, Praeger, 1975, as cited by Brody, *The Effectiveness of Sentencing: a review of the literature*, Home Office Research Study no. 35, London, Home Office, 1976.

McGuire, J., and P. Priestley, 'Reviewing "What Works?": past, present and future', in J. McGuire (ed.), *What Works: Reducing Reoffending*, Chichester, Wiley, 1995.

McHutchison, J., *NSW Corrective Service Industries and Offender Post-Release Employment*, Research Bulletin 14, Sydney, New South Wales Department of Corrective Services, 1991.

McLaren, K., *Reducing Reoffending: What Works Now*, Wellington, New Zealand Department of Justice, 1992.

McMillan, R. (pseudonym), 'What went wrong at Holloway?', *Prison Report*, 1996, no. 34, pp. 8–10.

Morris, A., C. Wilkinson, A. Tisi, J. Woodrow and A. Rockley, *Managing the Needs of Female Prisoners*, London, Home Office, 1995.

Motiuk, L., 'Targeting employment patterns to reduce offender risk and need', *Forum on Corrections Research*, 1996, vol. 8, no. 1, p. 24.

National Association for the Care and Resettlement of Offenders, *Opening the Doors: the resettlement of prisoners in the community*, London, NACRO, 1993.

National Audit Office, *Appropriation Accounts 1983–84. Vol. 6: Class IX Vote 8: Prisons, England and Wales (Home Office): Report of the Comptroller and Auditor General*, HC 614–VI, London, HMSO, 1984.

——*Home Office Prison Department; Objectives, Organisation and Management of the Prison Service Industries and Farms: report by the Comptroller and Auditor General*, HC 93, London, HMSO, 1987.

Penal Affairs Consortium, '*On the Record*': comments on the White Paper of June 1996, London, PAC, 1996.

——*The Crime (Sentences) Bill*, London, PAC, 1997.

Rajan, A., *1990s: Where Will the New Jobs Be?*, Tunbridge Wells, Institute of Careers Guidance and the Centre for Research in Employment and Technology in Europe, 1992.

Roberts, K., A. Barton, J. Buchanan and B. Goldson, *Evaluation of a Home Office Initiative to Help Offenders into Employment*, London, Home Office, 1996.

Ross, R.R., E.A. Fabiano and B. Ross, *Reasoning and Rehabilitation: a handbook for teaching cognitive skills*, Ottawa, The Cognitive Centre, 1989.

Skills and Enterprise Network, *Labour Market and Skill Trends 1992/93*, Nottingham, Employment Department, 1991.

——*Labour Market and Skill Trends 1997/98*, Nottingham, Department for Education and Employment, 1997.

Tilt, R., 'Rights, risks and rehabilitation 1996', *Criminal Justice*, 1996, vol. 14, no. 4, pp. 6–7.

Wells, J., 'Crime and unemployment', in K. Coates (ed.), *The Right to Work: the loss of our first freedom*, Nottingham, Spokesman, 1995, pp. 54–100.

Woodcock, J., *Report of the Inquiry into the Escape of Six Prisoners from the Special Security Unit at Whitemoor Prison, Cambridgeshire, on Friday 9th September 1994*, Cm 2741, London, HMSO, 1994.

Woolf, H., and S. Tumim, *Prison Disturbances April 1990: Report of an Inquiry*, Cm 1456, London, HMSO, 1991.

Index